Outcome-Oriented Public Management

A Responsibility-Based Approach to the New Public Management

A German Classic

T0344651

A volume in
Research in Public Management
Lawrence R. Jones, *Series Editor*

Research in Public Management

Lawrence R. Jones, *Series Editor*

Outcome-Oriented Public Management

A Responsibility-Based Approach to the New Public Management

Kuno Schedler
Isabella Proeller

INFORMATION AGE PUBLISHING, INC.
Charlotte, NC • www.infoagepub.com

ISBN: 978-1-61735-180-8 (paperback)
        978-1-61735-181-5 (hardcover)
        978-1-61735-182-2 (e-book)

Printed in the United States of America

Contents

PART **III**

Structural and Processual Elements in the Concept of OPM

PART **V**

Cultural Aspects in the Concept of OPM

PART **VI**

Reflections on the Model

Preface

The message of New Public Management did not reach Europe's German-speaking area before the early 1990s. In Germany, Austria and Switzerland, both practitioners and academics were searching for a new model according to which public administration could be organised and controlled. After the disappointing experiences of the 1980s, when Overhead Cost Analysis had tried to make public administration more efficient by means of a drastic cure—and failed pitifully—reformers sought to exploit staff motivation instead. Al Gore's "good people trapped in bad systems" furnished the symbolism that provided a favourable attitude towards New Public Management in the German-speaking countries.

However, New Public Management according to the US-American, British or New Zealand model was not suited to being introduced unmodified into the political and cultural context of the three countries. There was thus a demand for an adapted model that should include the specific contextual conditions of the German culture and language area and convert them into applicable recommendations for action. At the same time— and this appears to be decidedly relevant—the driving force behind the reforms was not politics but public administration itself. This was not a model which—like the original version of NPM—focused on technocratic measuring and monitoring systems that constituted the target area of the intended reforms; rather, it was slogans such as "let the managers manage" in conjunction with the "room to manoeuvre" offered by the one-line budget system that proved attractive to the often enthusiastic reformers in

Outcome-Oriented Public Management, pages xiii–xiv
Copyright © 2010 by Information Age Publishing
All rights of reproduction in any form reserved.

public administration. At last, they hoped, politics would provide clear-cut targets that the administration would be able to achieve in operative independence.

In comparison with New Public Management, the German-language version—Outcome-oriented Public Management (OPM)—which originated, and is chiefly applied, in Switzerland, values the attainment of outcomes over and above the technical provision of outputs. OPM is based on the assumption that public managers act responsibly, are intrinsically motivated and can rightly be trusted. In this context, it is only consistent that objectives are formulated and evaluated as results objectives. Particular attention is paid to the role of politics, which undergoes essential changes.

This volume is the English version of a book that was published for the first time in 2000 in German and has sold successfully: Kuno Schedler and Isabella Proeller, *New Public Management*, 4th ed., Berne: Paul Haupt, 2008. At present, it is in its fourth edition and is—as colleagues report to us—regarded as the German-language standard work for students of New Public Management. It describes OPM as an ideal model in the full knowledge that in practical applications, context-related adaptations will have to be made. It is intended to provide Continental European students with English-language access to OPM; it can serve other students as the source of an NPM variant that depends on a given context. Owing to its clear and simple explanation of the major elements of OPM, the book can also create an additional benefit for practitioners.

This version of the book has been made possible by the support of several people. Our sincere thanks go to Tony Häfliger and Vivien Blandford for the translation and to Labinot Demaj for the coordination and amendments. We would also like to thank Andrea Hug, Van Nguyen, Tobias Hänni and Karin Streule for their valuable contribution.

—**Kuno Schedler** and **Isabella Proeller**
St. Gallen and Potsdam, 2010

PART I

Introduction and Fundamentals

Public Administration and Outcome-Oriented Public Management

This chapter will first deal with the management situation in public administration in order to elucidate the background of public management. It will then be shown how New Public Management was developed as a reform model and how it gained international attention.

Administration? or Management? or Both?

It was the year 2001. The mayor of the city of Passau looked like a picture-book Bavarian: large, jovial, bearded, and a wily fox in politics. His city was his life. If we had to pick the mayor in a group of people, he would be our choice. Everything was as it should be, then; the City of Three Rivers was in the safe hands of a rock of immutable Bavarian nature.

The mayor of the city of Passau, however, was also a skilful manager. Within just under ten years, he and a handful of civil servants had turned his municipal administration inside out, aired the musty offices, activated

Outcome-Oriented Public Management, pages 3–35

the citizenry, schooled the politicians, and got rid of red tape. Thus he and his city became the epitome of innovative administrative reform, and he was visited by countless study groups and pilgrims looking for a new form of administration management.

Thanks to the introduction of its quality management, Passau was the first city to win the prestigious Quality Award of the Speyer University of Administrative Sciences for the second time. The jury's decision was reinforced by the greatly advanced efforts to enhance quality through citizen involvement. Passau had launched its first steps towards quality management as early as 1990 after Schmöller, the first mayor to represent the Social Democrats (SPD), had defeated a competitor from the Union of Christian Socialists (CSU). He seized the opportunity to deliberately involve the population in practical politics. What started out as an attempt to involve customers developed into the practice of administrative management.

The City of Passau opted for a mission statement to be drawn up. The development of this mission statement under the direction of an external consultant took place in workshops with the involvement of citizens, the municipal council and the administration. The first draft of the mission statement was published in the media, and citizens were called upon to provide feedback. Over 10,000 individual suggestions were submitted, appraised and incorporated. The mission statement was adopted in 1994; the completion of its implementation was scheduled for 2005. A survey revealed that thanks to their active participation, 75% of the population knew the mission statement well or very well. 80% believed that the objectives formulated in the mission statement could be attained by 2005.

For the mission statement to be implemented, 15 individual development plans were assigned to project groups. These, in turn, were made up of representatives of the citizenry, the government and the administration. Once their work was done, the project groups dissolved, and implementation began. In this process, the responsibility for resources was gradually decentralised. Administrative units were transformed into public enterprises and converted to accrual accounting; they defined their outputs and ascribed costs to individual outputs.

Simple customer feedback now ensures that each administrative unit is informed about how its customers experience it on a monthly basis. Self-organising staff groups receive this feedback and take measures to institute improvements wherever this is necessary. Customers express their gratitude by their constantly growing satisfaction.

The city thus became a service company—a success story that could have been lifted from a textbook, but work on the modernisation of the politico-administrative system will have to continue for a long time to come. Yet what is the role model, what ideal of administration and politics lies behind such developments? Can, may, should a public administration be led by management? What role must politics be able to play? What instruments do the actors in the political/administrative system require for such a development as happened in Passau to become possible and to be driven forward in a politically appropriate way?

Fundamentals

New Public Management (NPM) deals with the modernisation of public institutions and new forms of managing public administration. What is "new" in New Public Management is the institutional view of administration and its contact partners—and conceptual ideas of how such institutions should be steered. Particularly in the early stages of these kinds of reform, it was therefore called *Neues Steuerungsmodell* (New Control Model) in Germany and (homing in more on practical matters) *Wirkungsorientierte Verwaltungsführung* (Outcome-Oriented Public Management) in Switzerland and Austria. Both terms, however, focus on a specific aspect of modernisation according to the NPM type, namely governance and outcome orientation. Yet according to the pattern prevalent in Continental Europe, NPM seeks to be more than that: it aims at comprehensive reform. In an international comparison, this makes it more demanding than much that is or was aspired to elsewhere or at other times.

Definition 1.1:   New Public Management

New Public Management (NPM) is the generic term for an "overall movement" that has a globally standardised terminology and pursues administrative reforms based on an institutional view. A main characteristic of NPM reforms is the way they move political control from input-orientation to output-orientation.

The institution of public administration and its environment are the focus of the NPM perspective. To distinguish it from the more general term of "public management," which has also been used in Germany since around the mid-1990s (for instance in Damkowski & Precht, 1995), NPM has a more specific reform dialectic and does not only introduce management into the administration but integrates the administration into an environment that is intended to be outcome-oriented in nature.

The purpose of this book is to describe the particular Continental European version developed from "generic" NPM: Outcome-Oriented Public

Management (OPM). This term will be used throughout the book whenever this specific adaptation is referred to.

Before the reform measures and innovations of NPM can be depicted in more depth and detail, it is first necessary to generally describe the position of public administration within the social system and within the system of government organs. Moreover, the initial situation that gave rise to our considerations of public administration reform must be outlined.

The Functions of the State

The establishment of states, which has evolved differently in different societies, was supported by a characteristic that is peculiar to man: man as a zoon politikon is in need of human companionship and depends for his survival on a community based on the division of labour. The path from archaic forms of government to the territorial state and on to the modern multi-party and legislative states primarily shows that in every human community, certain functions of collective problem-solving were executed by an institution that can be called "state," regardless of whether it was actually constituted as such or merely bore that name.

Despite this seemingly natural phenomenon, questions such as what entitles the state to collect taxes through its administration evoke answers that differ depending on the prevalent and underlying notions and ideology of the state. Equally varied answers are given to the questions as to what the functions of the state are and in which areas it should be active.

The basic functions of the state in society can be diagrammatically portrayed as in Figure 1.1. Irrespective of the nature of specific political systems, a distinction can be made between four fundamental functions of the state. The state receives its immaterial basis through the democratic legitimation of its decisions and the generalised consensus about the form of society that is to be guaranteed. In order to be able to fulfil its functions, it raises funds in the form of taxes and duties to be paid out of economic production. The citizens accede to the state's demand for taxes and accept other government intrusions into their sphere of freedom since there is a certain individual obligation that arises from the social contract on which civil society and the state are based, and since the state possesses the means to force citizens to do their duty and to sanction them if they refuse to do so.

In return, the state guarantees the general conditions for private production, for instance through the guarantee of ownership, economic freedom and market regulations. In addition, it produces basic infrastructures such as the road network, which facilitate private production and reduce

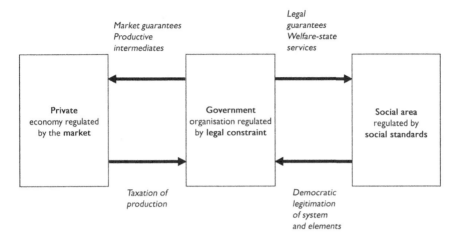

Figure 1.1   Elementary exchange relations between the general organisational areas of economy, state and society. *Source*: Linder (1983, p. 325).

transaction costs. Such projects allow for investments which private individuals or communities would not make or would not be capable of making. Also, the state is engaged in the social sector—i.e., in families, associations, etc.—to ensure a certain social order and a certain behaviour by underpinning social standards through laws and government means of coercion. Besides emphasising various social standards and rules, the state intervenes where social services are not available by making its own services available (Linder, 1983, p. 325).

The Legitimation of the State and its Action

There are several and varied reasons for the legitimation of the state. These reasons are numerous and in constitutional law and theory are based on a variety of legitimation theories; in the Continental European government systems, for example, republicanism and liberalism are of particular importance. Generally recognised reasons for legitimation have been accepted into the constitutions of our cultural sphere and now manifest themselves in principles of governance (Mastronardi, 2000).

In the *democratic principle*, state action is legitimated because it arises out of deliberative decision-making processes which run their course in directly or indirectly legitimated democratic institutions and transparent procedures.

States that are organised as *constitutional states* guarantee that private individuals are protected against the state, on the one hand through the fundamental rights, but on the other hand also through the requirement of legality. This requirement only permits the state to intervene anywhere if there is a legal basis, and it enables private individuals to defend themselves against government infringement by means of legal remedies.

In the last few decades, changes in state functions have caused these two traditional reasons for legitimation to be supplemented by a further legitimation requirement, namely *outcome orientation*. The activities of today's welfare state, which characterise it as a productive state, can no longer be justified by democratic and constitutional considerations alone; rather, their very nature requires legitimation on the strength of their impact on society.

In sum, it can be said that the traditional legitimation theories of constitutional and administrative law need not be renounced but have to be supplemented in order to integrate the various positions and claims made on the state into its legitimation basis. For this purpose, the notion of legitimation is subdivided, with recourse being made to the theory of three-layered legitimation (Czybulka, 1989, pp. 67ff.).

The legitimation of state action can be traced back to *popular sovereignty* in all democratic countries, irrespective of whether they are representative or direct democracies. Legitimation is thus vested in the citizens. Different levels of legitimation must be taken into consideration, however, when we notice that although citizens are perfectly satisfied with the state as such, they are sceptical of and dissatisfied with individual institutions such as the administration and the courts. This divide can be even more distinct between a basically positive attitude towards the state and dissatisfaction with individual services provided by public administration. These differences are what three-layered legitimation aims to illustrate. In the following chapters, overall legitimation will therefore be subdivided into basic, institutional and individual legitimation. Subsequently, the three different layers of legitimation will be interlinked. Particular emphasis will be placed on the fact that the notion of legitimation will not be used in the purely legal sense of authorisation under constitutional law or other laws; rather, legitimation is conceived of in the sense of "accepted" in this model, thus bearing a significance that is more in line with the everyday-language meaning of legitimate.

Basic Legitimation

With regard to basic legitimation, it is the fundamental consensus underlying the state that is the focus of interest. It serves to lay down fundamental aspects, which usually arise in situations of increased uncertainty (Frey & Kirchgässner, 1994, pp. 10ff.). The characteristic feature of the concept of fundamental consensus is a regulation of social problems and structures that is unaffected by short-term and particular interests. In this case, *legitimation is vested in the citizens*, who determine the general conditions that define the fundamental consensus through the exercise of their democratic rights. The *mode of legitimation* differs between individual countries depending on their individual conceptions of democracy. Generally, however, it consists of the election of politicians and government members by the people, on the one hand, and of further people's rights like the right to initiate legislation and referenda, on the other.

Institutional Legitimation

If citizens pass blanket judgements on, say, public administration, this concerns aspects that can be related to institutional legitimation. Public administration profits or suffers from its image, which also has an impact on the appraisal of specific contacts, and vice versa. What is striking is that the appreciation of government institutions in this context cannot be *directly* related to issues of the fundamental consensus or the individual citizens' appraisals of individual services provided by public administration. Instead, the focus here is on issues of the 'correct' organisation or the perception of competencies. In this case, *legitimation is vested in the politicians*. Accordingly, the *mode of legitimation* is created through the stipulation of a legal basis.

Individual Legitimation

If a citizen is engaged in a direct transaction process with a public institution, this takes place at the level of individual legitimation. The citizen takes on an additional role, namely that of a customer of public institutions. The differentiation between citizen and customer is an expression of a theoretical link between management theory and political science, which entails a danger of misunderstandings. In the language of law, the substantial differentiation between citizens and customers can at least partially be compared with the differentiation between general, abstract legal norms and individual, concrete legal acts. Whereas the general, abstract legal norms can be allocated to basic legitimation, individual, concrete legal acts only arise at the level of individual legitimation. Individual, concrete legal acts require a concrete relationship with an individual holder of rights. Similarly, a citizen only becomes a customer of public administration in the context of a concrete relationship. Individual legitimation is strongly subject to aspects of quality and refers to a customer's individual, subjective appraisal of individual services. At this level, then, *legitimation is vested in the customers*, and the subjective perception of services provided by public institutions serves as the *mode of legitimation*. It is self-explanatory that for this reason, the majority principle per se cannot apply within the domain of individual consensus (Czybulka, 1989, p. 68). This, however, need not prevent us from further pursuing the concept of three-layered legitimation.

Connections between the Legitimation Layers

The above explanations reveal that the layers of legitimation cannot be treated in isolation from each other. To the contrary, the different legitimation layers and the actors in which legitimation is vested are engaged in a multi-layered interaction process. Figure 1.2 outlines the relationships between the various layers of legitimation and the people who provide legitimation.

As mentioned above, individual legitimation is based on a subjective appraisal of a service provided by public administration. The yardsticks against which customers measure public services include experiences from business life (Hablützel, 1995, p. 501). The recognition of this fact is of fundamental importance since individual legitimation has an impact on both institutional and basic legitimation. The extent to which the impact shaped by individual experiences strengthens or weakens the state's basic legitimation is likely to depend on the explicit and/or implicit affirmation of individual legitimation, and vice versa.

If we compare this representation with the traditional democratically oriented model, we can infer that a basic consensus may be necessary for the legitimation of the state, but does not suffice to legitimate state action. Although it cannot be deduced from this that acceptance should be understood as the prerequisite for the legitimacy of state action (Würtenberger, 1996, p. 101), customers' individual acceptance should—against the background of three-layered legitimation—become a determining guide for the behaviour of public administration officials.

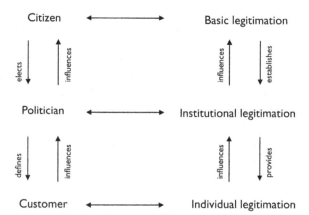

Figure 1.2 Differentiation between citizens' roles and state legitimation. *Source*: Schedler and Felix (2000).

An Ideological Antagonism: The Welfare State versus Neoliberalism

The role and function of the state in society is primarily determined by the conception of the state that is prevalent in a society. In the recent past, the predominant—and clashing—conceptions of the state in Western Europe have been the idea of the welfare state and the neoliberal conception of government. These two opposing conceptions shaped the quantitative development of the public sector in Europe and led to differing strategic government orientations. Thus the expansive growth of the state in the 1960s and 1970s was the result of the welfare state idea, whereas the consolidation stage of the 1980s, the heyday of privatisation, was driven by a neoliberal conception of the state (Naschold, 1995, p. 17).

The welfare state makes use of government resources to produce general welfare in society. Governments try to iron out social divides by means of state intervention. The state is an active, equalising and redistributing actor within society. Its political characteristics are an expansion of social services, social insurance and social rights.

According to Schäfer (1995, pp. 139f.), neoliberalism is, conversely, regarded as a variant of a conception of the market economy, which in essence is based on an intellectual ground that was prepared in the 1920s and 1930s. It has the following characteristic features: personal freedom as the fundamental standard, striving for gain as the economic driving force, competition, a call for standardisation, and stability in the government's regulatory policies. Its political characteristics are the call for the radical reprivatisation and economisation of functions exercised by the state. In neoliberalism, the role of the state is limited to the exercise of the actual core functions (i.e., making available the "genuine" public goods) and the guarantee of economic freedom. A conception of the state outlines what overriding objective citizens expect from the state and what purpose they assign to the state. The objectives and purposes ascribed to the two models outlined above differ substantially. Thus the objective of the neoliberal state is to establish an economy based on competition and to counteract any undesirable developments emerging within it—but nowhere else. By contrast, the welfare state pursues a normative and distributive objective based on the concept of solidarity. The purpose of the state is the establishment of a comprehensive system of government regulation and social compensation. These objectives and purposes provide the concrete foundation for the tasks to be fulfilled by the state, which ultimately define the range of the functions to be exercised by the state, as well as the ratio of government expenditure to the GDP.

Public Administration—The Implementing Arm of the State

The existence of public administration depends on the existence of a state. Public administration can only exist within a state. What is crucial here is that the state is able to make binding decisions in the execution of its purposes. The state and its administration have traditionally represented an organisation that has been set apart within society to a greater or lesser extent.

The delimitation of public administration from other organisations can be effected by reference to the purposes of the state, which determine the general services of the state for society. The formulation of these purposes, which as a rule are enshrined in the constitution, varies strongly in terms of concretisation with the result that they are often broken down into details in political decision-making processes. Public administration implements political decisions in individual cases and in its capacity as the interface between government and the citizenry (Becker, 1989, pp. 110f.).

Further, widespread approaches to the delimitation of public administration in the state derive from the system of the division of powers and define public administration as everything that is not legislation, jurisdiction and executive. Positively formulated approaches conceive of the administration as an implementing authority that is controlled by politics and checked by the judiciary. These definitions disregard the actual nature of the division of powers in European countries. A strict division of powers into legislature, judiciary and executive cannot be found in the current forms of government. Thus today's administration exerts a considerable influence on the legislature through its role in the preparation of policies.

A generally recognised definition of the term "public management" does not yet exist since the diversity of institutions makes it difficult for public management to be summed up in a comprehensive and precise definition. It is possible, however, for a list of features to be drawn up which characterise public administration and appear to circumscribe the term (Becker, 1989, p. 109; Reichard, 1987, p. 3): by preparing, implementing and monitoring political decisions and the actions based on them, public administration contributes towards the achievement of the purpose of the state and the fulfilment of the public functions arising from this purpose. It does this work in a special organisation made available by the state and determined by law, which in turn has the benefit of partially direct and partially indirect democratic legitimation.

The Model of Bureaucracy—The Organisation of Traditional Public Administration

In European countries, public administrations are organised and conceptualised as bureaucracies. In general usage, the term "bureaucracy" is not understood non-judgementally as a form of administrative structure, but used as a derogatory, indeed even accusatory description of the negative features of administration. This negative rating is caused by the insufficiencies and degeneracies that have entrenched themselves and spread in bureaucratically organised administrations. In spite of all this criticism, however, it must not be ignored that bureaucracy, too, has its attainments and advantages, and that its institution has made a substantial contribution towards the establishment of liberal and democratic constitutional orders.

Weber, who in the early 20th century conducted an extensive investigation of bureaucratic administrations, in essence described their modus operandi as follows (Weber, 1985, pp. 551f.):

1. There is a strict order of competence, which is determined by general standards.
2. Every office is firmly integrated in a hierarchy, and the rights and duties of individual offices and officials are precisely defined.
3. The discharge of an office is based on the principle that everything has to be written down, on the almost total separation between an official's office and private sphere and on the distinction between private ownership and administrative resources.
4. Every office requires special qualifications, which calls for generally regulated training and the assessment of officials.
5. An office is a full-time job. Careers proceed mechanically according to seniority.
6. In their work, officials have to comply with a specified system of rules, which ensure orderly procedures.

Weber arrived at this characterisation of bureaucracy through a systematic scientific analysis of forms of bureaucracy that were known in various cultures at various times throughout the world (Ju, 1986, p. 62). What is conceived of as Weberian bureaucracy is neither an invention of Weber's nor a doctrine propagated by him; rather, it is the result of his empirical investigations, which in an idealised representation resulted in a model of administration that Weber described as a rational bureaucratic ideal type (in the sense of an analytical categorisation).

Definition 1.2: Bureaucracy

The term *bureaucracy* nowadays particularly denotes state organisations and forms of organisations whose structures do not take their bearings from the market but follow the characteristics defined by Max Weber.

The Weberian form of public administration with the focus on the points listed above is reaching its limits in today's increasingly dynamic environment, which also calls upon public administration to show a growing degree of adaptability. The stability which Weberian bureaucracy deliberately aimed to achieve and preserve has lost its significance for the quality of administration: inflexibility towards the environment, uninterested and bureaucratic behaviour displayed by officials, and the dehumanisation of organisation, particularly at the lower levels of hierarchy (Frey, 1994, p. 25), have a devastating effect on the efficiency of public administration. The weaknesses and degeneracies of bureaucracies are leading to more and more calls to align bureaucratically organised administrations along a paradigm that is more appropriate to our age and focuses on different facets, with economic aspects being accorded greater significance. Aspects that were important in the previous bureaucratic model should be retained.

A Modern Conception of Public Administration

According to the modern conception, public administration should change from an administrative apparatus into a service provider. The previous formal control mechanisms should be replaced by the reorientation and the introduction of management instruments. The new form of public management implicitly requires a new conception of administration (or possibly only new insights into it). In the Weberian sense, public administration presented itself as an apparatus or a machine, which was in keeping with the then prevalent basic industrial trend in management, in which the theory of Taylorism was praised to the skies. Decision-making and processes were meant to be as "mechanised" as possible (Zehnder, 1989, p. 22). This conception is now increasingly being replaced by a representation of public administration as a dynamically complex social entity.

Public administration is embedded in a political, social and economic environment. The political system has a direct influence on the tasks and functions of administration. The relationship between administration and politics changed in the course of the last century. Whereas the traditional function of administration used to be limited to the implementation of political decisions in the sense of the traditional division of powers, it has gradually been extended into the field of policy-making everywhere. This shift, which is a change in the normatively required structure of the state (Mastronardi, 1998, p. 66), was primarily driven by the constantly growing and novel welfare-state functions assumed by government. Parliament, which in theory is supposed to be the actual centre of political opinion-making, is overtaxed and must leave substantial functions to the executive and the administration. Public administration has acquired a crucial role in political opinion-forming by introducing essential information for consensual solutions into the political decision-making process.

Public administration is not merely part of the political system but of society as a whole. The interface function between the state and the citizenry, in particular, requires that the administration is accepted by, and can justify itself to, the population, whose attitude is not static but subject to change as a consequence of shifting social values and ideas. Public administration faces these value systems in two ways. For one thing, the outputs generated by the administration, namely decisions and actions, make it clear that officials represent an elementary factor in the administrative process (Becker, 1989, p. 121). It is through them that value systems which exist in society are introduced into the administration and into its decisions and actions. Even though the officials' conduct remains within the framework of the law in accordance with the principle of legality, there is still latitude for discretion, action and conception which enables personal value systems to enter administrative processes. Then again, it must be noted with regard to the relationship between public administration and society that the state and thus also the administration have the possibility of creating value systems unilaterally. The state can, for instance, raise a problem from an individual to a public level, as it did with the discussion on abortion, and thus influence people's awareness of certain values or even provoke a value change in society.

Finally, the administration must expose itself increasingly to the market and thus to competition. Whereas in the traditional model, public administration was dominated by a pattern of regulation that was largely based on constitutional and democratic procedures and legal coercion, tasks are latterly also being fulfilled through (artificially created) market situations. The intention is to enhance the administration's competitiveness. For the administration, this means in the first instance that it acts as a competitor on a "service market," on the one hand, and as a customer in its relationship with suppliers on a buying market, on the other hand. Market mechanisms are meant to boost efficiency and effectiveness within the administration. The market and the state, i.e., public administration, are increasingly evolving into closely related systems.

Within the administration, there are three possible points of approach and channels of influence for its reorientation. These are the elements of an organisation which can be *formally* changed and influenced and in which change can be achieved by influencing formal elements:

- **Strategy**: In this context, strategy is not conceived of in the usual sense of the term as applied to it in general management literature. The notion of strategy used here covers all the elements that indicate the great thrust of action. The orientation of administration and its change towards certain *visions, tasks* or *objectives* is understood as a strategic element in this context.
- **Structure**: Structural elements constitute the *organisation of procedures and systems* within the administration, as well as *formal rules*. This also includes the general systemic conditions which were explicitly formulated with regard to the regulation of the organisation, such as *incentive systems, rules* and *regulations*.
- **Organisational capacity**: The *personnel* with their skills and knowledge, the *know-how* that exists within the organisation, as well as the *technical infrastructure* with its possibilities, together constitute the capacity of public administration.

It must be taken into account that the strategy, structure and capacity of an administration or of an administrative unit constitute formally regulated elements. They can be managed by deliberate actions and impulses. Thus a new organisational structure, for example, is launched through concerted transformation measures. These measures can be chosen with sufficient accuracy to consequently achieve the set objective, namely the new organisational structure. At the same time the structure, capacity and strategy influence each other. If, for instance, customer orientation is stipulated as a new strategy, then implicit adaptation processes will take place in the (micro) structures, for instance by "customer advisors" being appointed within the working groups. Simultaneously, officials undergo further training and inform themselves about what being customer advisors is all about; this, in turn, will change the capacity. All in all, however, how these relationships will evolve cannot be defined since such social processes cannot be organised like machines, nor can the courses they will take be easily predicted.

Conversely, the culture describes *informal* processes and interactions, which reflect the values and forms of these value systems that exist on account of the underlying fundamental premises. It is characteristic of the culture in this model that it is informally structured and cannot therefore be directly steered by deliberate intervention. This does not mean that the

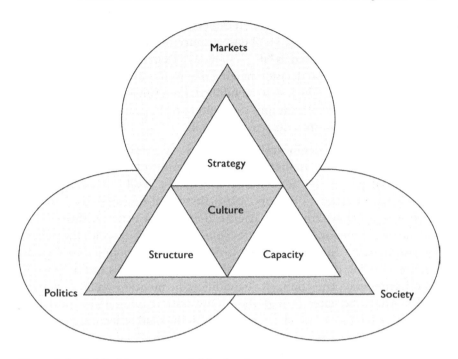

Figure 1.3   Public Management fields of action.

culture constitutes an immutable element because it also changes in step with the environment. The simple model is based on the assumption that exchange processes take place between the formal "intervention areas" and the culture, whose progression can only be predicted to a limited extent (Bleicher, 1991, p. 115). In the long-term perspective, the system tends towards an equilibrium. We may therefore surmise—without being aware of the exact course the processes will take—that any disharmonies between the individual elements and areas will be balanced out. In other words: if an organisation is ordered to accept structures that are not in keeping with the dominant culture, then either this culture will change or the formal structures will be circumvented in practice. This applies to both the bureaucracy model and to all the reform models that seek to replace it.

Public Administration Functions

The primary and original function of public administrations is the implementation of political decisions. Concrete administrative functions arise on the basis of the laws. Only when the substance of a political decision has been determined, i.e., has been laid down in the form of a statute, can tasks for implementation be derived from it. The laws can be conceived in different ways. Basically, a distinction can be made between finally and conditionally programmed law, i.e., between pure objectives and instructions that are usually formulated as "if . . . , then . . . ." Depending on their nature, the scope for action and decision-making that results for the administration can be very different. The task to be fulfilled, however, is described for both forms. The influence of statutory regulation on the administration will be examined in detail in the course of this book.

Descriptions of administrative functions are therefore not generally valid but can only be applied to specific administrations. However, certain fields of activity can be identified which exist in all European welfare states. Fleiner-Gerster (1980, pp. 397ff.) first of all distinguishes between the state's protective functions against internal and external threats. Besides defence functions and functions commonly associated with the police, this also includes functions for the protection of the population such as building control, food control, air traffic control, controls in the domain of environmental protection, etc. In addition, he mentions welfare state aspects in which the state, through the administration, fulfils a wide variety of functions, examples of which are functions in the field of securing people's livelihoods and other socially motivated insurance schemes, as well as of competition enforcement and energy supply.

Administrative activities are often divided up into law enforcement and service provision, with the former covering administrative functions by means of which the administration intervenes in individual people's rights, whereas the latter covers administrative acts with which the administration provides services—primarily economic and social—to citizens (Häfelin & Müller, 1998, p. 6).

Public administration has another important function besides the implementation of political decisions: it occupies a significant position in the context of policy-making. Politics depends on the specialist support provided by the administration in the preparation of the decision-making process. In this respect, the administration's task and service consists in supplying politics with information that it obtains from its implementation activities, thus providing members of parliament with the necessary basis for decision-making. Moreover, the administration is regularly entrusted with the preparation of draft bills, thus making a direct contribution to the political decision-making process. The contents of draft bills are not binding on parliaments but still force these chambers to discuss and debate them. In factual terms, the administration fulfils a political function here, since the selection of information is politics per se. This is even more significant as the administration has a substantial information advantage over politics.

Ethical Scales of Administrative Action: Utilitarianism versus the Ethics of Duties

As indicated above, the administration has a greater or lesser scope for action and decision-making in the execution of its functions, which it exploits (by itself or on the basis of external precepts and principles) in accordance with an underlying system of fundamental premises. In more recent discussions, a distinction has been made between two differing ethical positions from which administrative action can take its bearings, namely utilitarianism and the ethics of duties, also known as deontology.

Classic utilitarianism is characterised by a philosophy that perceives the foundation of ethical conduct in utility. The pursuit of happiness is among the highest-ranking human objectives. The evaluation criterion is always utility, which—depending on the form of utilitarianism—refers either to the benefit accruing to private individuals or to the greatest possible good for the greatest number of people. Good is what is useful. Utilitarian ethics dominates private law and constitutes the philosophical basis of the New Political Economy.

Conversely, the ethics of duties, which provides the foundation for Switzerland's public law and thus also for administrative action, proceeds from completely different criteria. It is based on a conception of the state which has been erected on the cornerstones of its rights and duties in relation to its citizens (and vice versa). In this case, compliance with strictly defined procedures overrides any results achieved in individual cases. In other words: politics also acts ethically if it acts pointlessly, if it creates no utility, as long as it adheres to the politically legitimated procedures, the assumption being that only a politically legitimated procedure can lead to an optimisation of general welfare. Against this background, the principles of democracy and the constitutional state gain considerably greater weight in the self-conception of the politico-administrative system than the principles of the productive and economic state.

In everyday administration, the deontological stance is made particularly clear by the instruments that are applied. Whereas instruments arising from a utilitarian position for the optimisation of efficiency and effectiveness, such as market mechanisms, will rarely be encountered in present-day administration, instruments arising from the ethics of duties, such as constitutional procedures and democratic processes, dominate actions and decision-making processes in public administration.

Crises in Public Administration

The following sections will examine the environment of public administration in more detail. The point is to reveal reasons for the failure of bureaucratic governance mechanisms while at the same time highlighting the changing demands made on administration. In analogy with the triangle model outlined above, the effects of change in society, politics and the market will be elucidated.

Social Change

The traditional structures, procedures and instruments of public administration no longer appear to be sufficiently efficient to confront the problem areas and requirements of state and society, which underwent a fundamental change in the last century (Budäus, 1995, p. 11). Since the early 20th century, when Weber conducted his survey of bureaucracy, society has changed from an industrialised society scarred by years of war and crisis into a modern information and consumer society. The pent-up demand of the war years has long been satisfied, and a certain prosperity has been attained. People have more spare time and are more highly educated than ever, and they make use of both these facts to reflect their own perception of values. Traditional values like religion, but also blind deference to authority, which certainly contributed towards the acceptance of bureaucracy, have decreased in significance.

The individualisation of society, which manifests itself, for instance, in the changing significance of social institutions such as the family, confronts administration and politics with new problem areas such as desocialisation and desolidarisation. However, Budäus (1995, pp. 13f.) perceives the actual problem that individualisation causes in public administration to be the fact that our politico-administrative system has been designed for bargaining concessions and negotiations with pluralistically organised interest organisations. Individualisation results in the emergence of a great number of small, particularised circles of interest. Some of these circles succeed in becoming clients of politics and pushing their particular interests through. The organisation of society in more individual and thus smaller and more numerous groups leads to an increase in the functions and expenditure of state and administration and calls for new forms of participation.

A second fundamental change is the development of information technology, which allows for an availability of data and information that would have been inconceivable a mere 20 years ago. Communication between the various levels of an organisation has been substantially facilitated by this technology. As a consequence of the permanent presence of extensive data volumes, characteristics of bureaucracy such as hierarchy and specialisation have decreased in significance. Storable knowledge is no longer a bottleneck factor today, which means that standard decisions no longer require any specialists.

In addition, the new ways of information processing have an influence on the formal organisation of bureaucracies, particularly on their hierarchical structure. The "proper channels" system appears outdated and inappropriate in this new environment. New technology makes it possible for responsibilities to be delegated to lower levels since information from various channels no longer only converges at the top but can be made available on a wide scale. In this new environment, hierarchies even hamper communication, information and management processes because information is passed on unnecessarily. Delegation is thus a simple consequence of technical information processing and results in a reduction of hierarchical orders of competence in favour of planning and monitoring concepts (Laux, 1993, pp. 342f.).

The Political Environment

The financial crisis that overtook most European countries in the late 1980s and the early 1990s is commonly regarded as the impulse and trigger that prompted politics and government to take stock and analyse reform potentials. Although the empty government coffers were merely a symptom of an increasingly recognised weakness of our functional and structural configuration of the state (Sachverständigenrat "Schlanker Staat," 1997, p. 5), it would appear that it was this very symptom that made both politics and the citizenry aware of the deficits and limits of our system for the first time. Throughout the preceding decades, steady growth and the constant expansion of the state covered up the bureaucratic organisations' decreasing ability to solve problems. These structural deficits, which are fostered by the traditional system, can no longer be funded. State bureaucracies are characterised by a high degree of continuity and have a tendency to grow. As early as the 1950s, an analysis by Parkinson (1957, p. 5) revealed that the number of jobs in public bureaucracies increased regardless of the volume of tasks to be fulfilled. According to Parkinson, the reason for this was the officials' thirst for power, which manifested itself, among other things, in the number of subordinates. This mechanism was able to prevail in state bureaucracies because a bureaucracy is able to influence the political leadership through its expertise and information advantages, and thus gain excessive weight. Today, however, the possibilities for the unrestrained growth of a bureaucracy no longer exist to the same extent owing to financial bottlenecks.

The general conditions and the socio-political challenges which an administrative organisation must be able to cope with have been transformed in step with general social change. In these circumstances, Weber's categorisation of bureaucracy as an ideal type (Weber, 1985, p. 550) is regarded more and more critically, and the traditional organisation model of public administration clashes with the problems occasioned by change. For one thing, we recognise today that a strict separation of politics and administration does not exist in bureaucratically organised administrations, either, but that both sides are interlinked and influence each other to a certain extent (Hughes, 1994, p. 44). It must be noted, however, that initially, bureaucratisation was primarily intended to stamp out corruption and nepotism whereas nowadaysm, the mutual exertion of influence should mainly consist in an exchange of information and the exploitation of the decision-making scope. Also, the appreciation of bureaucracy as being technically superior has been cast into doubt today for different reasons, such as information technology, the functions of administration in the productive state, etc.

Not least, all the organs of the state are exposed to increasing scepticism on the part of the population. Institutional legitimation appears to be feeble, which manifests itself in the fact that all the political organs are struggling against the citizens' disenchantment with the state while striving for their attention and commitment (Finger, 1997, p. 48). Public administration—the very aspect of government of which people have practical experience—often encourages or provokes a negative attitude towards the state. Dilatoriness, inefficiency and impersonality are features that many people associate with traditional administrations. For a long time, this model worked despite these shortcomings. It solved people's problems, it provided an elementary infrastructure, offered stability and conveyed an impression of fairness and social justice (Osborne & Gaebler, 1997, p. 25). This alone no longer appears to legitimate public administration today. What is increasingly called for is a good service quality, or, to put it differently, the individual legitimation of administrative work is gaining significance. Just as private individuals and private enterprises must accomplish more with less money within a shorter period of time, this is also required of public administration. For this reason, new public management forms are needed which help the administration to achieve this and to monitor the effects of administrative action better so as to counter the population's frustration and indifference.

What must also be mentioned are the development of the former Eastern Bloc countries and their importance for the configuration of the public sector. Developments in the East have affected the entire political discussion. Belief in the market was at first accorded excessive weight. The collapse of the socialist system enabled the market to emerge victorious from an ideological debate that had lasted for decades. However, the idealisation of the market increasingly weakened since the establishment of a counter-position to the plan was no longer necessary. The contest between two extreme positions had become immaterial and finally resulted in a less tense discussion about the configuration of the system. The fact that there were no ideologies left to defend paved the way for a constructive development of the market model into systems which were circumscribed by terms such as "the third way" or "managed competition" (cf. Chapter 8, Competition in Public Administration, pp. 149ff.).

The Market Environment

The more recent development of European markets has been characterised by globalisation, internationalisation and liberalisation. The consolidation of national markets into internationally or even globally integrated economic areas has resulted in sharper competitive pressure and encouraged the trend towards the concentration and international division of labour. The worldwide wave of liberalisation, which was triggered by organisations like GATT and the WTO, as well as by the economic opening of many developing countries, does not only provide enterprises with a larger potential sales market but also confronts them with greater competitive pressure. These changes primarily affect companies that are capable of influencing their market position through the choice of attractive general conditions and proximity to their international customers (Lütolf, 1997, pp. 75ff.).

The state and public administration have been affected by these changes in connection with locational competition. Today, efficient local authorities (Reichard, 1995, p. 21) as a network of public institutions are considered to be an important location attractiveness factor. Lengthy and laborious authorisation procedures result in higher costs for enterprises and influence their choice of location. The idea of "state sovereignty" (Lütolf, 1997, p. 85) has been debunked and replaced by the aspiration to see the administration as a service provider. Citizens and firms want to be treated as customers. An obstructive, slow and complicated administration may cause industrial and service companies to leave the area to the medium-to-long-term detriment of the material basis of the state organisation.

Locational competition has an impact on the relationship between market and administration with regard to the instruments of state action. Whereas traditionally the state used to operate with standard, unilateral sovereign acts in the shape of decrees or decisions, the significance of informal administrative actions is steadily gaining ground, and the state today often enters into arrangements and agreements and in so doing settles its concerns bilaterally, as a player with equal rights.

A Way Out of the Crisis

The bureaucratic model of administration, which has met the requirements of state and society for a long time, is increasingly revealing itself as weak and dysfunctional in today's changed environment. For the sake of consistency, the question must be raised as to whether and how public administration is able to observe and fulfil the functions of the state in a manner that is in keeping with the times without relinquishing any fundamental legitimation principles such as the principles of democracy and the constitutional state.

The Concept of the Guarantor State

It is striking that many concepts of government fail to treat public administration in the sense of a social system as a separate object of examination. Even though the administration is required to subordinate itself to politics, to participate in the preparation and enforcement of policies, and generally to act as the long arm of politics, its actual modus operandi is rarely subjected to scrutiny. In particular, the effect of different concepts of government on "daily working life" in administration is not taken into consideration.

Incremental adaptations to practical circumstances and experiences have imbued the modern state with a pragmatic understanding of government, which is rooted in various concepts of government that have become entrenched in recent times. The opposing principles that are addressed here are the previously sketched ideas of the welfare state and neoliberalism. Both models suffer from a central structural deficit: in practice, the welfare state is afflicted by *political failure* and an uncontrolled inflation of the

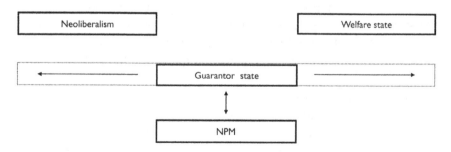

Figure 1.4 Reconciliation of the ideological antagonism as a basis for NPM.

government apparatus, which according to Riklin and Möckli (1983, p. 91) can even result in the endangerment of the constitutional state, democracy and federalism. Conversely, the competitive model of neoliberalism is afflicted by *market failure.* According to Schuppert (1989, p. 57) this has so far led to the emergence of new forms of self-organisation that cannot be controlled either through the market or through government regulation, namely the organisations in the so-called "third sector," the "non-profit sector." One form of control that aims to survive within the framework of the state is based on an understanding of government that seizes upon the central structural deficits of both approaches while departing from the level of ideology. It tries to draw, as it were, on those elements from both models which have been successful, but not without developing its very own, new understanding of government and the economy.

A synthesis of the two general principles results in a concept of government that is characterised by the replacement of "either/or" arguments by arguments that take both perspectives into consideration. The French organisation sociologist Michel Crozier wrote as early as 1987 that a modern state would have to be a *modest state* (cf. Finger & Ruchat, 1997, p. 32). According to Fischer and Thierstein (1995, p. 655) this is a new concept of politics and government that does not negate or abolish everything that

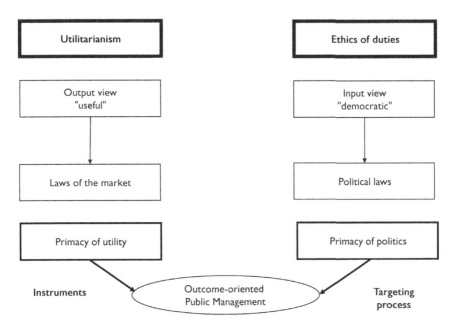

Figure 1.5 The legitimation sources of OPM. *Source*: Mastronardi and Schedler (1998).

preceded it but rather enters into a renewed partnership between the state and private individuals in addition to the traditional instruments; this idea can also be extended to a new partnership between government instances such as a confederation and its constituent polities. The outcome of this is the concept of the *guarantor state*:

1. The *range of tasks* to be fulfilled by government is subject to the decisions made by the political instances in the customary, democratically legitimated processes.
2. The government's *service depth* is limited in comparison with that of the welfare state; public services are only provided to fulfil the core functions of government responsibility *itself*. This limitation must not be equated with the neoliberal concept of a "mini-state" since government *responsibility* for certain welfare-guaranteeing functions is not discarded. The role of government in the development process, however, will be completely different: the state is meant to activate society to a greater extent by enabling and encouraging citizens/customers to participate in the provision of services (von Bandemer et al. 1995, pp. 58f.).
3. The guarantor *administration* that results from this acts in a target-oriented way but with more autonomy and more leeway for negotiations. The concrete definition of government functions is not decided on by the market but remains the result of a democratic process. These mechanisms are taken over by the new concept from the existing concept of the welfare state.
4. The borderlines between the state and the economy are not clearly drawn in the field of policy implementation; rather, they are characterised by overlaps. Inhabitants are *empowered* to create public goods themselves; public and private responsibilities are combined in public/private partnerships. Traditional authoritarian government thus changes into a partner, moderator and catalyst.
5. Into these fields of implementation, government deliberately introduces mechanisms which cause the highest degree of need satisfaction to be produced in the most efficient way, but without intending to enforce them through regulation. These mechanisms are taken over from market theory and adapted to specific situations.

The concept of the guarantor state leads to a notion of the politico-administrative system which can include elements of both the welfare state and neoliberalism. Outwardly, this becomes evident when both Sweden and the United Kingdom work with the same government concept while pursuing very different strategies. In the German-speaking area, there is no divide of the same dimensions but even here, projects have been initiated by governments of all political colours which today work with practically the same model (New Strategic Management, Outcome-Oriented Administration).

Definition 1.3: Guarantor state
In the concept of the *guarantor state*, the decision concerning the range of functions and the ideological configuration of government (neoliberal vs welfare state) is detached from the creation of the public services and the pursuit of functions. The range of functions is determined by political instances in democratic processes. In the fulfilment of its functions, government bears the responsibility for the guarantee of services in all areas of public functions but itself only provides the so-called core services of the state.

Administrative Responsibility in the Guarantor State

In order to take the step from an implementing administration towards a guarantor administration (Reichard, 1995, pp. 42f.), a new picture of the modus operandi of publication administration must be put in place. In a guarantor state, public administration bears the responsibility for securing the services based on democratically specified functions. In contrast to traditional administrative procedure, however, this does not mean at all that the actual execution of the task and the actual provision of the service, as well as its funding, must be organised exclusively within the administration. Instead, a distinction can be made between the responsibility categories proposed by Naschold et al. (1996, p. 102; a different structure of responsibility was created by Schuppert, 1998, pp. 421ff.):

- *responsibility for the guarantee* to ensure that a service will be provided as stipulated by objectives;
- *responsibility for funding* to ensure that the service provision will have a sound financial basis;
- *responsibility for execution* to ensure that the provision of the service is actually carried out.

The role of public administration in the fulfilment of functions depends on the category of responsibility to which a particular function belongs. In order to be able to react to differing requirements, public administration needs an organisation that enables it to act in accordance with the different categories of responsibility. This has led to the emergence of the model of the so-called *enabling authority*, particularly in the UK. The central element of this organisation is the establishment of an *awarding agency*. This agency is assigned performance objectives by the political leadership, and to attain these objectives enters into contracts with various (internal and external) suppliers.

In contrast to the bureaucratic model, which is hierarchical and self-contained, this assignment model admits of rational solutions in individual cases (for instance, according to categories of responsibility). However, this new structure also creates new incentives which have an impact on the self-perception of the administration. Evers et al. (2002) refer to social institutions to show that under a more market-oriented regime, public institutions develop into "social enterprises." What consequences this will have on the quality of services, particularly in the social sphere, remains open for the time being and must be subjected to close observation.

Public Governance

All these developments have a direct effect on the approaches to governance in the public sphere. Wherever the state is unable, or would like, to exercise control with the help of government power, it will look for alternative possibilities. It then becomes more and more important for the state to be able to employ the entire range of governance variants, i.e., that it is not only active on its own but, primarily, is able to activate others. These new forms of government activity have been examined under the heading of *public governance* ever since the late 1990s (Kooiman, 1999). A great deal is still being published on this issue, with the focus as a rule being on questions of political science. To delve further into this discussion would be beyond the scope of this publication. What is important in our view, however, is to indicate that public governance and the reform of public administration are not mutually exclusive but fertilise and complement each other both in conceptual terms and in administrative practice.

New Public Management as a Reform Model

In this atmosphere of strongly criticised public administration coupled with politics that was virtually floundering when it came to the governance of social developments, the model of a solution emerged which, on the basis of its simple message and its apparently radical course of action, held a great deal of attraction.

As a rule, reform programmes are a reaction to the perception of problem situations. A government that suffers from financial pressure will order cuts in expenditure. A government that suffers from acceptance problems among the citizenry will look for new forms of legitimation. With such a diversity of programmes, it cannot readily be assumed that a reform model with fairly homogeneous traits will be able to establish itself internationally for a specific period of time, bearing in mind the divergences between individual national situations. Yet the model of *New Public Management* virtually established itself—internationally in the late 1980s, and in the 1990s in the German-speaking area—as a standard model for modern administrations, as least as far as the rhetoric was concerned.

Exactly when this term was used for the first time is a bone of contention. However, it is likely to have been Rhodes (1991) in the early 1990s, who explicitly employed it as a term for a new approach to governance in administration. The point of departure was the need that was noticed in the developed world for a reform of public administration. On the quest for possible solutions that had not been dissipated by earlier reform projects, discoveries were made in various sources. For the German-speaking area, it was the descriptions of modern administration management in Dutch cities (Kickert, 2000) and at a national level in New Zealand (Hood, 1991; Boston et al., 1996), which local management scholars quickly took up and regarded as models. A great number of publications appeared about the various projects in the German-speaking area, such as practical cases primarily in connection with quality competitions by, among other, Hill and Klages (1993), but also conceptual approaches, for instance for public accounting and information systems by Lüder (Lüder, 1991; Lüder & Kampmann, 1993; Lüder, 1999), Budäus (1987, 1999), Schauer (1993, 2000) or Reinermann (1991, 1995; Reinermann & von Lucke, 2000).

Possibly the best known description of New Public Management is that by Christopher Hood, who lists the following points (Hood, 1991):

1. *'Hands-on' professional management*: active, visible, discretionary control in the public sector.
2. *Explicit standards and measures of performance*: goals, indicators of success, preferably expressed in quantitative terms.
3. *Greater emphasis on output controls*: resource allocation and rewards linked to measured performance.
4. *Shift to disaggregation of units in the public sector*: break-up of formerly monolithic units into smaller, decentralised and more independent units; working with global ("one-line") budgets; dealing with one another on an "arm's length" basis.
5. *Shift to greater competition in the public sector*: move to term contracts and public tendering procedures.

6. *Stress on private-sector styles of management practice*: move away from military/hierarchical styles, greater flexibility in hiring and rewards, greater use of PR techniques.
7. *Stress on greater discipline and parsimony in resource use*: cutting direct costs, raising labour discipline, resisting union demands.

Owing to closer international interconnections among actors in politics, consultancy firms and academic research, this new management approach spread more quickly and widely than had hardly ever been seen at an international level before. It must be emphasised, however, that although the elements of NPM were always described in the same or a similar way, the reality of implementation revealed vast differences (Pollitt & Bouckaert, 2000).

Publications and Rhetoric about New Public Management

Many contributions to the literature on NPM are normative in character. The term "normative" expresses the idea that these approaches raise certain solutions or ideas for solutions to the level of a norm, i.e., an element of reform that is worth imitating. However, these publications, which are conceived of as signposts for action, did not only devise their own content as a mission for the public sector but implicitly proceeded on the assumption of an ideal model of administration. An administration managed according to the first generation of NPM criteria is good, if as Buschor (1994) describes, it satisfies the three Es: Economy, Efficiency and Effectiveness. Later, in the course of an interdisciplinary debate on NPM, a number of further administrative quality features would be added, including, as in Bogumil (2003), the aspects of legality and legitimacy. Normative approaches are not limited to an analysis of conditions as they are but outline conditions as they should be.

Best-Practice Approaches

Best-practice research is often not primarily normative in character but aspires to a descriptive/analytical line of action. What it achieves in practice, however, is imitation, which turns the publication itself into a normative publication. The reason for this may well be found in the transdisciplinary reality of administrative reform. Political scientists tend to base their research on purely analytical methods, whereas—for professional reasons—lawyers and management scholars look for doctrines and norms (Bogumil & Jann, 2005). In particular, managers, who often work with graphs rather than concrete texts and whose yardstick for success is the practical feasibility of their concepts, have a tendency to adopt findings quickly if they appear to be useful for a practical solution to their problems and generally plausible. In point of fact, best practice is therefore a normative research approach no matter whether this is intended or not.

In the group of best-practice publications, roughly three perspectives can be discerned that are assumed by the authors:

The transmitters: they label a country (such as New Zealand) or a city (such as Tilburg) as exemplary and describe its governance practices. They cover a wide range, from detailed case studies (Boston et al., 1996; Herweijer & Mix, 1996) and analytical representations of ongoing developments (Aucoin, 1990; Hood, 1991) to attempts to make the practice of a model city (in this case, Christchurch) accessible for someone else's context (in this case, Switzerland) (Grünenfelder, 1997). The outstanding best-practice researchers of the North American region include Borins (1998a, 1998b), who explicitly refers to "local heroes" who transform the public sector. Even if the authors themselves often do not claim to have developed generally valid concepts, they still have that effect.

The international mediators: they assume an international macro-perspective by examining various practices in different countries and recommending that others should imitate them. It is primarily international organisations like the OECD (1996, 1997) or the World Bank (2001, 2003) who pursue this approach and try to induce other countries to imitate the successful practice they describe in their publications.

The national mediators: they are predominantly academics and consultants who, from the viewpoints of their own countries scan the world for examples that might furnish them with solutions to their own problems. They do not start out from one single model case but treat geographical sources quite eclectically, taking over ideas from all (allegedly successful) regions of the world. Most overviews of international developments in public management pursue this objective, a case in point being that of Banner and Reichard (1993), which was explicitly intended to provide the German reform with stimuli.

Best-practice approaches have the advantage that a depiction of practical examples often reveals that what was supposed to be impossible is in fact feasible. The authors try to evoke responses along the lines of "Anything you can do, I can do better." This course of action has evidently developed a great deal of mobilisation power at an international level, for which this method must be given credit. If we scrutinise it from a scientific angle, we will soon come across its weak points: how do we know, for example, that the examples that are laid out are really the best? Even competitions like that conducted by the Bertelsmann Foundation in 1993 to find "the world's best managed city" always only show an excerpt from reality. Even more weighty, however, is the charge of naivety with regard to the transfer of concepts: what may be best practice in one place may cause a lot of damage elsewhere.

Theoretically Conceptual Approaches

The theoretically conceptual approaches encompass the great number of publications which develop a certain management model on the basis of theoretical considerations and recommend it for implementation in a way that resembles the consultancy approach. Authors include the representatives of a generic management theory which assumes that there are hardly any differences between management in the private sector and the management of public institutions. The most prominent exponent of this group is most probably Peter Drucker, who claims that a good (standardised) management concept can serve to eliminate the grievances in both public administration (Drucker, 1980) and non-profit organisations (Drucker, 1990). He does not, however, supply convincing empirical evidence of this. Quite a substantial influence was also exerted by publications that presented their arguments on a theoretical/economic basis: Lane (2000), for instance, explicitly assumes a neoliberal stance and paints the picture of an NPM that has a correspondingly competition-oriented structure.

Reichard (1998a) warns against a naive adoption of private-sector concepts for the public sector—in our view, rightly so. In the Anglo-Saxon discussion, it was particularly the empowerment of public managers vis-à-vis the politicians that was criticised, which went hand in hand with the decentralisation and autonomisation of administrative units. The concept of *managerialism*—regardless of how vague it has become by now (Grüning, 2000)—symbolises this critical attitude (Pollitt, 1990).

The Analysis of Processual Elements

Authors who choose this focus are more interested in the reform process, the reasons behind it and the mechanisms that accompany it, than in the substance of reform. Barzelay (2001), for example, views administrative reform as a political programme ("reform policy") among many others and develops a method of how such policies can be analysed and discussed. Important considerations concerning this perspective can also be found in policy research, which investigates the question as to how policies cross national boundaries or what influence policies of supranational organisations have on national developments (Knill, 2001).

It is particularly against the background of the motives and interests of NPM that questions concerning processes of change come into their own. Pollitt (1993), for example, asks whether the managerialism of NPM primarily effected cost cuts or whether it was also possible to change the culture. Schick (1996) examines the changes in governance processes during the reform in New Zealand and compares them with experience from the USA. More recently, particular attention has been attracted by the integration of information technology into everyday administration. Here, an important contribution is made by structuration theory, which visualises the interconnections of the structures of an organisation and the actions pursued by that organisation's members. A consequence of this is that today, a distinction is made between *objective technology* and *enacted technology* and that the focus is on the question as to how organisations can be prompted to make sensible use of technology (Fountain, 2001).

The Interdisciplinary View of Reform

The literature on New Public Management is as extensive as that on any other issue that has been the object of academic debate over almost 30 years. Differences of opinion exist as much as neutral analyses, recipes as much as reflections and debates, and a narrow focus as much as holistic perspectives. It is therefore of particular importance to students of public management to point out an author's perspective in every case. In what context does he propose his arguments? From which discipline does he come? What is his target public? What research paradigm does he apply? Only when these questions of perspective have been cleared up can it be appraised how much of what he has written is in fact relevant to one's own context and issues.

Public administration is an object of study in various disciplines, with each discipline examining public administration on the basis of its own rationality. The diversity of rationalities in academic disciplines gives rise to the existence of views of public administration that differ a great deal and even seem to be incompatible with each other. With regard to administration, it is the rationalities of management, the law, political science and economics that are most important, along with the specific rationalities of the profession that dominate the public task in question.

In sum, it may be said that New Public Management is not a theory in its own right but a concept with different theoretical and empirical influences. All in all, NPM is better described as an international pattern of reforms with a wide variety of divergences and influences. The most important sources of the first generation were political approaches based on general conceptual considerations. Thatcherism in the UK was followed by an ideology that is today labelled neoliberalism; the reorientation of *public governance* in New Zealand (as extensive reforms would undoubtedly be called now, whereas at the time they were called New Public Management—which again illustrates the relativity of academic branding) was based on conceptual fragments of New Institutional Economics and management theory; and the new governance models of Dutch cities took their bearings from the new organisation ideas of the 1970s private sector (concern-division model). Not infrequently, then, partial ideas of theoretical concepts were blended with pragmatic opportunities to create local NPM models whose practical implementation shows only little common ground. Yet this may well have been the reason why New Public Management has achieved so much that is good in so many countries.

Discuss

The model of three-layer legitimation distinguishes between the roles of the citizen, the politician and the customer. What further roles could or should be defined in order to get a clear idea of individual people's relationships with the state?

The NPM model represented here attempts to combine deontological and utilitarian elements. How must this attempt be rated?

The guarantor state is depicted as a concept that admits of both welfare-state and neoliberal policies and is therefore beyond these great ideological disputes. But is it as neutral as it has been described?

Public management is interdisciplinary and must therefore find its way in various rationalities. How can this situation be dealt with in practical or academic reality?

Further Readings

Lyn Jr, Laurence E. (1996). *Public Management as Art, Science and Profession*. Chicago: University of Chicago.

Osborne, Stephen P. (2010). *The new public governance?: Emerging perspectives on the theory and practice of public governance*. London: Routledge.

Pollit, C. (2010). *New Public Management in Europe: Adaption and alternatives*. New York: Palgrave Macmillan.

Hughes, O. E. (2003). *Public Management and administration, an introduction*. Houndmills: Palgrave Macmillan.

Pollitt, C., Bouckaert, G. (2004). *Public Management Reform: A comparative analysis* (2nd ed.). Oxford: Oxford University Press.

2

Theoretical Foundations and Fundamental Premises of NPM

Whenever scientists develop concepts or theories, they base them on partially implicitly defined ideas about how reality works and is structured. An idea of the natural order of our society and its subsystems constitutes a necessary prerequisite for the logical development of a theory. NPM has based its concept on a number of assumptions concerning reality. In order to understand and structure these assumptions, we will first focus on the theoretical foundations on which NPM has been built. This will be followed by some of the assumptions concerning the understanding of reality in NPM. They are called the *fundamental premises* of NPM.

The Theoretical Foundations of NPM

As outlined in the previous chapter, NPM is a concept which has evolved and has been developed under the influence of a variety of theoretical and practical experiences. Here, the focus will primarily be aimed at the theoretical concepts and models whose ideas informed the concept of NPM.

Outcome-Oriented Public Management, pages 37–45
Copyright © 2010 by Information Age Publishing
All rights of reproduction in any form reserved.

Generally speaking, the theoretical roots of NPM are primarily considered to be in two theoretical currents: NPM is traced back to ideas of public choice theory and managerialism (Aucoin, 1990; Grüning, 2000; Lynn, 2005; Reichard, 1996). Looked at and analysed more closely, a reduction to these two approaches is simplifying and provides only a rough and diagrammatic sketch of the numerous influences and development thrusts as described at the end of Chapter 1. In his analysis of the theoretical foundations of NPM, Grüning (2000, p. 413) arrives at the conclusion that the practical elements that are subsumed in the model of NPM were influenced by a great number of theoretical approaches. According to him, the greatest significance must be accorded to public choice theory and the approaches of public management; however, important influences also came from classical and neoclassical economics, as well as from policy analysis. The most important conclusions and results of public choice theory and public management will be briefly discussed below with regard to their influence on NPM.

Public choice transposes the theory of rational decisions, which originated in economics, onto political phenomena. It is therefore also termed political economics. Public choice is concerned with incentive structures and decision-making processes which play a part in the provision of, and the decisions concerning, services in the political environment as opposed to those in the market. It is a characteristic of this approach to accept methodical individualism with the model of the *homo œconomicus* who acts rationally and is guided by self-interest. This results in the assumption that in the politico-administrative field, too, all the individuals including officials and politicians are out to maximise benefit. One of the studies that is relevant to the influence on NPM is Niskanen's (1971) study of bureaucracy and representative democracy, in which he demonstrates that as a rule, bureaucracies do not produce their services in the interest of optimising welfare and that the greatest benefit for officials results from budget maximisation. The structures of majority democracies and bureaucracies do not only prompt rationally acting people to strive for profit but primarily also incline them to rent-seeking (Krueger, 1974; Tullock, 1967). *Rent-seeking* denotes a behaviour displayed by participants in the market that aims to obtain perks through the exploitation of power or information advantages (for example through influence exerted on government control instances) in order to secure a largely non-performance-related income ("rent"). Examples include monopoly rents but also the provision of public goods to certain groups. The theory of rent-seeking shows that the sum-total of political activity can be interpreted as a fight for the attainment of such rents. Politicians safeguard their re-election by the consideration of certain interest groups, which, in turn, obtain rents as long as the costs of the exertion of political influence are lower than the benefits attained. Any additional costs this causes for the general public are spread among many people and are hardly perceptible in individual cases, so no one needs fear any sanctions. In their core, the results of public choice theory show that the structures of majority democracies and bureaucracies do not only lead towards a constant expansion of the state but also cause enormous losses in welfare resulting from inefficiencies and waste inherent in the system.

To limit the possibilities of rent-seeking, and thus the damage it causes, proponents of public choice theory call for the limitation of the extent of state activity (Buchanan, 1967; Niskanen, 1971). Since public choice supporters are convinced that every state action involves inefficiencies and welfare losses, the only possibility of curbing welfare losses is a limitation of state activity. Another thrust is the demand for a break-up of the monopolistic structures of state service provision and the creation of possibilities for state goods to be evaluated on the market. The monopolistic negotiation power of administrative units should be broken up since it is instrumental in the enforcement of budget maximisation strategies. Alternative forms of state service provisions are proposed which contribute towards an improvement in efficiency and make use of the forces of competition. Besides competitive tendering, such proposals include internal offsetting, outcome-oriented funding models, but also global funding systems with incentives for surplus utilisation (Demsetz, 1988; Downs, 1967; Niskanen, 1971). These two important conclusions and demands of public choice theory are reflected in individual elements of the NPM toolbox, such as the NPM methods and instruments of privatisation and outsourcing, but also the division of roles among funder, procurer and provider, which occupies a prominent position in NPM (cf. Chapter 4, Separation of Funder, Buyer and Provider, pp. 75ff.).

The approaches of public management are considered to be the second important current. They point in the direction of improving, and thus debureaucratising, the capacities of modern organisations by means of management structures and approaches (Aucoin, 1990). The central question in public management is therefore how managers in the public sector can intervene with a guiding hand, and what techniques they can apply to make their organisation successful (Grüning, 2000; Kettl, 1991; Lynn, 1996; Metcalfe & Richards, 1987). The influence of public management on NPM therefore generally lies in the reinforcement of and emphasis on management aspects in the public sector and manifests itself in the adoption of various management techniques and approaches in NPM.

Thus the question more likely to arise here is how NPM differs from public management or whether NPM is not in fact an "approach" of public management. An answer to this question cannot be unequivocal; according to the views advocated in this book, however, it can be summarised as follows. Owing to what it aims to achieve, NPM may indeed be largely viewed as part of the public management school of thought. One of the reasons for this position can be found in the course of time: ever since the beginnings of NPM in the 1980s and 1990s, elements of the national NPM agendas have become everyday business, and NPM instruments and techniques are often part of a well-known repertoire of public management. A differentiation between NPM and other approaches of public management and what is new in *New* Public Management had and still has a rhetorical-symbolic and an objective component. To begin with, the point was to draw people's attention by the "packaging" and propagation of this approach as new and sometimes revolutionary, thus projecting the necessity of a novel approach to control that would not only proceed in increments. Since NPM did not evolve out of theoretical public management, either, but was often developed by practitioners, this positioning was credible and authentic. In objective terms, a differentiation between NPM and public management can be seen in the fact that compared to many other aspects of public management, NPM provided a (pre)selected set of instruments. This toolbox was filled with many management techniques and instruments but—as discussed earlier on—also with results of other theoretical and practical schools of thought.

An analysis of the substance of NPM demonstrates, in sum, that its individual elements had indeed been known before NPM and had come from various theoretical sources. In NPM, they were combined and fitted together into a cohesive governance model. An analysis of its theoretical foundations does not only reveal what was known and what was new, but also provides important pointers to possible tensions and contradictions that emerged from this combination. After all, some of the individual theoretical currents are based on greatly differing basic assumptions and directions, which then also underpin the way individual elements function. Thus Aucoin (1990, p. 115) points out that the actions recommended by public choice theory and managerialism, as well as the assumptions on which they are based, result in deviations or even contradictions in the implementation of individual ideas. Thanks to a knowledge of the theoretical foundations, people can be sensitised to these tensions, which must not simply be understood as "misconceptions" but also represent a characteristic of modern governance systems.

Fundamental Premises

Under the heading of "fundamental premises," a few central assumptions and ideas on which NPM is based will now be addressed. These fundamental premises express value propositions and appraisals which are helpful for an understanding and classification of the concept.

An Optimistic View of Humanity

The idea of the fundamental nature of man exerts a strong influence on the concept and the ideas of NPM. Although every human being has his/her own character and acts in accordance with his/her experiences, the NPM model still contains generalised assumptions about human predispositions and behaviour patterns which are of crucial significance for the model to work in practice.

The Continental European version of NPM is based on an optimistic view of humanity which can be equated with McGregor's Theory Y (1960, pp. 45ff.). It proceeds from the following basic assumptions:

- People basically require no external motivation to do well at work, i.e., their motivation is intrinsic. They are ready and able to adapt to new situations in order to learn lessons from their own work.
- People act responsibly and appreciate having a certain amount of leeway to make their own decisions.
- People at different hierarchical levels are basically equal but are shaped by their functions.
- People are "complex men" who look for a task they can identify with, while at the same time looking for a social environment into which they can integrate.
- The predisposition to a relatively high degree of imagination, discernment and inventiveness for the solution of organisational problems is widespread in the population and not limited to individual elites.

In keeping with this view, NPM administration does not work through bureaucratic control and the threat of adverse consequences in cases of misconduct, but primarily relies on the personal responsibility of those involved (cf. also Behn, 1995). This view of humanity also underpins a number of modern management approaches but is in clear contradiction to assumptions of the public choice theory and the principal/agent theory, as well as to rationalist management models such as Taylorism. Although the international NPM literature frequently refers to *accountability*, German-speaking countries adopted this notion only to a limited extent. Instead in Europe, it is the concept of *responsibility* that is at the centre of more modern organisational considerations of administration. In this respect, NPM is in line with the views of more recent management theory, which is also breaking loose from the extrinsically motivated view of humanity propounded by Taylorism and is developing management forms for intrinsically motivated people.

In NPM, externally visible products of this view of humanity include an organisational structure that does not emphasise individual control and supervision, but focuses on effect and goal attainment. Members of staff are motivated to do target-oriented work through checks on goal attainment rather than, say, working hours.

This view of humanity alone ultimately enables NPM to establish a governance system that is based on contracts. The fundamental condition of a contract is trust. Only people who embrace an optimistic view of humanity believe in the efficiency of contracts. Conversely, distrustful people will cover their backs and bureaucratise administration.

The State and Administration Are Necessary

The state and its administration are institutions without which society is inconceivable. The state is inextricably linked with human societies and their coexistence. The fundamental premise that the state and public administration are necessary for a society to function (i.e., to coexist in peace) has a substantial influence on the arguments that buttress NPM: there is no intention to "abolish" the state or to forcibly reduce it through radical (full) privatisation; rather, NPM intends to strengthen its function by creating new competencies and leaner structures in order to adapt it to present-day requirements.

Besides considerations that are more strongly informed by political philosophy, practical experiences in, say, the UK and the US support the perception that privatisation is not the panacea for all the modern problems of the state (Naschold, 1995, pp. 32ff.). Rather, NPM aims to identify and solve problems that are inherent in the system of public administration. State responsibility is not relinquished, as would be the case with privatisation. The extent of this responsibility, however, is subject to decisions made by politics.

The Problems to be Solved in Administration Are Efficiency and Effectiveness, not Legality or Legitimation

The subjective perception of an organisation's main problems can usually be identified from the approaches pursued to solve them. If we have problems with democracy, a project for the advancement of democracy will be launched. If the proportion of female managers is too low, a programme for the promotion of women will be initiated.

The fact that NPM does not primarily deal with legality and legitimacy implies that these have a solid basis in "NPM prototypes." The main problem of our administration is not considered to be legality or (democratic) legitimation, but a lack of efficiency and effectiveness.

We could go even further: the *fundamental prerequisite* for NPM to work is its integration into a state structure that is in a position to implement the rules of NPM in a fair and predictable manner. In the European context, this would mean that a regulated and controllable administrative system and a stable political system would be expected to be in place. Only on such a basis can NPM be established and implemented. In a Western view, "implementing legitimation" is contingent on democratic legitimation (Schedler & Felix, 2000). Countries which are not democratically organised in the Western sense of the term will come up with different definitions of the legitimatory basis of NPM, yet the use of instruments that are typical of NPM is often still possible and leads to an increase in efficiency and effectiveness. The proposed new forms of governance are contingent on goal-setting and control mechanisms that are adapted to them, including external audits through an audit office. The assumption that the state in its basic form is in place and acts legitimately is thus a fundamental premise of NPM.

Rational Public Management is Possible

If administration is a complex social system which functions according to the same patterns as other organisations, it can be inferred that a form of management that works on the basis of management rationality must be possible in administration, too. On the cornerstone of this fundamental premise, NPM intends to reinforce management rationality by introducing management instruments into public administration. In the Anglo-Saxon world, the term used for this is *managerialism*, which includes all the measures required to strengthen management.

Although it is emphasised time and again that vague objectives which are difficult to operationalise are particularly typical of the public sector (cf. for instance Buschor, 1992, p. 210), NPM tacitly assumes that administration pursues clear-cut objectives. The idea of management by target agreements, which has been successfully used in the individual sector for years, is reflected in the performance agreements between institutions that are typical of NPM. Only clearly formulated and operationalised objectives allow for the compliance with such agreements to be monitored.

At the same time, this fundamental premise implies that private-sector experience can be transposed onto public administration at least in parts. Management instruments that have proved successful with service companies, for example, should also benefit administration. This does not mean to say that the private sector as such is always more efficient than the public sector. However, NPM adapts successful concepts and instruments for the purposes of administration.

Competition Results in More Efficiency and Effectiveness Than Planning and Control

In economic theory, the effects of the market and competition have been subject to extensive research. The insight that functioning competition leads to an efficient distribution of scarce resources has been widely accepted. This nexus is also tacitly assumed by NPM, which concludes from it that the internal and allocative efficiency of service production increases in proportion to competitive pressure. In keeping with this theory, NPM attempts to install the widest possible range of market mechanisms in the public sector.

This favourable basic attitude towards market mechanisms is justified against the background of the grievances in today's public administrations. Numerous observations and studies provide evidence of the fact that the principles on which decisions in the public sector are often based do not always guarantee the productivity of public services (Badelt, 1987, p. 55).

Politics and Administration Are Able to Learn

Many critics emphasise that NPM is not compatible with the processes in politics and administration that are customary today and that it is therefore bound to end in failure. This is tantamount to saying that NPM should adapt to existing conditions in politics (and thus, at least partially, in administration). However, NPM is based on the fundamental premise that political processes and structures can be changed, too. Politics and administration are perceived as learning systems which adapt to changing environmental conditions, albeit often slowly. The more openly these systems are constructed in relation to their environment, the faster those learning processes will progress.

We will show in the course of this book that reforms do not take place in a vacuum. Changes are always based on that which exists, and possibilities are limited to what those who are involved will approve. Even so, the adaptability of politico-administrative systems must not be underestimated.

Discuss

 What tensions and contradictions result for NPM from the two important sources, i.e., public choice theory and managerialism, and how do they have to be treated?

 Do the above-mentioned fundamental premises of NPM generally apply to reality or are there situations, disciplines and branches of administration to which these fundamental premises are not applicable?

 To what extent do the fundamental premises of NPM differ from those of Taylorism and Max Weber's theory of bureaucracy?

 What further fundamental premises for modern administrative management would you formulate yourself?

Further Readings

Niskanen, Jr. W. A. (2007). *Bureaucracy and representative government.* Chicago: Aldine Transaction.

Kooiman, J., Eliassen, K. (1987). *Managing Public Organizations—Lessons form a Contemporary European Experience.* London: Sage.

Grüning, G., Sandford, B. (1998). Origin and theoretical basis of the New Public Management. In *Managementforschung* (8th ed.). New York: de Gruyter.

Hood, C. (2005). Public Management: The word, the movement, the science. In *Oxford Handbook of Public Management* (pp. 7–26). Oxford: Oxford University Press.

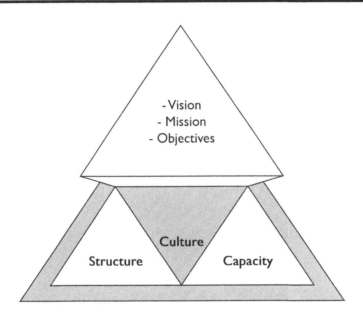

PART **II**

Strategic Elements in the Concept of NPM

3

The Strategy of NPM

This chapter will investigate the orientation of the field of action of strategy as perceived by NPM. The concept of strategy as a formal influence channel of processes of change in the sense of the model presented above contains elements such as an organisation's vision, mission and strategic objectives. They specify the direction of a public institution's development and, in so doing, always try to unite the essence and the actors in organised strategy processes. They do this with the help of instruments of strategic management (Schedler & Siegel, 2005).

The following sections will present the strategic elements of NPM which are crucial for this specific development direction of administrative reforms.

The Vision of "Human Administration" and of the "State as a Service Provider"

In management theory, a vision is the general guiding principle that constitutes the origin of entrepreneurial activity (Bleicher, 1991, p. 75). The vision of modern public management is first of all the idea of the configura-

Outcome-Oriented Public Management, pages 49–66
Copyright © 2010 by Information Age Publishing

tion of public administration as a "*human administration*" as opposed to the machine-like, depersonalised view of the bureaucratic model. In particular, "*human administration*" should be characterised by the involvement and consideration of elements of individual relationships between administration and stakeholders, as well as by a deliberate adoption of the human factor in the management model. Human administration wants to see satisfied citizens, customers and staff. This view requires that administration does not only work with precision, constancy and independence, but that it also has to make efforts to gain the acceptance of customers, citizens and its own staff. What is vital here is an orientation towards actual needs, which find expression on all three legitimation layers. Within the politically determined framework, needs should become an essential yardstick against which to measure administrative action without, however, supplanting existing criteria like legal security and legal equality.

The vision of modern administration is often described in terms of rather bold parallels with the private sector. The idea of the state as a *service provider* is intended to express the transposition of various concepts and instruments derived from the private sector and adapted to public administration. This transfer of concepts is meant to contribute towards more effective, efficient and citizen-oriented public administration. This aspect of the vision of modern administration according to NPM should be understood under the heading of "*town and country as service providers*."

"Human administration" and "town and country as service providers" complement each other to constitute the overall vision of administration. Whereas the idea of "human administration" is strongly geared towards present-day legitimation problems of traditional administration, it simultaneously disregards the lacking awareness of efficiency. To make clear that "human administration" is not intended to advertise a modern "welfare institution," it is contrasted with the image of a "*service provider.*" This metaphor is meant to illustrate that modern administration is expected to provide good-quality services to customers and principals. The extent to which administrative areas can be run with a service provision mentality depends on the type of the prevailing administrative function.

This vision embodies the modern view of administration, which is based on outcome orientation towards the common good, as well as on fundamental constitutional and democratic legitimation. This picture takes into account general conditions that are conducive to customer-oriented, efficient and effective service provision and avail themselves of suitable organisational structures, instruments, functions and members of staff to achieve this purpose.

Processes and Actors: Normative-Strategic Management

The distinction between normative, strategic and operative management tasks propounded by management theory (Bleicher, 1991, pp. 52ff.) can also help public management to align the activities of the entire system with essential aims and directions in order to make them more efficient. These "roles determined by management functions" are intended to replace the hierarchy and operative division of labour in the Taylorist sense that are widespread in bureaucracy.

The Distribution of Competence between Politics and Administration in NPM

A functional division of labour is not a feature of the traditional configuration of state organisation. The constitutional laws of Continental European states provide a distribution of competence between government and parliament through the separation of powers; however, practices vary substantially from country to country. The differentiation between legislation and the application of law contains some fundamental elements of the role allocation demanded by NPM.

The separation of management functions in NPM is often represented in simplified terms, as follows: parliaments and political bodies are meant to specify the "*what*," i.e., the strategic objectives, and the administration determines the "*how*" of achieving the objectives thus formulated. This functional division, however, does not sufficiently take into account the various incentive structures of politicians and the administration. Whereas the administration, and its top in particular, is able to identify the role of a management organ that should lead in accordance with legal and economic principles, the goal and incentive system prevalent in politics is plural in nature.

Politics and management constitute two worlds with different thought patterns, conceptualities, and sanctioning and rewarding mechanisms. This results in rationalities of thought and action which differ for politics and management. What is politically rational may strike management as irrational. Whereas management makes decisions based on fact, politics depends on majorities to drive its concerns home. Majorities, in turn, tend to be the result of complex negotiation processes, in which consent and rejection are bartered for things that are often only loosely connected. Politics and management are frequently equally target-oriented; only the way towards the goal can differ fundamentally. The art of leadership in the politico-administrative system consists in drawing the best out of both worlds by means of skilful combination.

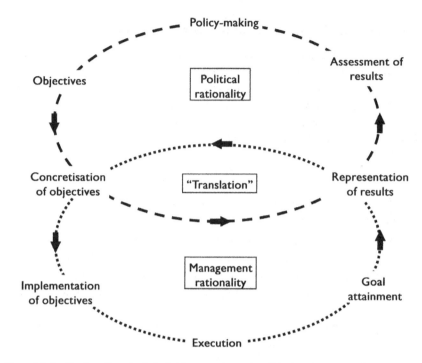

Figure 3.1 Rationality model: the integration of politics and management.

Figure 3.1 illustrates that there are two different decision-making circuits in administration and politics, which ideally overlap. However, this requires a so-called "translation function": political precepts must be dismantled into management-relevant objectives and, conversely, the results of administrative production must be categorised in terms of political aspects.

The way in which the parliament of the Swiss Canton of Zurich governs the canton's upper level secondary schools and colleges (known as *Gymnasium*, *Fachoberschulen* and *Berufsoberschulen*) may be regarded as an example that is typical of NPM. Parliament approves of one single sum for a one-line budget. The use and allocation of these funds to various types of schools and items of expenditure are in the competence of the executive and its subordinate administrative units. Coupled with the one-line budget is a performance agreement, which specifies the outcome to be achieved, and the output to be delivered, by the executive. Results indicators enable parliament to check whether the results stipulated in the performance agreement have been attained. An outcome indicator referring to the *Gymnasium*-type schools, i.e., the schools preparing pupils for university, that was included in the 1999 cantonal budget was the percentage of school-leavers who had obtained a university degree seven years later. Subsequently, this triggered off lengthy political discussions about what the purpose of the final *Gymnasium* examination actually was. Finally, a majority was won by that political group that opposed the idea that every young person who passed a *Matura* or *Abitur* examination should take up studies at university, so this indicator was dropped the following year.

Role Assignment According to Administrative Units

The assignment of roles to specific administrative units is strongly determined by the configuration of the government system. In parliamentary systems as they are known in Europe, it is the system of how the executive is constituted, in particular, that has a decisive impact on the relationship between the government and parliament. In a concordance system such as is in operation in Switzerland and most of the *Länder* in Austria, and in which the central political executive is made up of all the major parties represented in parliament, parliament is effectively able to exercise a control function over the executive. For role assignment under NPM, this means that parliament can assume a role of its own. In such a case, parliament will specify the outcome while the executive determines the concomitant output.

In competition systems, where the executive is formed by the parliamentary majority, i.e., by the government parties, the distribution of interests entails parliamentary control being exercised by the opposition only (Pede, 1999, p. 67). The "political merger" between the executive and the parliamentary majority, in which the executive has a predominating presence (Öhlinger, 1997, p. 149), leads to a situation whereby the desired outcome is effectively determined by the government or by individual ministers. The determination of the outcomes at ministerial level also takes into account the fact that a government in competitive systems has to be classified as a political organ owing to the incentive and responsibility structures. In the administration itself, the translation into output targets (concretisation of objectives) should be carried out by the top-level administrators and/or the heads of administrative units. With regard to the control mechanism, the role of parliament can be limited to the control function exercised by the opposition.

The Essence: The Strategic Objectives of NPM

NPM aims to improve the management and performance processes in public administration by the concerted inclusion of entrepreneurial and market-economic elements. All the various national forms of NPM share certain central principles, which can be formulated as individual objectives of NPM.

Such an objective is constituted by the reinforcement of the leadership function of parliament that was called for in the previous chapter and which should be achieved through strong concentration on strategic tasks. Further objectives will now be described below.

Customer Orientation

The term "customer" and any associations connected with it were originally strongly influenced by the distribution activities of private enterprises. The transposition of the notion of customers to the public sector is a *metaphor* for the postulated opening of administration towards citizens' concerns. It continues to lead to misunderstandings since the identification of customers and their role in the context of public services is not immediately apparent. The difficulty with the transposition of the notion of customer to public administration becomes particularly clear with examples from the field of law enforcement. Thus the question arises as to whether a publican can be stripped of his licence in a customer-friendly manner, or whether the customers of the police are citizens or criminals. The private sector's customer concept, then, cannot be transposed to the public sector without any modifications.

Transposition to Public Administration

In countries with democratic constitutions, the citizens are indirectly the principals of state service provision. According to the idea of NPM, they assume an additional role in certain situations, namely that of customers. In parts, the circle of customers is more extensive than that of the citizenry since customer status is not contingent upon nationality, age and gender. Public administration is called upon to take its bearings from the specific requirements that its customers have expressed in surveys conducted in this field. The introduction of a customer's perspective, however, is neither intended to challenge the fact that laws and procedures still have to be complied with, nor is it meant to transform customers one-dimensionally into the measure of all things. Rather, customers can be used to *monitor the range of services* and the *quality of the services on offer* (Bertelsmann-Stiftung & Saarländisches Ministerium des Inneren, 1996, p. 20).

People's role as customers is therefore added to their role as citizens at the level of implementing legitimation (but does not replace it!). The customer metaphor is meant to support the service provider mentality in administration.

It must be kept in mind that the private sector does not fulfil each and every customer's wish. *Conventions* to which we have long become accustomed stipulate the limits to customer expectations. It is a matter of course, for instance, that we do not take any products out of a shop without paying for them. The balance of interests between the seller and buyer of a product or service is established through the price. A customer's legitimate expectation in the private sector is limited to enforcing the seller's performance of the (purchasing) agreement, i.e., those who pay can take the product away. Taking away goods without payment would be an illegitimate expectation. Yet there remain two typical elements of the private-sector customer concept that must be perceived in a differentiated way for the public sector: *exit* and *voice*, i.e., walking away from a supplier and contradicting him, are not available without restriction to individual recipients of services in the state environment (for details, cf. Bogumil et al., 2001).

What is typical of the public sector is the division of roles between principals (i.e., the citizens) and the recipients of services (i.e., the customers). The principals define the customers' legitimate expectations in a democratic procedure. The administration is under an obligation to offer customers optimal services within the limits of their legitimate expectations.

Customer Identification

Who, then, are the customers and particular target groups of an administrative unit? The answer to this question is crucial to a customer-oriented form of administration. The circle of customers and their requirements differ greatly depending on which area a public unit works in. Even though the customer's role and position cannot be defined unequivocally and universally for the entire public sector, this does not mean that certain areas of the administration are able to exempt themselves from customer-orientation. In this context, it is often rather too quickly asserted that the notion of customers is inappropriate to this or that domain or that in certain domains, there are no customers but, if anything, clients.[1]

Definition 3.1: Customers

Customers of an administrative unit are people who individually accept services from it or improve the outcome of an output through activities of their own.

---

1. The use of the term "client" as opposed to "customer" illustrates that the people concerned do not face the administration as partners with equal rights but instead are dependent on the services provided by the administration. Typically, the term "client" is readily given preference in areas such as social insurance and the health service.

Klages (1998, pp. 125f.) proposes the following course of action for the differentiation of the customers of an administrative unit. To begin with, he makes a distinction between customers inside and outside the administration. In a next step, he distinguishes between "citizens" in general and particular "target groups" of the administration, after which he differentiates between customers in terms of the type of their relationships with the administration. This last, important step allows for the determination of areas and possibilities of influence for a variety of customer groups. Shand and Arnberg (1996) distinguish between seven different types of customers, who all make different demands on a service. The consideration of the type of relationship is an essential element of customer orientation in NPM and is also likely to differentiate this customer orientation from private customer relations.

The Meaning of Customer Orientation

The strong increase in the significance of the individual legitimation of administrative activities makes a deliberate management of services for customers a necessity. However, the location of customer orientation in the layer of individual legitimation is also expressive of the fact that customer interests cannot override citizens' interests at the level of fundamental legitimation. Rather, interests and stakeholders, who include the direct customers, should be weighed up in a balanced manner. In this way, citizens decide on the principle whereby the state is active in a certain area, as well as deciding on the extent and the outcome of these activities. Citizens determine, as it were, who may be a customer and what services he or she may expect. By contrast, customers exert an influence on the concrete form of these activities, i.e., the product.

Nonetheless, customer orientation in public administration remains a multidimensional concept. The various meanings and procedures that are associated with the concept of customer orientation are evidence of this (Klages, 1998, p. 124). The bandwidth of what administration staff understand by customer orientation today was illustrated by a study conducted at the University of St.Gallen. Whereas for some members of staff, customer orientation meant putting themselves in the customer's place, others conceived of customer orientation as having to explain the (unalterable) situation to their customers as best as possible. This shows how vague and unclear the meaning of customer orientation in connection with NPM can be within the same administrative unit. Thus the heads of administrative units would be well advised to define, together with their staff, what conception of customer orientation is appropriate to, and desirable in, their specific environment.

Outcome Orientation

Traditional public administration is managed and led through inputs. The underlying logic implies the following mechanism: the allocation of various inputs such as funds, personnel, equipment, etc., ensures that the administration will work in certain areas. This mechanism, which attempts to guide administrative action through the dosage of resources, gives rise to some corollaries that are not conducive to the system. As a consequence of asymmetrical information between the provider of resources (parliament) and the user of resources (the administrative unit), the incentives in the input-oriented system are such that it is not always attractive for the administrative unit to work efficiently and effectively. If an administrative unit succeeds in reducing its annual consumption of resources, a traditional budget will then allocate a correspondingly lower amount of funds to it the following year. Economically inspired work is punished by budget cuts, as it were. This explains phenomena such as "December fever," a term that describes the behaviour of authorities which during the last month of the year spend all their budgeted resources regardless of requirements in order to avoid a budget cut.

The central element in NPM is therefore a shift from input orientation to outcome orientation (cf. Chapter 6, Figure 6.1). The debating point and the yardstick against which to measure administrative action should no longer be the available means of production, but the outputs (products) that have been delivered or the outcomes achieved by such outputs. This means that political control has to be effected through results targets. This is backed by the consideration that ultimately, the outcomes are the goal that the state wants to attain, and not just administrative action.

Definition 3.2:   Outputs and Outcomes

Outputs represent the direct result of administrative activities from the perspective of third parties, i.e., external recipients of services. *Outcomes* are the indirect result of the provision of one or several services by the administration. Through a great number of different, mostly internal activities, the administration provides services to its recipients, which trigger off certain outcomes within these recipients or in their environment.

Outputs or Outcomes

For a long time there was uncertainty as to whether the outcome-oriented target values for administrative action should be defined in terms of outputs (products) or outcomes. In reform discussions, the target debate was long dominated by the output level. In more recent discussions, however, a shift has been recognised from outputs to the actual *outcomes* of administrative action (Hill, 1996, p. 33). In Switzerland, the going term was *"Outcome-Oriented Public Management"* right from the start (Buschor, 1993).

In principle, administrative action should take its bearings from outcomes since the task of the state has only been fulfilled once the desired outcomes have been achieved (Brinckmann, 1994, p. 173). The great difficulty with outcome orientation lies in the provision of evidence of valid cause/effect relations. It is sometimes impossible, or requires extreme research efforts, for a certain outcome to be measured and for the change that has been discovered to be traced back to a certain cause.

Outcomes can often only be recognised in the long term, which makes it even more difficult to measure and record them. Thus even if outcomes were the conceptually superior targets, we still frequently lack the necessary analytical instruments today. For this reason, NPM still often limits itself to output orientation. To attain the actual goal of outcome orientation, the administration has to gain experience and turn its efforts in this direction, for in conceptual terms, output orientation is only a type of "interim level" on the way to outcome orientation. The connections between activities and results can be represented as in Figure 3.2.

Reading aid: *Read upper row from left to right. The boxes of the lower rows explain the connections with the upper rows and provide examples.*

Within the sequence that ranges from the production of outputs to the realisation of outcomes through government measures, causal connections have always been suspected to occur which can be diagrammatically represented in so-called *functional chains* (Figure 3.3). In the pertinent international discussion, it is increasingly a feedback model that is gaining the upper hand, which on the basis of needs defines objectives that have an impact on the allocation of resources, trigger off activities and finally lead to outcomes. In the short term, these outputs spark off interim outcomes in third parties, which in the long term lead to final outcomes. Ultimately, the purpose of all this is to create such results in order to solve certain socioeconomic problems.

Implications of Outcome Orientation

Outcome-oriented management of public administration calls for new instruments and resources. Management by means of outcomes will only

By means of a great number of internal *acitivities*	the administration produces *outputs* for service recipients,	which triggers off certain indirect *outcomes* in these service recipients or in their environment.
Activities are the daily work in administration that is not delivered to third parties.	Outputs are the direct effect of a set of activities that can be seen by third parties. As a rule, it is aggregated into products.	Outcomes are the indirect result of the delivery of one or more outputs provided by the administration.
Examples:	**Examples:**	**Examples:**
Working on the objection files in connection with a planning application	Decision on the objection lodged against the planning permission	Compliance with building regulations in construction work
Drawing up a reconstruction plan	Noise-reduction measures in a street	Reduction of noise emissions
Procuring teaching aids	Lessons taught at school	Success of a class in a test
Preliminary examination of a patient	Therapy conducted in hospital	Recovery, improvment in the quality of life
Investigations in the case of a welfare recipient	Agreement drawn up with the welfare recipient	Reintegration, orderly living conditions

Figure 3.2 Activities, outputs, outcomes.

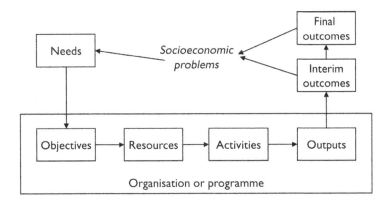

Figure 3.3 Functional chain. *Source*: Pollitt and Bouckaert (2000).

be possible if these are made measureable. The need for such information cannot be satisfied by traditional control and finance instruments. Any effective management by means of outcomes therefore requires a combination of financial accounting and performance management (cf. Chapter 7, Financial and Management Accounting, pp. 133ff.).

Outcome orientation must be reflected in the incentive system for staff. Output targets must likewise be found in the measurement/assessment system (Fairbanks, 1994, p. 117). The administrative units' responsibility for outcomes should support this.

Outcome orientation is also a central prerequisite for the introduction of many NPM instruments. The introduction of competition mechanisms (cf. Chapter 8, Competition Mechanisms in Public Administration, pp. 152ff.), for instance, is only possible once the different types of outputs generated by various public and private providers can be compared. Input data are unsuitable as a reference basis since every provider works with different combinations of resources. Only the product can be used as a criterion to assess an output and admits of comparison with other alternatives (Adamaschek, 1997, p. 42).

Efficiency and Effectiveness

In the context of performance measurement, a differentiation into three levels has established itself internationally: the so-called 3-E model (Figure 3.4). This model, too, is based on the functional chain but primarily refers to the three elements of resources, outputs and outcomes. It is based on the following three Es:

> *Economy* is achieved when the necessary resources can be procured with the smallest possible outlay of funds.
> *Efficiency* is achieved when specified outputs are delivered with the smallest possible use of resources.
> *Effectiveness* is achieved when specific outcomes are triggered off with the smallest possible volume of outputs.

It is necessary for all three Es to stand side by side as indicators for the measurement of the performance of outcome-oriented management. Economy alone cannot be the measure of all things but must be considered in conjunction with efficiency and effectiveness.

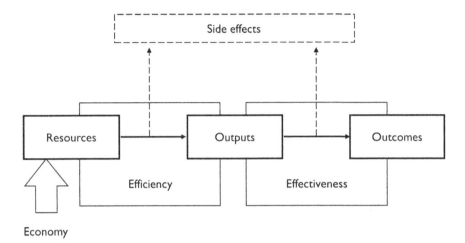

Figure 3.4   3-E model for outcome orientation.

Quality Orientation

The discussion of results, products and objectives gave rise to a debate on the quality of public outputs in many places. For a long time, NPM models themselves focused on the creation of the framework conditions and structures of a new organisation of administration without developing the new scope for action that would emerge in an administrative unit or any instructions for the exploitation of this new scope. In order to achieve more efficiency and effectiveness in public service production, however, processes and structures inside the administration must also be objects of modernisation. In conjunction with the customer orientation of NPM, which was explained above, it is necessary for an extensive quality management and quality awareness to be introduced into public administration.

Quality in the Public Sector

In public institutions, the notion of quality is traditionally primarily equated with legitimacy and correctness. Its extension to user and customer orientation adds some completely new elements to it which many of the people involved find unfamiliar: recipients of services become customers and may have expectations regarding administrative outputs. This means that it is not only *how an output is produced within the administration that is of importance, but also what benefit the customers can derive from it.*

Definition 3.3: Quality

Quality denotes the satisfaction of expectations and requirements (ISO 9000, 1999, p. 12).

However, it is a peculiarity of the public sector that the quality of public administration is circumscribed by several dimensions. In terms of the classic categorisation that Garvin (1984, pp. 25ff.) developed for the private sector, we can distinguish between the following quality dimensions for public institutions (cf. also Oppen, 1995, pp. 43ff.):

- **Output-related quality:** differences in quality are defined by a product's differing attributes. This includes the output itself (the "naked" product) but also the way in which the product is delivered to customers, as well as the additional services that are connected with it, i.e., the service system (Belz et al., 1991, p. 12).
- **Customer-related quality:** this covers the service producer's objectives of producing an *impact* on service recipients (as a rule, benefit) and includes customer satisfaction, but also an intended change in customer behaviour or skills.
- **Process-related quality:** this indicates the extent of process security (few mistakes) and process optimisation (speed, efficiency) and also includes the issue of lawful and correct service production.
- **Political quality:** in its capacity as the principal, politics assesses the quality of an output on the basis of the benefit that this output provides to politics. Here, the objective benefit for society is one component (for instance, an improvement in the standard of living, security), while another is social benefit (for example, social peace or cohesion in a community). Political quality is often predicated on the appropriateness of government measures.

A comprehensive quality management thus deals with questions of efficiency, effectiveness and the appropriateness of outputs produced by the state.

Quality Management Models

A glance into the past reveals that the concept of quality in private-sector organisations has had a turbulent history (Seghezzi, 1996, pp. 16ff.). A first "generation" of quality management was based on a static quality assurance that was purely limited to compliance with technical standards. Only with increasing competition and the consequent shift from a sellers' to a buyers' market did it become evident that far more components had to be taken into account by quality-conscious organisations. The competition was not won by the most perfect solution, but by the solution that was best able to satisfy customer requirements. It became clear that quality did not only depend on technology and process control, but also involved aspects such as the customers' view, personnel orientation and leadership. This resulted in the concept of Total Quality Management. A transposition of TQM, which has its roots in the private sector, to the public sector is thus also contingent on an analogous and extensive interpretation of quality that far exceeds "customer-oriented quality".

In practice, public administration works with various quality models, each of which tackles the issue from a different perspective (Felix, 2003). The three that are known best are briefly outlined below.

The *International Organization for Standardisation* (ISO) developed a standard for quality management (ISO 9000) with which a public administration can be certified. It focuses on the definition of and compliance with optimised processes and is considered to be a good entry point into quality management.

The Business Excellence Model of the *European Foundation for Quality Management* (EFQM Model) is regarded as the comprehensive model of a quality management that covers virtually all fields of action of public management. Certification is not possible with EFQM; rather, audits are conducted and a number of points are awarded. The European Quality Award can then be granted on the strength of these points.

Finally, the EFQM Model provided the European Union and its member countries with the basis for the development of the so-called *Common Assessment Framework* (CAF), which is very specifically attuned to the requirements of public-sector quality management. The European Institute for Public Administration (EIPA) has continued to develop the model and has distributed it in Europe ever since 2001.

NPM and Quality Management

NPM has a symbiotic relationship with quality management. Whereas NPM primarily focuses on the management of public institutions, i.e., prefers an interinstitutional view, quality management aims to improve the processes and measures within an organisation, i.e., constitutes an intrainstitutional view. For many administrations, quality management is the only way of satisfying the distinctly tighter output requirements that NPM confronts them with.

Conceptually, NPM and quality management are related in that both focus on the results of administrative action. NPM concentrates on socioeconomic problems that have to be solved with the results of administrative action, whereas quality management concentrates on the results experienced by the customers of administration. The functional chain described above establishes the connection between these two levels.

Competition Orientation

NPM is characterised by a systematic inclusion of the notion of competition in all areas of government activity. Since public administration, or leastwise its core, usually operates in a monopolist market, a competitive self-control mechanism used to be lacking. Irrespective of the staff's technical and management level and qualifications, a lack of competition in public and private organisations is conducive to more efforts being directed at the satisfaction of one's own organisation's requirements rather than customer requirements (Adamaschek, 1997, p. 25).

The objectives described so far and the reform proposals of NPM that were derived from them, such as quality, customer and outcome orientation, are incapable of changing the administration's monopoly situation. Although each of these objectives makes a contribution to a reorientation of administration that should not be underestimated, an environment must additionally be generated that integrates the other reform objectives and further increases the effectiveness of administration. This should be achieved through the introduction of competition and market-like structures (cf. Chapter 8, Competition in Public Administration, pp. 149ff.).

Market Mechanisms in Public Administration

NPM clearly aims to create market-like situations in as many areas of administration as possible. Naturally, the creation of a market environment is less fraught with difficulty in service-provision administration than it is in implementing administration. Since there are areas in public administration where no actual competition can be caused to develop between (public and private) providers, NPM envisages a number of instruments with which competition-like situations can be simulated. These instruments include pure cost/output comparison with third parties, competitive tendering or genuine awards of contracts to third parties (cf. Chapter 8, Competition Mechanisms in Public Administration, pp. 152ff.).

A comparison of German and international administrative reforms demonstrates that market and competition orientation are accorded a relatively low significance in German reforms. The idea of administration as a guarantor does not appear to have found roots there. Efforts to create competition between public and private providers and to outsource tasks were kept within limits. The creation of internal (quasi) competition, such as the intermunicipal benchmark test launched by the Bertelsmann Foundation, is the most widespread instrument of competition orientation in Germany (Reichard, 1997, p. 59).

NPM and Privatisation

Competition orientation in NPM is tantamount to a reinforcement of the state rather than a call for radical privatisation. In terms of the guarantor state described above, it is the job of the state to organise and maintain competition for public goods in its area of responsibility. In contrast to (material) privatisation, government retains the responsibility for the provision of the output and for the production of this output in a competitive situation.

Different countries use different strategies to try to create a competitive environment. In an internationally comparative study, Naschold (1995a, p. 84; 1997, p. 28) identified various forms of the marketisation of public functions. Whereas in the UK, for example, private-sector competition markets were pushed through compulsory competitive tendering, Christchurch and Phoenix preferred forms of planned competition between private and public providers. A further form of marketisation was chosen by Hämeenlinna (Finland), which was to make use of flexible legal structures (within public administration) to achieve a management flexibility that would result in cost cuts and cost shifting.

So far, the experiences and findings of this study imply that formal privatisations and legal structures alone are unlikely to trigger the hoped-for self-regulation mechanisms of competition. Only a working, permanent competition will result in more efficiency and effectiveness. In areas where market structures can be made use of, competition between private and public providers turned out to be most advantageous with regard to price, quality and customer orientation from the customers'/citizens' point of view. Generally, it is an operative and real-time feedback mechanism between citizens/customers and producers/administration that is especially important, which is why preference should not be systematically given to one type of competition mechanism (Naschold, 1995a, pp. 84f.; 1997, pp. 29f.).

Since in the New Zealand of the 1980s, which played a pioneering role in NPM, an enormous privatisation and liberalisation wave took place, NPM is often equated with privatisation. This, however, is an error: New Public Management actually requires institutions that are managed along these lines to still remain in the public sector.

Discuss

Q NPM is based on politicians' willingness to concentrate on so-called relevant questions and political course-setting. Is this assumption correct? Do politicians actually want to make transparent political decisions at all?

Q Public administration should behave in a customer-oriented way, i.e., it should assess its service provision more from the service recipients' point of view. What dangers and opportunities does the administration's customer orientation offer from the perspectives of the four disciplines, Management, Law, Political Science and Economics?

Q Politics is meant to control outcomes, public management is meant to control outputs. This distribution of competence is rather revolutionary for the German-speaking area. How do you rate this distribution against the background of your own experience?

Q Why has the management view of quality not become widespread in public administration so far? Are there any parallels between the development of quality management in the private and public sectors?

Q NPM clearly distances itself from (material) privatisation. How can this dissociation be explained? Where are the differences, where are the similarities?

Further Readings

Pollitt, C., Bouckaert, G. (2004). *Public Management Reform: A comparative analysis* (2nd ed.) (Chapter 4.) . Oxford: Oxford University Press.

Hood, C. (1991). A Public Management for all Seasons? *Public Administration, 69*, 3–19.

Osborne, D., Gabler, T. (1992). *Reinventing Government: How the Entrepreneurial spirit is transforming the public sector* (9th ed.). Reading: Addison-Wesley.

PART **III**

*Structural and Processual Elements
in the Concept of OPM*

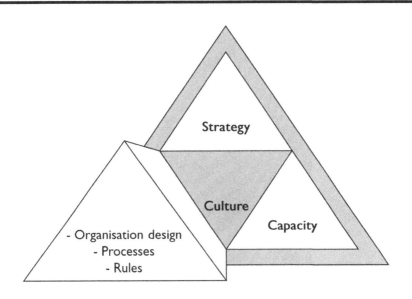

4

The Decentralisation of the Management and Organisation Structure

Hallmarks of the New Management and Organisation Structure

As a rule, today's structures and processes of public administration are geared to achieving the highest possible degree of security and a balance of risk in action. The attainment of the best possible results appears to play a subordinate role. Outcome-Oriented Public Management attempts to change this by consistently bringing structures into line with an output-oriented philosophy.

The fundamental strategy of outcome-oriented forms of organisation in public administration aims at an *extension of the responsibility* of administrative units. All the reforms—regardless of whether they take place in Australia, New Zealand or the USA—are backed by the idea that someone can only work efficiently and effectively if they are responsible for their actions and have to bear the consequences. For this reason, the goal is a form of organisation whose structure is similar to that of a multicorporate enterprise (such as a management holding company). The following characteristics are considered to be ideal in type:

Outcome-Oriented Public Management, pages 69–92
Copyright © 2010 by Information Age Publishing
All rights of reproduction in any form reserved.

- Ministries and administrative units are structured according to output groups, i.e., the organisation of public administration is aligned with customers and outputs rather than traditional bureaucratic influences. The number of ministries and specialist administrative units is kept as low as possible.
- Functions, outputs, production processes, markets and target groups that belong together are subsumed in manageable organisational units, which are responsible for their results, in order to create unequivocal responsibilities and optimal administrative processes.
- The responsibility for previous tasks of interministerial units is largely delegated to administrative units. The tasks of interministerial units with a coordinating function are combined in a staff office (*central coordination service*), which reports directly to the top-level administrators. Interadministrative services can still be offered centrally but must be regularly funded by internal settlements whose acceptance and amounts are fixed in the budgeting process (cf. Chapter 4, Interministerial and Multicorporate Functions, pp. 86ff.).
- Competencies and responsibilities are divided up between three levels, namely those of the output funder, the output buyer and the provider, and new roles are defined for the institutions (cf. Chapter 4, Separation of Funder, Buyer and Provider, pp. 75ff.).
- Control is basically executed through performance agreements and one-line budgets. To monitor compliance with these, control units must be set up.
- A well-structured control and information system that is more strongly based on results indicators ensures the political and administrative management of the decentralised units.
- Comprehensive quality control is already stipulated in the performance agreements and ensured by the control units.

Outcome-Oriented Public Management aims to create administrative units that largely organise themselves autonomously and constantly adapt to the changing nature of their environments. To ensure that this is possible, such units should not fall short of a minimum size.

Political Leadership and Administrative Management

The organisational structure required by OPM attempts to transpose ideas of private-sector *corporate management* to public administration in order to enhance the latter's controllability and capacity to act in a way that is similar to that of a multicorporate enterprise. As addressed before (cf. Chapter 3, The Distribution of Competence between Politics and Administration in NPM, pp. 51ff.), this calls for a clarification of the *roles of politics and the administration*, but also for the introduction of an actual management level in public administration. For the political levels, this entails a new conception of their roles, which should have an impact on the activities of political bodies (fewer operative and more strategic-normative functions). Owing to the alignment of control with output groups and the simultaneous global allocation of funds, political interest will shift from the detailed specification and monitoring of credit lines to the output side of administration. At first sight, this might look like a loss of political influence. Closer scrutiny of the information and decision-making possibilities reveals, however, that parliaments will have more influence on outputs actually generated by the administration than was the case previously. Experience gained from projects demonstrates that politicians have new possibilities that they never expected themselves—cost-cutting measures in particular acquire an unforeseen quality when detailed budgets are no longer the only information that is available but debates focus on the public value created by specific output groups, the definition of quality standards or the outsourcing of output groups to the private sector.

This realignment of the political organs in the sense of OPM requires that these organs should make more *finally programmed decisions*, i.e., decisions concerning the "what?" and "what for?" rather than the "how?" This, however, is hindered by some central structural problems of the political system. Whereas the processes and mechanisms of the political system are based on representative-democratic leadership with democratic representation mechanisms, OPM aims to allocate roles and responsibilities to politics and the administration. The separation of roles thus envisaged results in conceptual tensions between political and administrative control at their interface (cf. Chapter 3, The Distribution of Competence between Politics and Administration in NPM, pp. 51ff. and Figure 3.1). International comparisons reveal various examples of how the entire governance structure can be configured in order to surmount these tensions. An international analysis conducted by Naschold (1997, p. 324) shows that the notion of managerialism is predominant in most of the cities that were investigated. Public management thus also appears to dominate politics. The opposite example of political hegemony was also in evidence. A contractual relationship between politics and administration was only discovered in one single city, whereas a relationship of mutual exchange between politics and administration is more widespread.

At a municipal level, the reason for the difficult assertion of the focus of politics and administration on their new roles also appears to be found in a limited scope of action on the part of politics. Although municipalities are entitled to self-administration in certain areas, their scope of action is rather small; this results in a situation whereby local politics is characterised by a very high degree of powerlessness and helplessness. As Bogumil (1997, p. 36; cf. also Kleindienst, 1999, p. 108) pointed out, the basically modest decision-making scope of local politics automatically gives rise to a neglect of political target discussions, which in turn develops its own momentum of meddling with technically ongoing administrative business. In keeping with Naschold's findings, this aspect illustrates that the focus on strategic and operative concerns will not come out of thin air; rather, politicians and administrators will have to strive for it deliberately and from their own conviction.

Decentralised, Flat Organisation

The most outstanding *structural* change introduced by OPM is an *increased decentralisation* combined with the establishment of a *high degree of autonomy for the decentralised unit* with its own management and decision-making structures (cf. Chapter 4, The Level of the Providers, pp. 83ff. and Figure 4.4). Its differentiation from centralisation is not only structural, but also cultural in nature:

> Centralization is characterized by the use of before-the-fact controls, by rules and regulations that specify what must be done as well as how, when, where, and by whom.
>
> Decentralization is characterized by after-the-fact controls, by rewards and performance targets that are high enough to elicit the best efforts from an organization's personnel. (Thompson & Jones, 1994, p. 21)

A prerequisite for the autonomy of an administrative unit is a clearly demarcated remit which can be approached and shaped in an entrepreneurial spirit (Gomez, 1981, p. 110). In public administration, this is countervailed by two trends: for one thing, the principle of the division of labour has struck particularly deep roots in administration; for another, politically sensitive tasks are often deliberately assigned to various units in order to achieve a balancing effect, i.e., to prevent power from being concentrated in any particular area. It is obvious that this is bound to impede efficiency. It is therefore necessary to create more "enterprises within the enterprise" in administration (Gomez, 1981, p. 110), where the discretion accorded to the units depends on both their internal structures and the development of their envi-

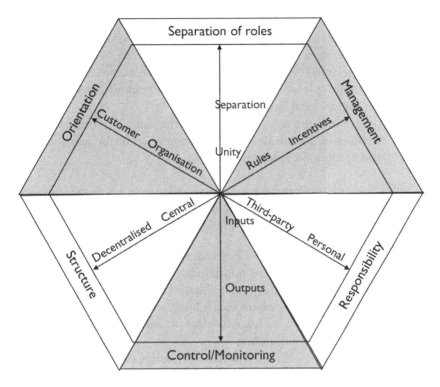

Figure 4.1 Dimensions of decentralisation in OPM.

ronments, and is likely to vary with these. From a cybernetic point of view, it is perfectly justifiable to reduce the discretion of these output centres in times of crisis, whereas it can be extended during an economic boom.

The necessary steps of decentralisation do not only concern the structure of administration but must be understood in a wider sense. As illustrated in Figure 4.1, the politico-administrative system must turn away from its centralist orientation in six different dimensions, some of which have already been touched upon:

- The structures will become more decentralised, as will be demonstrated in this chapter.
- (Centralist) inward orientation will be replaced by (decentralised) customer orientation.
- The (centralist) unity of principals and agents will be decentralised by a separation of roles—though not necessarily following the economistic perspective of agency theory.

- Management through incentives will allow for decentralised approaches to solutions, whereas management through rules creates a tendency towards strong centralisation.
- The personal responsibility of operative units and members of staff will replace the centralist third-part responsibility of the upper hierarchical levels.
- Centralist input control and monitoring will be transformed into a system of decentralised output orientation by the management and accountancy auditing bodies.

Once these considerations have been applied in full, this will lead to an organisational structuration into *centres of responsibility*, whose introduction is contingent on the satisfaction of the following requirements:

1. Autonomous decision-making concerning revenue and expenditure.
2. Delegation of the full responsibility for economic activities to the centre of responsibility (for both good and bad results).
3. Limitation of government control to:
   - the stipulation of the performance objectives and the regulation of output funding,
   - the issuance of instructions to guarantee that the performance is achieved,
   - pricing to the extent to which output costs cannot be determined by the market (monopoly outputs, outputs in the field of the social economy; public value),
   - checks on transgressions of the limits of discretion in law enforcement,
   - monitoring the accounts and prevention of uneconomic outputs.

These requirements, which are listed as preconditions for the creation of centres of responsibility in public administration, are largely in line with the concept of OPM. At the same time, it must be said that these are very far-reaching forms of decentralisation; in practice, the application of all three points listed above tends to be the exception rather than the rule (cf. also Jann, 2005).

Decentralised structures result in substantial *advantages* for public administration (Budäus, 1995, p. 56):

- a reduction of complexity;
- the creation of transparency;
- the allocatability of costs to outputs;
- the establishment of a basis for one-line budgeting;

- the congruence of decision-making and responsibility, which can be achieved through the union of specialist responsibility and the responsibility for resources;
- possibilities for the institutionalisation of functional mechanisms that are similar to competition.

However, decentralisation also carries the danger that possibilities of control are lost. This gives rise to a centrifugal tendency that causes administrative units to arrogate more and more independence to themselves, which in turn leads to a less than optimal fulfilment of tasks. For this reason, new internal coordination mechanisms must be put in place which prevent excessive detachment and enable administration to develop in a coordinated way. This will be the subject of the next chapter (cf. Chapter 4, Remarks on the Separation of Roles in Different Government Systems and Polities, pp. 77ff.).

The requirement of an improved monitoring of results entails substantial innovations in management accounting for the structures of administration. These activities will have to be reinforced and, primarily, to be coordinated at each hierarchical level, which will not least constitute one of the main functions of the central control unit. This is not to argue the case for an expensive parallel organisation with additional personnel. However, personnel must be designated who are given the competence to deal with these tasks and will have to build up the necessary know-how.

When we look at this structure (Figure 4.2), which appears to be rather elaborate at first sight, we must bear in mind that it replaces many decision-making channels since in the OPM model, a great deal that previously ended up in the in-tray of the top-level administrators has already been decided upon at the level of the provider. If an administration succeeds in limiting management accounting to what is strictly necessary and establishing a lean organisation in this field, too, then substantial process simplifications may be expected. The detailed form of management accounting will be looked at more closely in one of the following chapters (cf. Chapter 7, Financial and Management Accounting, pp. 133ff.).

Separation of Funder, Buyer and Provider

In a traditionally organised administration, decisions are largely made centrally. Competencies are concentrated at the top even though they can be delegated by the top-level administrators. Ultimately, the top hierarchical levels are mostly even consulted on detailed decisions.

In OPM, these chunks of competence are separated into funders, buyers and providers of outputs. According to the traditional view, public admin-

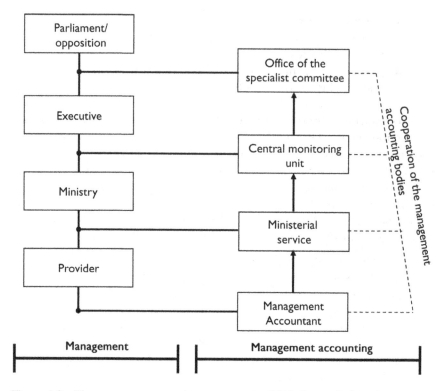

Figure 4.2 Management accounting structure in OPM. *Source*: Egli and Käch (1995, p. 177).

istration is simultaneously and monopolistically funder, supplier and buyer. This personal union makes *price negotiations* unnecessary. The—often only— remaining control mechanism for the expenditure incurred by the adminis- tration is the annual budget. The frequently vaunted view that public-sector outputs do not have a price may well be traced back to that fact.

This separation creates an internal or—depending on the administrative unit's nature—external market with suppliers and buyers. Even if there is only one buyer (for instance, the ministry), more than one supplier may appear on the market. Inside the administration, a bilateral monopoly may occur (this is the case when the market consists of only one buyer and one supplier) if the principal is an authority which fulfils a law-enforcement function (for example, the police). In such cases, a separation between supplier and buyer does not result in a free pricing process but in a clear demarcation between long-term output planning, strategic objectives and their implementation. The linking elements are budgets, in which funds are allocated as lump sums (*one-line budgets*) if at all possible, as well as performance agreements.

The internal customer/supplier relations also have an aspect of quality. In its capacity as an internal customer, the buying administrative unit will carry out a quality control as soon as it has received the output or activity[1] of another administrative unit, and it will complain if the output does not satisfy the desired criteria. In this way, numerous interim quality inspections take place before an output is ultimately passed on to the service recipients outside the administration.

The principle of separating output funders, buyers and producers brings about substantial changes in the organisational structure of the politico-administrative system. A clear-cut separation into pure functions is not always possible, but as a rule distinct *focal points* can be defined.

The new structure envisages three separate levels. The separation of functions illustrated in Figure 4.3 serves as a model; particularly in large-scale administrations, the output buyer's role can also be delegated to individual authorities. Moreover, the figure ignores the fact that there are also horizontal buyer/supplier relations (for example, in the area of interministerial service delivery), which results in an indirect form of funding.

Remarks on the Separation of Roles in Different Government Systems and Polities

This book aims to illustrate the concept of OPM as generally as possible rather than with reference to the peculiarities of specific countries. However, borderlines will be drawn with regard to the structure of the politico-administrative systems. When it comes to separating the roles according to OPM at national and sub-national levels, it is particularly the executive system that has a great influence. Whereas in competition systems, the executive is formed by a parliamentary majority party or coalition, it may be directly elected at the sub-national level of coalition systems. The differing power structures and power-balancing structures that result from this in competition systems tend to run along a "fault line" between government (parties) and the opposition, whereas in coalition systems they are established between parliament and the executive and are less dependent on affiliation to political parties (cf. Chapter 3, The Distribution of Competence

---

1 Whether we speak of an output or an activity depends on the relevant observation unit. If a single office is considered to be the relevant observation unit, then all the outputs which it passes on to its internal customers (other offices) and external customers are outputs in the sense of products. If, however, the entire administration is regarded as the relevant observation unit, then all the outputs that are supplied to internal offices are activities, and only those going to external service recipients are products (cf. Figure 64, p. 144).

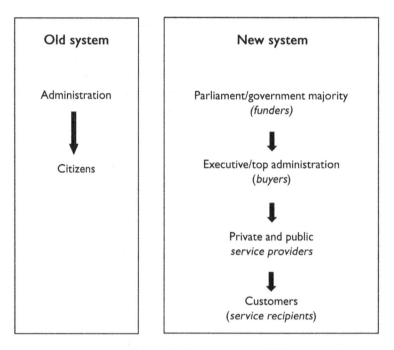

Figure 4.3 Separation of funders, buyers and providers.

between Politics and Administration in NPM, pp. 51ff.). Although cabinet members are the political heads of ministries or chancelleries, the different executive systems cause their members to have different conceptions of both their roles and themselves, which has a considerable effect on the separation of roles according to OPM. Added to this, there is often no authority to issue directives or guidelines between members of the executive. At the same time, in some countries, ministries do not have the post of a top civil servant who is in overall charge of the administration, in contrast with other countries, where officials in the position of secretaries or undersecretaries of state fulfill an internal management function throughout their ministries.

In connection with the discussion about the separation of roles in OPM, these differences between the systems have a particular effect on the allocation of the role of the buyer of public services, i.e., on the level that is responsible for the conclusion of performance agreements with the output-providing units.

The situation at the level of municipalities and municipal administrations is different yet again. Thus, say, the direct election of a mayor may provide him or her with a very independent role that is relatively free from the council's constraint. The output buyer's role is therefore often to be found in the executive.

An example will serve to illustrate how the roles of politics and administration, i.e., funder and buyer, can be shaped. In practice, the initial attempts to assign roles at the top of the administration were fraught with some difficulty. In Australia, for example, a first reform wave tried to involve ministers in the management responsibility for the administration. This attempt failed, which is why subsequently the rule was established that ministers should only be involved in the actual management to the extent demanded by the clear stipulation of political directions and the formulation of concrete results objectives. The actual responsibility for the management of the administration was devolved on the managers inside the administration. This division of tasks was structurally supported by an institutional separation of ministries that provided ministers with political advice, and executing agencies charged with the delivery of government outputs. The responsibility and accountability structures were configured accordingly. The managers of the agencies report to the ministers via the ministries and are accountable to the minister for the achievement of the operative objectives; the ministers, on their part, are accountable to parliament for the ministries' work and the agencies' performance (Zifcak, 1994, p. 75). In this example the ministries, which monitor the attainment of the performance targets, are the central control instance in the role of the output buyer. The ministers themselves, as well as a large part of their ministries, are also *politically* active and thus work more in support of the funders' level than of the buyers' level.

These preliminary remarks are intended to alert readers to the fact that in the following sections devoted to a discussion of an assignment of roles, it will always be necessary to visualise the nature of the polity under scrutiny.

The Level of Funders
The level of funders is where the general objectives of administrative policy are determined. This is done in various harmonisation and negotiation processes and is reflected in, for instance, the context of codification and law-making processes, as well as in annual budget decisions in which financial resources are allocated to different domains.

The organs and representatives of the level of output funders are the citizens and—depending on system-specific differences—the elected representatives of the people such as parliaments and executives. They are termed output funders because they have an authoritative influence on the supply and funding of public goods (outputs). Thus it is usually in the competence of parliament to make decisions regarding the utilisation of taxpayers' money and to fix fees, levies and other prices for public services. Its funding decisions are usually closely related to the determination of the supply, i.e., to the question as to which services are offered by the public sector and to what extent. Since the output funders are by no means always also service recipients, this results in interlinkages and role conflicts between customers and output funders.

The separation of roles in OPM primarily refers to an assignment of tasks in the context of the administrative control process. Accordingly, the role definition should chiefly be of assistance in the creation and application of the control instruments, information and processes with whose help policy objectives can be mapped and achieved in the implementing arm of the government, i.e., the system of public administration. The definition of a funder role, then, emphasises the following three aspects of coordination: to start with, it is the output funder's tasks to set out focal points and realignments in the production of administrative outputs. Then it is highlighted that the budget process performs a central coordination function that serves to push the political objectives through and to exercise overall control of the administration. Finally, the designation as a funder also points to the significance of an evaluation of benefits and results to establish whether the objectives have been attained or even only what effects have been achieved with certain items of expenditure.

The question arises as to what changes OPM entails for the level of output funders. Here, a distinction must be made between this level's institutionalised organs such as parliaments and executives, and the general public, i.e., the citizenry. In the former's case, they persist in their previous structures. The control instruments, specifically the nature of budget bills, change in accordance with outcome-oriented requirements. Experience gained from projects in Continental Europe reveals that after the transitional stage and once the control instruments have been adapted, budget debates can be observed to shift from individual financial items to medium-term-oriented performance discussions (for effects of OPM, cf. Rieder & Furrer, 2000; Rieder & Lehmann, 2002).

The question as to what changes OPM would entail for citizens usually elicits a brief answer: the democratic instruments should not be encroached upon; primarily, citizens should receive a better service as customers of the administration. Moreover, citizens would not only be able to exercise their rights and have to fulfil their duties, but would be increasingly involved in the political decision-making process by means of periodic *surveys* and other forms of participative inclusion. However, there might well be crucial changes for citizens depending on the make-up of the model. The spectrum of conceivable interventions is wide and ranges from rather informal adaptations to a possible reorganisation of direct-democratic instruments, which are available to a higher or lower degree in different government systems. This happened in the Swiss Canton of Solothurn in 2004, when the so-called *performance initiative* was enacted as a new people's right (Finanzdepartement Solothurn, 2003). Moreover, the previous layout of the annual accounts of a polity are likely to look distinctly different, as the annual reports from New Zealand, Germany and other countries demonstrate. Detailed lists of account items are replaced by a representation of the polity's objectives, so outputs and global financial expenditure look more attractive to the residents. The administrative outputs and their outcomes are depicted in a transparent and comprehensible way, so much so that in some countries such annual reports even sell in bookshops.

The Level of the Output Buyers

Output buyers bear the responsibility for compliance with the performance budget vis-à-vis the output funder and are responsible for the provision of the various tasks and outputs of the public sector. In this context, it is immaterial whether they want to buy the products from third parties or to have them produced by the administration since, according to OPM, the output buyers should be granted an extensive implementation competence with regard to the way in which they procure outputs (*make-or-buy*). However, they bear the political responsibility for the outputs in respect of their quality, quantity, availability in time, and access for customers—they are the *guarantors* for the correct provision of outputs. Thus they have to exercise the *management responsibility* in cases of deviation from and non-compliance with contracts and they are compelled to select and monitor their providers well.

In organisational terms, the output buyers' level is located in the top level of the administration in the German-speaking countries, with the output buyers' role being assigned to different management positions in different systems (cf. Chapter 4, Remarks on the Separation of Roles in Different Government Systems and Polities, pp. 77ff.). Depending on the structure and size of the polity, ministries or major authorities and administrative units may assume central responsibility for the procurement of outputs for customers.

For one thing, the designation "buyer" enshrines the differentiation between guarantee and provision, which OPM strongly emphasises in comparison with the traditional model, on the structural level. An output buyer is responsible for the provision and supply of public services in accordance with the output funder's requirements. At the same time, however, the buyer's role serves to emphasise that the primary interest is in outcomes and outputs and that this level's self-conception is not limited to that of a "supreme producer" but must be understood as a critical and judicious mediator between funder and producer or, to use another term, as a "smart buyer" (Kettl, 1993). The buyer's label, however, should not make us forget that the top-level administrators still exercise a classic management function. Top-level administrators in ministries, authorities and administrative units remain the interface between politics and the administration. They are responsible for the management of the polity. According to OPM, the top administrative level does not intervene in the administration's operative business to the same extent as is the case in the traditional model. It still exerts a great influence on the form and contents of agreements. Irrespective of all the freedom that is intended to be accorded to administrative units, top-level administrators remain the supreme management body and thus in many cases make the final decision in management issues (for instance by the stipulation of standards for personnel work). Besides, the top-level administrators exercise representative functions and introduce concerns voiced by parliament or council into the administration.

Changes brought about by the separation of roles at this level affect both a factual-objective dimension and, primarily a structural-organisational one. It may be assumed that here, too, discussions and harmonisation processes will increasingly home in on essential issues. In a classic bureaucracy, too many decisions concerning details are taken to the top administrative bodies with the result that essential decisions are not infrequently delayed. This increasing focus on essential matters is achieved through an extensive delegation of operative management responsibility to operative units, as well as by standardised coordination through instruments such as performance agreements.

Gradually, a new know-how for the preparation and monitoring of contracts with providers will evolve in the output-buyer units, which are organised as separate departments. These support services fulfil all the functions that are required for the management of the output buyers' level, i.e., also interministerial functions that were previously carried out by the ministries' own administrative units. In particular, these functions refer to the area of management accounting and can be described in more detail, as follows:

- analyses of existing structures and processes in the authority in question;
- competitive tendering if or when new quotations for contracts must be obtained;

- assessment of the quotations, and preparation of the selection decision by the ministerial/administrative leadership;
- preparation of the contracts with the providers;
- monitoring the providers' contractual performance;
- compilation and evaluation of the providers' financial statements;
- drawing-up of financial reports for the output buyers' attention;
- preparation of measures in cases of extraordinary incidents;
- general management support for the top-level administrators.

The Level of the Providers

Provider is the designation of an organisational unit which produces products, i.e., outputs, at stipulated conditions and delivers them to the customers. The providers' level is in a contractual relationship with the buyers. It is accountable to the output buyers for the production of outputs and for compliance with the specifications, and it bears the operative responsibility.

In *organisational* terms, the level of providers covers a very heterogeneous and wide range of organisations. To begin with, this includes administrative units with *implementing functions*. Moreover, it extends to external organisations that have been entrusted with the production of public services by means of contracts and agreements. These may be administrative organisations of other polities, privatised and outsourced organisations, but particularly also private and charitable organisations. The unit's legal form, and its position as an institution or organisation is immaterial for its role as a provider; only its function as a producer of public services for the relevant polity is of interest. Providers often take on tasks that do not only have a service-provision nature but are connected with law-enforcement functions. Depending on the situation, they may also be accorded the competence to issue guidelines for third parties. It is also conceivable that providers, on their part, instruct further persons or institutions to become involved in output production. This possibility must be created for comparatively large-scale task domains in order to achieve the highest possible degree of flexibility.

OPM causes changes to output-producing administrative units in that they are granted a high degree of autonomy, but at the same time also more responsibility. In OPM, providers are expected not only to produce outputs, but also to assume entrepreneurial responsibility for the organisational unit. Besides having to do their job properly, they are also increasingly confronted with, and assessed according to, results. The incentive that providers receive for this change consists in greater discretion and a transfer of control structures to results. Experience with reform projects shows

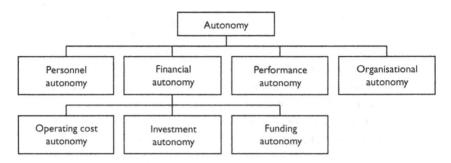

Figure 4.4 Autonomy areas of providers. *Source*: in analogy with Dubs (1996, p. 12).

that the greatest changes are felt by the senior and medium management levels of these organisational units (Rieder, 2006).

For administrative units, operative autonomy means that they are able to make independent decisions on how they want to produce a certain range of agreed outputs. As can be seen in Figure 4.4, decision-making autonomy concerns various areas of management, including personnel decisions regarding, say, employment, promotion or training, but also decisions concerning the application of financial resources and the procurement of material resources. Consequently, staffing schedules, which are now subject to parliamentary approval, *can* still be used as an instrument of administrative control but will lose their influence as an instrument of political control because they are a classic input regulation and thus run counter to the system.

Even though administrative units are described as being at an "operative level," their designation as centres of responsibility is accompanied by an increase in their management function. The more autonomous an administrative unit is, the more important it is for it to give itself a strategy of its own (cf. the widespread use of mission statements in the corporate world) of how it is able to fulfil its performance agreement. Thus strategic issues play an important part at this level, too.

As the autonomy of providers increases, and as control on the basis of results in accorded a stronger position, the question arises as to what the differences between providers from different sectors consist of. A crucial difference between units of public administration and third parties is the fact that these providers work "in the shadow of the hierarchy." This means that the hierarchical structures and traditional control mechanisms such as the authority to issue directives, chains of command and the duty of obedience are still in place and are applied if need be. Thus providers of public administration are subject to a more layered and denser set of control instruments than non-government parties. All in all it becomes apparent that the make-up and selection of providers has undergone little change through OPM.

The Model of the Enabling Authority

Against the background of the concept of the guarantor state outlined at the beginning of the book, the separation of roles described above leads to a new concept of administration. The concept of the *enabling authority*, which has widely gained ground in the UK and New Zealand in particular (Reichard, 1995, pp. 11ff.), constitutes a model of administration in which the idea of a guarantor can be realised and which clearly separates the actors' roles for this purpose:

Figure 4.5 reflects the level of municipal administration in the German government system, and the explanations below are based on the same example, which furnishes a concrete illustration of the organisational configuration of an enabling authority.

In analogy with the distinction between guarantee and implementation, the enabling authority divides German municipal administration into

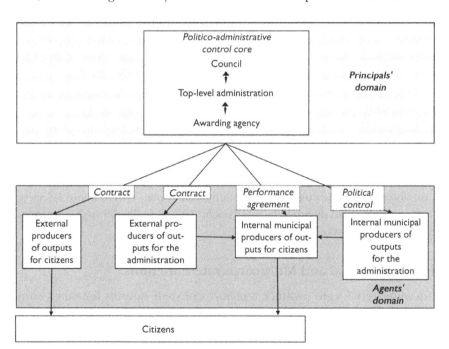

Figure 4.5 Model of the enabling authority. *Source*: Reichard (1998, p. 123).

two. In the principals' domain, the representative body (the council) and the top-level administrators determine the municipality's performance objectives and programmes, make the necessary financial resources available and generally monitor the process of goal attainment and the utilisation of resources. These tasks correspond to the role of the output funder. The "awarding agency," which assumes the output buyer's role and thus is still part of the principal's domain, translates the politically stipulated performance programmes into concrete assignments that concern individual specialist outputs to be produced.

Definition 4.1: Enabling authority

An *enabling authority* is characterised by a bisection of the administrative organisation into a principal's and an agent's domain. The principal's domain consists of the politico-administrative leadership and an award agency, which guarantees that the politically stipulated outputs are made available to agreed specifications. The role of agent can be assumed by administrative units, privatised units or any third party.

The awarding agency awards the contracts to the "most effectively priced" supplier from the agent's domain, which is made up of the various specialist and service units of the municipal authority, as well as of external suppliers. The award agency then also assumes the role of the support services and monitors the process of output production, intervenes if need be and regularly reports to the control core (Reichard, 1998, pp. 122f.).

The vision of a radically realised enabling authority is described by Reichard (1995, pp. 42f.) as the idea of a municipality that works like a pure *holding company* without its own production division and therefore purchases all outputs, i.e., internal services and services to be delivered to the citizen, from external suppliers. This statement must not be misunderstood to mean that it is OPM's supreme aim to make government output production obsolete. To the contrary, OPM aims to set up an efficient and effective output production in order to finally achieve politically defined outcomes, the public value (cf. Moore, 1995).

Interministerial and Multicorporate Functions

Interministerial units produce a majority of their outputs for other units inside the administration, i.e., for *internal* customers. Interministerial outputs thus do not directly benefit the population; rather, they support the rest of the administration in the fulfilment of their tasks. Examples of interministerial units are the finance administration, central organisation units, central IT services, procurement and personnel units. In traditional administration, interministerial functions are usually centralised, at least in comparatively big administrative units, and they are exercised by internal providers for a majority of the other administrative units. (Reichard, 1987, p. 170). As it is, interministerial units—which are often also called *resource units* because they make central decisions concerning the various resources such as personnel, funds and IT throughout the administration—occupy a very powerful position. The above-mentioned separation of roles into output funders, buyers and producers, combined with the concomitant call for a decentralised responsibility for resources, also changes the functional profile and the organisational integration of the interministerial units in OPM.

Functions and Control Mechanisms of Interministerial Units

As a rule, the activities of interministerial units are divided up into two types of functions, which are often amalgamated in terms of organisation but are controlled in different ways:

- *Coordination functions*: This area covers all the tasks that are necessary for the coordination of the administration as an organisation. This is where decisions are made on communication standards, the provision of data, a uniform visual identity, management principles and other areas to be coordinated. In financial management, for example, these tasks include planning, budgeting and external reporting.
- *Service tasks*: This area covers all the tasks that are offered as services to other administrative units. These tasks include material procurement, advice on personnel matters, training schemes, legal investigations and IT support, but also services with regard to accountancy and payment transactions.

Coordination tasks stem from the structure of public administration, which is based on the division of labour, and from the specialisation of its individual parts. Their purpose is to realise the coherence and controllability of the overall administration and to produce synergy effects in the interest of the management of the entire organisation. This requires a uniform orientation throughout the administration, and as a rule these tasks are organised in a centralist and hierarchical fashion. In the traditional organisation of administration, this centralisation is located in the interministerial units.

Conversely, service tasks are requested by (mostly internal) customers, i.e., there is a demand for such services. When it comes to providing them, there is the basic option of either doing so internally or externally, through third parties. This results in two important distinctions with regard to service tasks at the interministerial level. Firstly, the demanders—the administrative units—have to ask themselves whether they are able to choose their supplier freely. In many cases, they are in fact constrained to acquire certain services from internal suppliers. Secondly, the suppliers of internal services—often the interministerial units—have to define whether they can choose what they want to offer or whether they are obliged to provide certain services. Naturally, compulsory services are largely products that the private sector would not generate without government intervention. At the same time it is understood that outputs which have to be acquired from an interministerial unit actually have to be delivered by that unit. To this extent, there is a *congruence of duties* with regard to demand and supply.

According to OPM, service tasks should be controlled through a market-like mechanism which as a rule is based on the supplier's free choice and corresponding charges for services. In the case of services that an internal buyer has freely chosen to purchase, the supplier of these services is in competition with other—external –potential providers. In the case of services that internal buyers are obliged to purchase, market-like mechanisms should be used to ensure efficiency. Services that are purchased internally are debited to the administrative unit that buys them. In organisational terms, internal providers thus resemble service centres.

Basically, it is also conceivable in OPM that an organisational unit takes on both coordination and service tasks. With this constellation, the challenge is to ensure that the exercise of coordination tasks does not lead to a distortion of competition in the service tasks, thus undermining the market-like control of service tasks. Competition mechanisms will not come to fruition if the compulsory purchase of services from internal suppliers is abolished while the specifications for services (coordination tasks) can still be stipulated by one of the suppliers. What is needed here is a consistent separation of tasks.

An example may serve to illustrate the problem: an administration decides that the IT hardware will no longer have to be bought compulsorily from the central IT department but that this competence will be delegated instead. The IT department will then become a service company within the administration that is in competition with external suppliers. Owing to its profound knowledge of the administration, it will still have a competitive edge, but it will be compelled to set its price/benefit offers at a level that will enable it to compete with private suppliers.

Organisational Structure and Decentralised Responsibility for Resources

OPM aims to achieve an extensive organisational congruence between tasks, competencies and responsibility for specialist areas. The separation into output funders, buyers and producers that are interlinked by contacts makes this principle a reality. The reorientation also has an impact on the organisational positions of interministerial units.

In the traditional organisation of administration, interministerial units have a certain right to issue directives to specialist units; for example, the central personnel office may not only draw up employment contracts and formulate job requirements but also establish binding principles for personnel assessment. The exaggerated centralisation of interministerial functions in many authorities erodes responsibility in the specialist units because although they are provided with human, financial and other resources for output production by the central units, the responsibility for the management and utilisation of those resources is not passed on to them but remains at the interministerial level. In contrast, OPM aims to loosen the reins as regards the use of resources but to make the administrative units more strongly responsible for the results.

The decentralisation of the management structure must go hand in hand with a *decentralisation of the responsibility for resources*. The specialist administrative unit—i.e., the provider—is allocated a certain budget out of which all expenditure must be covered. This administrative unit is thus not only given the responsibility for the financial resources but also for all other resources such as personnel and IT. Consequently, it receives a substantially extended responsibility for how it organises the way in which it exercises its function.

Decentralised responsibility for resources should not and cannot result in a complete dissolution of interministerial functions. Rather, what is aimed at is a balanced reintegration of organisational, personnel and budgetary issues into the specialist units. Coordination and service tasks which, from the point of view of the overall governance of the polity, are better provided centrally, will remain centralised. The necessary assessments essentially take their bearings from the aspects listed in Figure 4.6.

In Detmold in Germany's North Rhine-Westphalia, the introduction of decentralised responsibility for resources led to a new division of tasks among

Advantages:	Disadvantages:
• Higher degree of specialisation and professionalisation of the members of staff concerned • Improvement in the central control of the operation • Uniformity and equal treatment	• Distance from specialist units • Erosion of responsibility in specialist units • Delayed decision-making processes • Lack of willingness to be of service

Figure 4.6 Aspects of the centralisation of interministerial functions. *Source*: Reichard (1987, p. 170).

the specialist and interministerial units. Thus the heads of the specialist units were able to exercise substantial personnel competencies from 1995. Even at that time, they were able to make decisions regarding the promotion and dismissal of officials up to a certain seniority, employment on expiry of the probation period, administrative leave and the fixing of regular weekly working hours. From an organisational point of view, this was tantamount to a re-integration of tasks that had been the province of the personnel department at the interministerial level into the specialist units (Bertelsmann Stiftung & Saarländisches Ministerium des Inneren Band 4, 1997, pp. 58f.).

Effects and Consequences of the New Management and Organisation Structure

The hope that the decentralisation described above would introduce more cost-conscious behaviour into public administration has largely been fulfilled so far. More recent evaluations in Switzerland make clear that this—besides being an improvement in customer and performance orientation—is probably the most immediate effect of OPM (cf. Rieder & Lehmann, 2002). However, it also creates new problems that will have to be solved:

- Many administrative units are not (yet) used to handling their autonomy. Wrong reactions thus lead to inefficiencies.
- Ministries often do not conceive of themselves as output buyers as is provided for in the OPM concept. In practice, they tend to behave like advocates of their administrative units rather than as management and control institutions.
- The negotiation of internal outputs and the decisions on whether their purchase is compulsory or optional is labour-intensive and initially prolongs the budgeting processes.

- The political bodies often experience difficulty finding their way around the new structures and processes—or else they completely refuse to adapt.
- Many projects overshoot the desired goal, and perfectionism occasionally results in rather peculiar outcomes.

It also transpires that the weaknesses of the corporate model that are well-known in the private sector come to light in the public sector too. The coordination of the newly autonomous providers (administrative units), in particular, is a great challenge. The centrifugal forces of decentralisation jeopardise the principle of thinking for the common good. They are apt to increase the administration's focus on its own business. Ultimately, the challenge consists in finding the proper balance between efficiency and central output provision (which is typical of, for instance, the area of ICT) and effectiveness and decentralised, correctly adjusted solutions.

Discuss

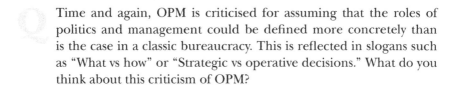

Time and again, OPM is criticised for assuming that the roles of politics and management could be defined more concretely than is the case in a classic bureaucracy. This is reflected in slogans such as "What vs how" or "Strategic vs operative decisions." What do you think about this criticism of OPM?

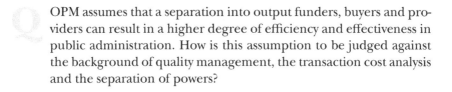

OPM assumes that a separation into output funders, buyers and providers can result in a higher degree of efficiency and effectiveness in public administration. How is this assumption to be judged against the background of quality management, the transaction cost analysis and the separation of powers?

Interministerial functions can be judged according to various criteria and be centralised or decentralised. How would you proceed if you had to determine, for instance, which functions of the personnel department would be exercised from the centre and which would be decentralised?

Further Readings

Bouckaert, G., Peters, B. G., Verhoest, K. (2010). *The coordination of public sector organizations: Shifting patterns of public management.* New York: Palgrave Macmillan.

Ferlie, E., Lynn, L., Pollit, C. (2005). Decentralization: a central concept in contemporary public management. In *The Oxford handbook of public management* (pp. 371–97). Oxford: Oxford university press.

Pollitt, C., Talbot, C., Caulfield, J., Smullen, A. (2004). *Agencies: How governments do things through semi-autonomous agencies.* Basingstoke: Palgrave Macmillen.

5

Organisation from the Points of View of Customers and Quality

The traditional organisation of public administration is a fact-oriented, functionally structured staff-line organisation with strict hierarchies, which enables politically elected people to be democratically accountable. The motivation behind the present-day structures is thus a clear-cut attribution of political responsibility and the control of the administration. This concept of administration has no room for customers. If, however, we jettison this inside view and position ourselves on the customers' side, then this view, too, reveals a deficit of public administration: its function-oriented structure leads to substantial coordination problems.

Having a *functional* organisation means that those people work together in a unit who have similar competencies or tasks. In the private sector, these are departments like research and development, marketing or sales. Public administrations, too, are often structured according to competencies; in the area of planning permission, for example, these are the spe-

Outcome-Oriented Public Management, pages 93–100
Copyright © 2010 by Information Age Publishing
All rights of reproduction in any form reserved.

cialist administrative units for water, land, air, construction safety or fire prevention.

A so-called "90° turn" in the perception of organisations in the 1990s led to a situation whereby organisational efforts no longer focused on vertical hierarchical structures, but on horizontal process structures. *Process-oriented* organisations are additionally encouraged by modern information technologies—any form of introducing a digital file management system would not make sense if the relevant administrative processes had not been analysed and optimised beforehand.

Finally, *customer-oriented* organisation changes the system from a self-referential one to an open and responsive one. It concentrates on customers, aiming to achieve as high as possible a degree of service and support quality through the establishment of customer support teams. Again, the central challenge is and remains coordination.

In today's public administration, different types of coordination can be found that vary with regard to the extent of customer-orientation. In the following sections, these types of coordination will be presented in order of ascending customer orientation.

Coordination by Customers

Let us assume that the administration wants to persevere in structures of functional specialisation. In this case, complex problems such as planning permission require coordination between the individual relevant administrative units to be effected by an external unit. Traditionally, this is the applicant: a planning application is split up into individual specialised applications so that each administrative unit will only have to deal with the part with which it is concerned. This has advantages for the administration: it makes internal coordination unnecessary, and each specialist unit can retain its own pure perspective. For customers, however, it has a disadvantage, namely that they have to make a pilgrimage from office to office (the so-called *Behördenrallye* in German) until all the necessary components of the permission have been collected. In extreme cases, in may even happen that administrative units are not in agreement with each other and argue out their disputes in legal proceedings at the applicant's expense.

In organisational terms, all the administration does is to outsource coordination (particularly coordination costs and risks) to applicants. It is obvious that this form of organisation favours the idea of "il faut cultiver son jardin" inside the administration and is thus a system which tends to hamper holistic problem solutions.

Coordination by Intermediaries

To counter these problems, organisations have been established in many places which relieve certain customer groups of these coordination tasks. The countless self-help organisations and associations very often do not merely represent their members' interests in practice but also constitute a professional interface with public administration. For instance, they often collect the administration's own telephone directories so that the competent officials can be rung directly, or they make available all the forms that are necessary for an application. Self-help organisations and associations thus factually take on the role of translators for their customers because the administration has become incomprehensible and thus inaccessible to the latter—which is a very dangerous development from a democratic point of view. In Switzerland as in other countries, all administrations are therefore required by federal law to coordinate their relations with citizens (cf. also Hubmann Trächsel, 1995).

One-Stop Concept

The one-stop concept strives to offer all the services of a polity in one single (geographical) place. Originally, the concept was developed to make the administration accessible to people who did not have the necessary educational background or did not have the time to contact the various administrative units directly. Accordingly, so-called "one-stop shops" were set up in Australia in the 1970s (cf. Wettenhall & Kimber o.J.). Their purpose was

1. to provide poor people with easier access to social benefits in the knowledge that it was precisely these needy people who found it most difficult to discover the right administrative unit for their specific problems, the result of which was a factual discrimination against penurious and poorly educated people by the bureaucratic system,
2. to shift the reference points and the decisions nearer to customers,
3. to improve coordination between official units, and
4. to provide politicians and civil servants with support and guidelines to enable them to make better decisions.

The concept of the first *one-stop shop* proved so revolutionary for the traditional hierarchical administration culture that the shop was closed in the mid-1980s. The idea survived, however, and similar approaches can nowadays be observed at the municipal level, in particular. With the OPM, this—primarily socially motivated—idea has received a new impetus and a new quality. Not only the socially less well off, but all the customers of public administration should now have easier, more comprehensible and more courteous access to the administration. In the meantime, it has become an actual hallmark of citizen-friendly municipalities to set up a citizens' advice bureau or a municipal office in which virtually all the business with administration can be transacted in one single location.

For the administration concerned, this means that an interface with customers is established that has to possess enormous generalist knowledge. If the citizens' advice bureau is not merely intended to be a trumped-up information desk which then refers applicants to other administrative units, but to have on-site decision-making competencies, then this constitutes a breach with the functional structure of administration. In organisational terms, such a reorientation can practically only be solved with an intelligent data-processing system that enables customer advisers to access the most important fundamental documents and data. In the context of electronic government (cf. Chapter 11, Development of a Conceptual Frame for e-Government, pp. 200ff.), the one-stop concept is also known as *single window access*. This, however, does not solve the problem with the structure of administration that arose in Australia. Ultimately, such projects rarely fail because of technical issues; as a rule, the cause of a potential failure resides in the resistance put up by those involved. However, the topic of administrative culture will be treated later on (cf. Chapter 12, pp. 209ff.).

A conversion to a citizens' advice bureau is often conducted in stages. The Berlin-Köpenick district, for example, tackled its projects in three stages:

Stage 1: Specialists from the specialist units were gathered in one place; to begin with, they worked exclusively in their respective fields.
At the same time, the team members trained each other; this was done during those working hours when the office was not open to the public.

Stage 2: On completion of this "generalisation" of the team, the *first come, first served* principle could be introduced since each and every member of staff was able, and was intended to be able, to treat all the business at the same level.

Stage 3: Further offers could then be integrated in addition, and new decentralised citizens' advice bureaux could be opened up.

As a rule, the experience gained with citizens' advice bureaux is extremely positive (Lenk, 1992, pp. 570) and the workload of specialist units can be substantially reduced by means of competent preparation. The citizens' advice bureaux thus often do not merely take on a sorting function but constitute that professional interface with the specialist units which, if it is not in place, is formed by self-help organisations (cf. above).

These one-stop shops are known in many countries, and the concept has been included in public administration reforms even in developing countries. Opening hours and the range of services differ widely.

Customer-Segment-Oriented Organisation

The orientation of the whole organisation goes one step further if it takes its bearings from predefined customer segments. The Office of Environmental Protection (AFU) of the Canton of St.Gallen in Switzerland, for example, has carried out such a conversion in order to be able to provide its customers with optimal services.

Until its reform project, the AFU was traditionally bureaucratically organised—i.e., according to the various relevant functional laws—or media-oriented, as this was called in the AFU. Land, water and air, etc., were the organisational criteria. The reform project now aimed to align the AFU's core processes with customer requirements, thus achieving a lasting change. For this purpose, four main customer groups were identified: the public administration, nature and environment organisations, trade and industry, and municipalities and infrastructure. The AFU's internal organisation was converted and brought into line with these customer groups and products. Today, the departments are structured into Law and Environmental Impact Assessments, Environmental Resources, Industrial Environmental Protection, and Infrastructure and Energy. This now provides customers from the individual groups with a place to go where they are given support and advice. The various specialists had to be trained to become specialised generalists.

Customer and Quality Orientation in the Life-Cycle of Output Production

The ideal-typical form of process-oriented organisation assumes that there is a value chain that goes "from customer to customer." Extensive service quality management starts with the customers' requirements and the expectations they place in a service, and it ends with the provision of the service or rather, the way in which customers perceive it (Parasuraman et al., 1985). In between, the process moves into the administration and then out of it again. It is therefore not sufficient if a public administration only organises itself optimally; rather, the customers' possibilities and technical systems must also always be taken into account. Moreover, the administration must ensure the customer orientation of its own organisation with a wide range of measures such as customer panels, citizens' charters and quality circles, etc.

TABLE 5.1   Customer and Quality Orientation in the Value Chain

Process elements	Possible measures of customer and quality orientation
Customers' requirements: service expectations	Ascertainment of service expectations, e.g., by a customer
Definition of customers' legitimate demands	Exertion of influence on demands through the communication of the quality level that can be expected, e.g., through citizens' charters
Definition of the service on offer: service specifications	Involvement of customers in service specifications, e.g., through quality circles or prosumer models
Production of the service	Information to customers about the status and further procedures of service production, e.g., in the context of CRM models
Service provision: service perception	Ascertainment and monitoring of service perception, e.g., through customer surveys

An administration is therefore able to organise the constant improvement of its own service quality by, among other things, systematically bringing customer and quality orientation to bear on the individual stages of the service process. In comparison with the private sector, it is conspicuous that a step called "Definition of customers' legitimate demands" has been introduced. This is done for two reasons: for one thing, it must be made clear that customer orientation must not be equated with boundless demands on the part of the citizens. For another, however, citizens' "consumers' rights" (Promberger et al., 2001) must be deliberately strengthened by making an authority's promises and obligations to provide services transparent.

Customer surveys are particularly highly valued in OPM, for they double as an instrument of quality management and furnish indicators about the impact of administrative action. For this reason, it is well worth every public administration discussing the issue of customer surveys in detail. However, the principle applies that any survey must be conducted with the top-level administrators' declared intention to actually implement any changes that will be necessary.

For the purpose of further-reaching quality development, it is recommendable that surveys of service perception should not only extend to customers but also be conducted among the administration's own staff. There are often great differences in what customers and administrative staff regard as good service quality in public administration. Administrators frequently have the wrong ideas about the quality that their customers expect. Germann (2004) reveals in the context of a job placement programme that administrative staff generally occupy themselves too little with their customers' requirements and focus more on the fulfilment of their legal functions.

To make the quality gap between customers' and administrative employees' expectations transparent, Koci (2005) developed a method of interviewing both stakeholder groups simultaneously and then comparing the results with the help of so-called *linkage research*. The study makes clear that in many service situations of public administration, the personalities of officials and customers play an important role. They put their stamp on the image and mutual expectations from which service quality emerges. Higher job satisfaction in the administration usually goes hand in hand with higher customer satisfaction, i.e., both values exert a mutual influence on each other. In addition, Koci demonstrates, with the example of a government social insurance scheme, that there are indeed great differences between the expectations of officials and customers that are worth shedding some light on.

A survey with this systematic structure enables the top-level administration to optimise its own value chain in respect of quality. In addition, the alignment of the organisation with customer needs—which ideally results in a higher degree of customer satisfaction—is generally described as positive for the administration since better satisfied customers lodge fewer complaints and appeals, which all in all results in more efficient service provisions and delivery.

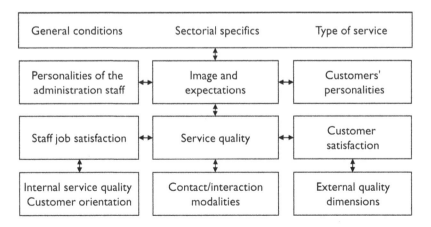

Figure 5.1 Service quality and customer orientation. *Source*: Koci (2005).

Discuss

Q If you had to specifically implement the one-stop idea in a municipality, how would you organise a citizens' advice bureau or a municipal office? What services could be offered in one single place?

Q What arguments speak against concentrating all the administration's contacts with citizens in one single place?

Q Can the one-stop concept also be implemented at the level of the federal administration? What examples exist of this?

Q Assuming you had to organise a kick-off workshop for an integrated customer and staff survey: what points would have to be addressed in such a workshop? What decisions would you have to agree on before you could proceed with the survey?

Further Readings

Bovaird, T., Löffler, E. (Eds.). (2009). Quality management in public sector organizations. In *Public Management and Governance* (pp. 165–180). New York: Oxford University Press.

Schedler, K., Helmuth, U. (2009). Process management in public sector organizations. In *Public Management and Governance* (pp. 181–203). New York: Oxford University Press.

Hampy, J. C., Hammer, M. (1993). *Reengineering the corporation.* New York: Harper Business.

6

Outcome-Oriented Control through Performance Agreements

Possibly the most outstanding change that has been initiated by OPM is a restructuring of control processes in public administration. It is not without reason that in Germany, the term *New Control Model* was coined for this (KGSt, 1993).

In the traditional system of (bureaucratic) administration, *functions* are defined that have to be exercised by government. The *legal foundations* which are necessary for this and without which administrative action would be illegitimate are created in democratic processes. The *resources* that enable the administration to become active are made available in the annually revolving budgeting procedure where spending competencies are allocated and personnel plans are adopted. In the context of production processes, managers here speak of so-called *inputs*. This type of control is therefore often called *input control*.

The replacement of a pure concentration on inputs by *outcome orientation* can be regarded as the *basic tenet* of the new type of control. All the

Outcome-Oriented Public Management, pages 101–126
Copyright © 2010 by Information Age Publishing
101

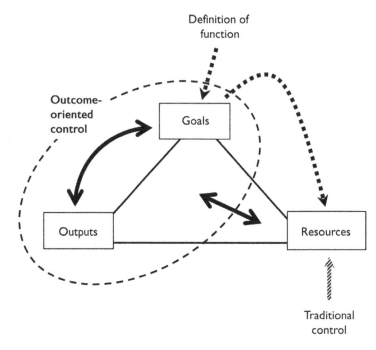

Figure 6.1   Outcome-oriented control.

consequent rules, rearrangements and instruments derive from the tenet, and their suitability can be measured against it. The objects of control are thus not the resources but the administration's products (outputs). Whereas traditional control assumed that there was a (direct or indirect) nexus between the resources and the attainment of goals, OPM only establishes this nexus through the definition of outputs. On this basis, certain financial resources can be made available for outputs or outcomes by *calculating* their consumption of resources. Resources are allocated in correlation with outputs or outcomes, and not as a control factor in their own right. Control becomes more direct, and the political instances have stronger possibilities of influencing the *results*—for instance, whether the stipulated objectives have been attained.

The Control Process in OPM

Public administration produces a wide variety of outputs such as education, opinions, applications of law, services and information. They all originate from certain requirements which become part of the administration's output range owing to either direct customer demand (in the case of the services) or political objectives (in the case of compulsory outputs). As in every organisation whose behaviour can be considered target-oriented, this results in a production process of one form or another which, from a management point of view, has to be "controlled."

The control process depicted below is highly simplified for reasons of clarity. In reality, the service provision and delivery processes do not take place in such clear steps, either in terms of time or in terms of substance; rather, they influence each other. They are informed by external effects— for instance by influences from other actors within the political system— and interlinked with surrounding systems such as ecology, technology, society and the economy, which means that these simple causalities will only rarely be found. Nonetheless, the graph is still capable of illustrating the basic processes of the production of administrative outputs and of providing a theoretical analysis of these processes.

This view of public administration as an output producer may look unusual at first sight. Parallels are drawn with *physical* production although the administration's outputs are often not purely material and thus not quanti-

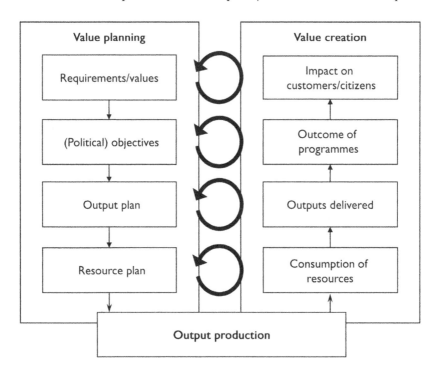

Figure 6.2 The control process in the politico-administrative system. *Source*: in analogy with Mäder and Schedler (1994, p. 58).

fiable to the same extent. The exponents of *performance measurement* are well aware of these differences. Yet the representation of the control process as a thought model is extremely useful for it helps us to structure the complex interconnections.

Value Planning

In the representation of the control process, it is assumed that certain *objectives* are formulated in the state on the basis of the *requirements and values* of the various groups of customers and stakeholders. These objectives lead to an *output plan*, which ideally should enable the objectives to be attained. Once the output plan has been drawn up, a *resource plan* can be computed with the help of performance budgeting, which should be sufficient for the production of the planned outputs provided that the resources are put to efficient use. These processes are component parts of the planning process in the politico-administrative system and ideally result in a *programme*, i.e., in an inherently consistent combination of all the above planning elements.

Requirements

The requirements the administration is expected to deal with can be asserted in a variety of ways. The traditional path leads through the political parties and the representatives of the people in parliaments and councils, who introduce people's requirements into the politico-administrative system. Moreover, the *citizens* themselves are given an opportunity in many places to introduce their requirements directly into politics through initiatives, referenda and other democratic instruments. In principle, these manifestations of *public interest* are not affected by OPM (although there may be a formal impact), and it remains a function of politics and administration to follow up the public interest as prospectively as possible.

Requirements, however, also manifest themselves in a closer, more immediate connection with the *product* at issue. This microeconomic and management-oriented view then raises questions as to why citizens are prepared to spend taxpayers' money on this product, how their decision is motivated, for whom certain outputs should be produced, and what overriding purpose these outputs have.

Above and beyond the original motives, we can also ask how *customers'* requirements and values have changed and what problems customers generally have with the outputs of public administration. An increase in crime in a city, for example, gives rise to a greater need for physical security, and present-day unemployment changes the need for social security. Other influences again may cause requirements to disappear completely.

Objectives

Again and again, the process of setting objectives in public administration is described as extremely difficult since the goal structures are said to be considerably more blurred, have many more dimensions and are heterogeneously controlled by stakeholders (Buschor, 1992, p. 210). This may well be why it is not in all areas by far that clear objectives are set so the administration has to follow its own precepts. However, administrative activities that are not target-oriented can easily become *ineffective*. For this reason, two different sets of objectives must be determined for each output: *the superordinate objective as such (outcome objectives) and the specific (operative) objectives necessary for its attainment (output objectives)* for the period under consideration.

Wherever objectives have been set—such as a reduction of the crime rate in a city by xy per cent—they are quite frequently measured today. This, however, also applies the other way round: wherever objectives are easy to measure, they are regularly set today. Consequently, there is a lack of objectives in areas that are often more difficult to measure, which leads to a situation whereby their attainment is not measured and thus not checked either. Such areas are then declared factual taboo zones for any form of outcome orientation. However, the results of an activity are among the most important success factors of both *service-provision* and *law-enforcement* administration and have to be consistently recorded even though this is not always easy. In this connection, *performance measurement* is accorded a great deal of significance (Congressional Budget Office, 1993, p. 4) since it must be clarified whether the efforts made by the administration have really met and satisfied its principals' requirements. This means that civil servants have to be aware of their principals' requirements, which will constitute the foundation for the political decision to set certain objectives for the administration.

The traditionally input-oriented view prevalent in public administration is particularly persistent and disruptive in the process of defining objectives. Even practised advisers have to keep in mind at all times that objectives are not circumscribed by resources or the "how" of output production but by concrete results. Politicians who lead their administration through outcome and output objectives are called upon to improve their competence to ask the relevant questions, which in this context may include the following:

- ▪ For outcome objectives:
  - – What is the purpose of an activity?
  - – What will have to be achieved in the long term with the creation of this output?
  - – What developments are aimed at?
- ▪ For output objectives:
  - – What will have to be achieved in the period under consideration?
  - – What quality standards are aimed at in the period under consideration?
  - – What efficiency dimensions will have to be attained in the period under consideration?
  - – What quantity of outputs will be produced?
  - – What quantity of outputs will be delivered?
  - – What benefit should be reaped from an output and by which customers?

The differences between the two approaches to defining an objective are evident. Although the formulation of outcome-oriented objectives can cause considerable difficulties at times, great weight must still be attached to a correct result. As will have to be demonstrated later, these objectives are the basis for the establishment of performance indicators, through which the provider's success is measured and the contract is controlled.

Objectives are defined in an iterative process which continually incorporates information from the outside and compares individual steps with previous results. The following procedures can be noted as a grid:

1. For the administration to determine the purpose of its own activity (the "mission statement"), it can base its considerations on the legislator's intention that is pursued by the task. To this end, many administrations can have recourse to the results developed in their definition of the function (particularly of the purpose).
2. The outputs established in the output definition are now placed in the context of this overall task. What contributions will the outputs make to the fulfilment of the purpose?
3. Critical success factors are performance elements that will categorically have to be satisfied for the purpose to be achieved. These critical success factors must be taken into consideration for a first cluster of objectives to be defined.
4. The cluster of objectives is then subjected to the two following questions: a) are the objectives necessary (i.e., the purpose can-

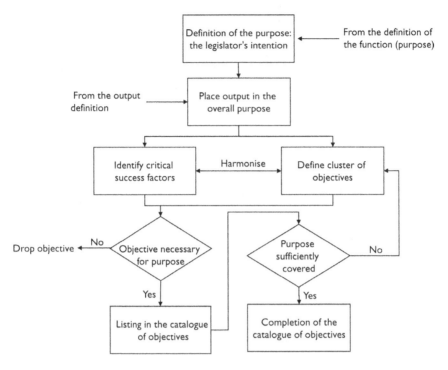

Figure 6.3 The definition process for objectives.

not be fulfilled unless each and every one of these objectives has been attained), and b) do these objectives cover the purpose sufficiently (i.e., when all the objectives have been attained, will the purpose also have been achieved)?

5. The catalogue of objectives can be regarded as completed if the cluster of objectives satisfies these two conditions.

The question of the establishment of priorities and posteriorities is also part of the setting of objectives. In the past, various methods were developed for this, but not all of them have found their way into practice. As Becker (1989, p. 769) put it, there are various models of prioritising that help decision-makers solve their problems, but there is one thing they cannot do: they are not capable of relieving decision-makers of the problems of assessing what is more important, less important or equally important for them. Prioritising methods facilitate this process because they are systematically rational procedures. One example of political prioritising is constituted by the *high impact agencies* in the US. In the context of the National Partnership for Reinventing Government—the national administration reform project headed by the then Vice-President Al Gore—the federal administration was supposed to be restructured in a customer- and outcome-oriented way. Initially, activities concentrated on the so-called high impact agencies. Administrative units were identified which had *the greatest* impact on the public image of the federal administration. These units were obliged to attain certain objectives during the next few years. The point of this course of action was to achieve clearly visible and palpable results with the *very first* reform efforts.

Outputs

Public administrations that have not yet come into contact with reforms often completely lack *output orientation*. The traditional system of public administration encourages the actors to think in terms of financial and material resources, personnel ceilings and credit lines. It tends to be bureaucratically oriented, i.e., processes and rules are in many cases accorded more weight than actual results. There may be a certain justification in this since—as is often argued—the administration is more accountable to the general public for its utilisation of the latter's money than is a private firm for the utilisation of its equity. Shareholders would be unlikely to cast doubt on the system of private enterprise because a joint-stock company's accountant has embezzled some money. If this happens in the administration, however, many taxpayers feel compelled to find the administrative system guilty on a point of principle. The fact that public administration is oriented towards resources and rules is therefore also a consequence of greater *risk aversion* against the background of critical citizens. Thus it would be erroneous to propagate a complete disregard of the input side in favour of results alone.

OPM attempts to integrate all the aspects of the control process into its considerations. Nonetheless, it places relatively great weight on the output side, which may give the impression that it focuses *exclusively* on results. This can be explained by the fact that an output focus has the greatest development potential and that we expect an extension of this new approach to yield positive effects. In the medium to long term, a balanced weighting is of great significance for public administration. Owing to a strong concentration of both external and internal effects, the resource side and the volume side are not disregarded in OPM, either.

The *traditional* focus on processes in public administration assumes that certain functions are performed through certain activities with certain resources (money, personnel, material resources, time). In this model, *output* is defined by the number, intensity and quality of the activities, a majority of which are controlled through the resources. In the model of

OPM, too, certain functions (often the same ones) are performed, but the focus is on the outputs that the administration produces with its resources. In the model, control is effected through the definition of the outputs and through measurable objectives for the fulfilment of tasks.

The new, output-oriented instruments allow for various goals to be pursued:

- citizens can be informed about the value for money they receive from the state;
- the money flows can be identified and checked, and effectiveness and efficiency can be measured and assessed;
- the quality of the political instances' possibilities of control can be improved and thus new scopes of action can be created for the parliament/council and the top-level administration;
- the responsibilities of the parliament/council, the top-level administration and the administrative units can be clearly demarcated;
- complete information can be supplied for strategic and operative planning in good time in order to enable the administration to react to deviations with immediate effect.

Output properties. An output *leaves* the administrative unit that is responsible for it as a completed entity. This explanation implies that there is a difference between activities and outputs which is great enough to influence the administration's control system (cf. Figure 6.4). In fact this step means that each administrative unit concentrates more consciously on its actual *volume*, i.e., on those output units that leave its own area.

An output thus has four properties that can be used for its determination:

1. It is produced or refined in an administrative unit, or a unit is responsible for its production or refinement according to the instruction of the competent administrative unit.
2. It satisfies a requirement on the part of third parties (customers), i.e., output production is not an end in itself but creates a benefit for customers.
3. It is delivered to third parties, i.e., it leaves the administrative unit.
4. It is suitable for use as an auxiliary quantity for control in the politico-administrative system.

In practice, a distinction is made between internal and external outputs. Internal outputs go to customers inside the administration (but outside the producing administrative unit), whereas external outputs leave the

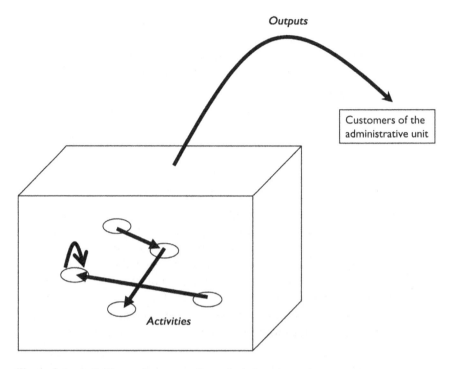

Figure 6.4   Activities and outputs of an administrative unit.

administration. There are some consequences that can be deduced from these four output properties.

Re point 1: Outputs are *produced* in the administration or on its behalf, with *one unit* assuming the responsibility for each output. Pure articles of trade do not count as outputs. This can be illustrated with the example of the purchase of materials: paper, pencils, office equipment, etc., are not outputs produced by the materials management unit, but the services they involve, such as supply and delivery to offices, can be defined as outputs in this sense.

Re point 2: The requirement that an output must cover a need expressed by third parties becomes significant if, say, a part of an administrative unit's activities consists in creating a good image of itself among the general public. Such PR measures make sense when it comes to influencing the distribution of scarce resources in favour of one's own activities. To accept them as one of the unit's outputs, however, would be tantamount to describing the exertion of this influence as an external need, which is hardly likely to be the case. There is a second reason for this requirement, namely the necessity of defining this need and of establishing clarity as to whether it is indeed capable of creating the expected benefit.

Re point 3: If the output is delivered to third parties, this means that it leaves the unit where it was produced. If, for instance, an office of environmental protection conducts measurements in the environment which serve to monitor the effectiveness of its own measures (such as a change in regulations concerning flue gas filters), this need not be an output. It can quite as easily be defined as a quality assurance measure on the administrative unit's own premises, which means that it is not delivered to third parties. If, however, such measurements are periodically published and used as quality data for the general public, then these publications would be outputs, whilst the measurements themselves would be part of the output requirement for the preparation of the publication.

Re point 4: For managing and coordinating purposes, the output fulfils a wide variety of functions:

- It constitutes the basis for the definition, stipulation, measurement and monitoring of results.
- It serves as a basis for costing and for the allocation of resources (performance budget).
- It is a medium-term item of planning (cf. Chapter 6, The Integrated Tasks and Finance Plan, pp. 118ff.)
- It defines the level of the exertion of political influence by consolidating outputs for parliamentary decisions, while keeping more detailed output definitions for internal management purposes.
- It serves as a basis for the formulation of policies (outcome objectives) and measures (output objectives), as well as for their evaluation (results indicators).

Against this background, output definition is not a purely technical procedure but part of policy-making and thus of vital political interest. It is more an art than a science, and it must not be perfected to excess. Practical experience gained in trial projects has so far demonstrated that politics is usually excluded from these processes; as a rule, outputs (and indicators) are defined by experts inside the administration. This has clearly discernible positive effects in that it creates a new outcome and output awareness among administrative staff. Ideally, the question of the creation of public value through administrative outputs replaces the pure efficiency orientation for which OPM is often reproached. This serves to justify the fact that until now, output definition has remained a process that is predominantly inherent in the administration.

However, OPM must in the foreseeable future find ways and means to subject outputs and indicators to a democratic examination and, if need be, to redefine them. Ultimately, outputs defined in this manner are a main instrument of interrational translation and control at the interface between politics and administration. As a provisional aid for the assessment of output definitions, the following criteria can be mentioned that must be satisfied by a good solution:

- **Customers' view:** An output should be defined from the point of view of the customer and not from that of the administrative unit that produces it. For example, outputs should also bring together different providers if they are delivered to customers as homogeneous services. The check question in practice could be: Is this what the inexpert customer on the other side of the counter receives from the administration?
- **Relevance:** An output should be relevant to operative output control, whereas for political control, outputs should be consolidated into larger categories in order to avoid information overflow. This precludes too great a complexity of detail (rule of thumb: 3–4 output categories for political use, and a maximum of 8 outputs for administrative control should be sufficient for a medium-sized administrative unit). At the same time, this means that the establishment of focal points for the benefit of manageability is more important than detailed completeness.
- **Task view:** An output must contribute towards the administrative unit's fulfilment of a task for the general public (outputs must be in *conformity with the objectives*).

An administrative unit can use output definitions as an opportunity to subject its own activities to a fundamental check (what tasks are actually in demand? what outputs could be better produced by third parties?).

Output definition as a process.   The act of output definition is a process that public administration and politics are unaccustomed to. For this reason, it is particularly important that in essence, those involved conduct the process themselves. Firstly, they know their own tasks best, and secondly, output definition requires exactly that change in thinking that OPM as a whole aims at. Moreover, efforts should be made whenever possible to involve politicians in this output definition process as well. In this way the administration can be prevented from applying a purely administrative

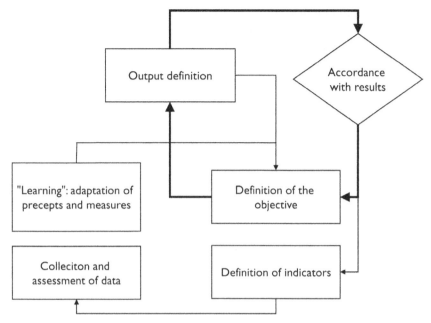

Figure 6.5   The double loop of the output definition.

rationality in order to create the foundation on which political discussions should then take place.

In a *pragmatic output definition*, the actual situation serves to provide a picture of the present-day output in the guise of the new control elements. Outputs, objectives and indicators are practically inseparable. At the same time, it is indispensable for those involved in the definition process to bear in mind at all times the result to be achieved by this function (planned situation). Figure 6.5 gives the impression that this process can be systematised, but a caveat must be expressed against false expectations: only constant feedback combined with improvement and learning processes will result in an output range that satisfies the high level of requirements.

An output is defined in several conceptual steps:

1. First, the customer groups that are relevant to the administrative unit are analysed.
2. Then the relevant organisation is identified, i.e., the point in time when an output "leaves the administrative unit where it has been produced."

3. Subsequently, contacts with third parties are analysed, and the outputs these customers obtain from the administrative unit in question are then recorded.
4. Finally, the various outputs are combined in such a way that they satisfy the requirements of an output (cf. above).

Once these first preparatory steps have been completed, the output definitions must be tested. The two most important questions in this context are:

- Do the defined outputs have a useful effect? (In particular: have we not defined excessively detailed activities as outputs?)
- Can the activities of an administrative unit be sensibly controlled through the defined outputs, i.e., does a performance agreement for the administrative unit on the basis of these outputs make sense?

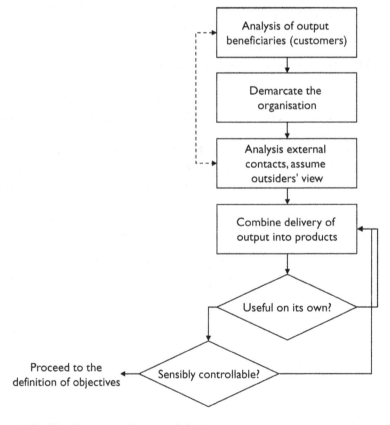

Figure 6.6 The first steps of output definition.

Experience shows that it is simpler to proceed from larger categories towards detailed outputs. Then, objectives and indicators can be defined for each output (cf. Chapter 7, Indices for Public Management, pp. 140ff.).

Setting up outputs for political use. For the purposes of budgeting and reporting to the parliament/council, it is necessary to combine these still fairly detailed outputs in groups. This is done to prevent the political instances from being inundated with information and is done in terms of a purely linear condensation.

Definition 6.1: Outputs grouped

For political use, outputs are grouped so that they constitute a strategic unit with a clear orientation within one field of tasks. These output groups cover an entire field of tasks in a manageable number (Brühlmeier et al., 1998, pp. 301f.).

Since, as a rule, parliament is expected to control its resolutions at the level of output groups, these must not be too heterogeneous. An output group thus combines outputs with a shared orientation that is geared as clearly as possible to a political programme or to measures with an unequivocal outcome objective.

Resource Plan

In essence, the resource plan is a demand plan for the production of the desired outputs. This resource plan does not only refer to financial issues but also to personnel, material and investment-related concerns.

Although under OPM, legally binding detailed budgets and employment plans are abandoned, these planning activities will naturally have to continue in the administrative units. The managers will have to occupy themselves with this task, as they have to in every private firm, in order to exercise their responsibility—indeed, owing to the decentralisation of competencies, an administrative unit will no longer be able to refer to a central precept but will have to decide on its own what resources it needs in what amounts and at what point in time. Thus the resource plan is highly significant for management purposes and will have to be integrated into cost/output accounting.

Output Production

With the resources that are allocated on the basis of the plan, the administration produces a certain number of outputs of a certain quality and at a certain time. In the model under review, the production of outputs by the administration appears as a *black box*, because it pivots around questions of "how," about which the administrative unit should make its own decision.

The consideration of output production answers questions concerning the administrative units' organisation of processes and structures which, however, do not (any longer) affect the relationship between the top-level administration and the administrative unit since according to the principle of *decentralisation*, the administrative units are themselves responsible for their own organisation. However, the top-level administration or the ministry in its capacity as the supervisory body may have a certain interest in the processes going on in administrative units, namely when they should be optimised. If no comparative data with other organisations are available, then such details can be clarified in surveys.

Value Creation and Measurement

Output production in the administration results in a *consumption of resources*, which can and should be compared with the resource plan. An analysis of actual consumption also refers to all the factors of output production. The financial side of resource consumption is of particular interest, and thus costing is accorded great value.

The outputs that are actually produced are usually measured *quantitatively*, as well as being checked for compliance with the specified *quality standards*. The *winter road maintenance* programme could result in an output whereby *x* kilometres of national roads are cleared of snow on *y* days, with *z* per cent of the road being cleared within 4 hours.

Various outputs are often combined into a *programme*, whose *outcome* for the environment in general or the environment of the administration can be ascertained and compared with the political objectives. The outcome of snow clearance could be a reduction of accidents, of public transport delays or of damage to roads in spring.

The addressees of the administrative output (*customers*) experience these programmes and their results against the background of their needs and values. The *impact* of administrative output can therefore differ from its *outcome*, which is more easy to express in objective terms. Particularly the latter two factors (*impact* and *outcome*) are hardly recorded and differentiated in practice although they are of great importance for the inhabitants' satisfaction with the administration. Under certain conditions, quality can be reduced—for instance, snow clearing within eight hours instead of four—

without achieving a significant impact if customers of public transport accept delays as a consequence of bad weather.

The Three Levels of Control

Control in the state is exercised within different periodicities and with different instruments. Mastronardi (1999) defines three so-called rails of control:

- The *normative control level* of law-making stipulates government tasks and the principle of their fulfilment for an unlimited period of time.
- The *level of medium-term planning* is geared to future developments. As a rule, it extends to between 4 and 6 years and, in a traditional control system, includes the finance plan and–usually separately—sectoral plans.
- The *level of annual control* covers the coming year. In a traditional control system, it includes the budget.

In this chapter, we will limit ourselves to the two levels of medium-term planning and annual control (for the normative control level cf. Chapter 9, pp. 169ff.). Both medium-term planning and annual control always combine the financial side with the output and outcome side of government activity. From the medium-term perspective, a distinction can be made between two elements: the executive's priority programme, and the integrated tasks and finance plan. From the annual perspective, politics exercises control through a combination of performance targets and one-line budgets, usually called performance budgets. They constitute the cornerstones for the general and annual contracts (performance agreements) with internal and external output providers.

The Executive's Priority Programme

As a rule, the executive's priority programme is published at the beginning of a legislature. It contains all the causes that the executive wants to take up without, however, claiming to be exhaustive. It is politically motivated and serves to enhance the executive's profile. Whether such a priority programme has to be published depends on a country's political system. In Switzerland, so-called legislature programmes or legislature objectives are customary and are expected. In other countries, programmes are used for other forms of political profile enhancement.

The Integrated Tasks and Finance Plan

An integrated tasks and finance plan (ITFP) is drawn up by the executive alongside the priority programme and thereafter at least once a year. It constitutes the instrument for the presentation of costs, outputs and outcomes in the medium-term, i.e., for four to six years. The ITFP is a rolling plan, i.e., any change (for instance through political resolutions or external factors) is recorded, and the ITFP is periodically adapted. Every decision made by parliament should therefore be examined for its outcomes in the ITFP and be made transparent.

The ITFP contains at least the following information (Brühlmeier et al., 2001):

a. the forecast and intended development of tasks, i.e., of their central output and outcome indicators structured according to task areas;
b. the forecast and intended development of finances, i.e., of the annual financial objectives;
c. the measures necessary to correct the forecast development and to achieve the intended development, including changes in the law, target dates and responsibilities;
d. the future problem areas and the scope for action that still exists today.

Since the ITFP is not limited to a fixed period (it "keeps rolling along," as it were), a final report is unnecessary. However, the recipients of the information—in this case, parliament and the executive—should still be able to check the ITFP for its reliability; after all, it serves as a general orientation for the assessment of developments.

Annual Performance Budget

The performance budget allocates a one-line budget and a performance agreement for certain outputs to each administrative unit. Today, the one-line budget, which is adopted by parliament, has two different legal forms:

The *output budget* reports net costs or net expenditure of certain outputs or task areas. In this form, it is adopted as legally binding. Subsequently, shifts between outputs and task areas are only possible through supplementary credit lines or amending resolutions.

In the *unit budget* (e.g., the administrative units' budget), net costs or net expenditure are allocated to certain units and adopted as legally binding. Although financial data are reported per output, they have no legally binding effect, and shifts of funds between the outputs of an administrative unit are perfectly admissible as long as the agreed output is produced. The crucial value is the amount per unit (contractual amount).

Thus budget sovereignty remains with parliament under OPM, too. This means that parliament can determine what funds are used for what purposes; only the way in which the funds are bound (*legal specification*) is changed, as described above.

The performance budget is accompanied by a reporting system that mirrors the planned figures. Today's forms of financial statement—often divided up into the accounts and an administrative report, i.e., separated according to finances and outputs—must be fundamentally revised—in our opinion in favour of a form that would contain an integrated report on finances, outputs and outcomes every year.

Figure 6.7 illustrates diagrammatically how we conceive of the interaction between the various control options. All the elements are embedded in the constitution and in law. The mission statement provides the overriding visions for the polity, which ideally are reflected in the executive's priority programme, in the integrated tasks and finance plan and in the performance budgets.

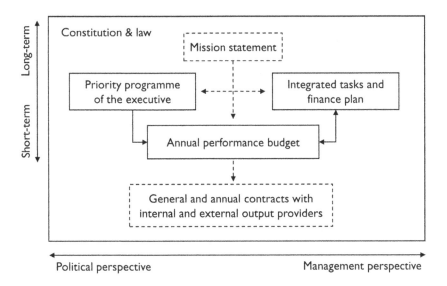

Figure 6.7 Interaction between the instruments of political control.

Contract Management

Output control is considered to be a central issue in OPM. It can be exercised in various ways; however, the dominant element is the advance stipulation of expected outputs. This can be done with the help of performance contracts, although in practice you can also find individual cases as hierarchical precepts or as orders for outputs.

Definition 6.2:   Contract management
The concept of *contract management* provides for target agreements to be concluded between administrative units at different hierarchical levels but also between administrative units and external organisations. The components of this control mechanism are one-line budgets and performance agreements (Neisser & Hammerschmid, 1998, p. 568).

The previously strict division into decision-making tiers, with the superior instance being able to issue instructions to inferior units, is replaced by increased communication between—albeit not completely equal—partners (Hill, 1994, p. 309). Quasi contracts, so-called performance agreements, are intended to replace hierarchical instructions. This approach implies a new orientation for top-level administration: the cost/output ratio is not governed by directives issued from on high but by decision-making processes in a spirit of partnership. When operative decisions are left to output providers, contracts will furnish the guidelines for output production. They cover quality, quantity, availability in time, as well as the contractually agreed funds that are available to the provider. The subject matter of the contract is legitimated by agreements concluded at higher hierarchical levels, in which condensed precepts are stipulated.

Definition 6.3:   Performance agreement
The term *performance agreement* denotes all the orders, contracts and agreements that regulate tasks, competencies and responsibilities between politics, top-level administration, administrative units and third parties. Performance agreements specify the supraordinate and operative goals, the outputs to be produced and the resources to be made available for this purpose. Inside the administration, performance agreements fulfil the function of management agreements; in relations with third parties, they are contracts.

It is incumbent on the political level, i.e., parliament or the council, to lay down politically normative goals in a strategic plan. The funds are approved as lump sums (i.e., as a net amount), and the calculation of these funds has to be disclosed. Top-level administration and the ministries are responsible for the formulation of performance agreements for the administration. Now, the interactions of performance control and financial control can assume widely differing forms.

The details of performance agreements must be formulated with regard to concrete applications. What is essential, however, is that performance agreements at all levels—like output planning previously—must be *prepared* by the ministries at national level and by top-level administration at municipal level as that is where the know-how is located.

This gives rise to a *model of a procedure* which, however, must be adapted in analogy with the structures of a municipality, a *Land* or the national government:

1. As is the case now, the *award agencies* in coordination with the providers carry out the preparatory planning work for the consolidated performance budget. This process is *interlinked* and possesses components of both the top-down and the bottom-up process.
2. Taking into consideration the various political initiatives in parliaments or councils and the precepts issued by the executive or top-level administration, and on the basis of the preparatory work done by the award agencies such as the ministries, a central unit draws up the consolidated *performance budget* for the new year for the attention of the political bodies.
3. The executive or top-level administration adapts the *performance agreements* for the specialist units on the basis of the adopted performance budget. It is now up to the award agencies, if need be, to conclude *contracts* with external providers for the production of goods and services and to monitor their performance.

The conclusion of contracts can be founded on two pillars: a general contract of several years' duration (as a rule, four years) governs the fundamental relationship between the award agency and providers. It constitutes a medium-term framework for business relations. An additional annual contract then covers the detailed specifications about outputs with regard to volume, quality, financial associations and the sum-total of the funds contractually agreed for that year. Moreover, it lists special annual objectives that may result from special projects.

In everyday administrative life, the process of agreements at a contractual level will largely be characterised by minor adaptations to the contracts. If fundamental changes are in the offing or if better overall conditions are

General contract
1. References to general provisions (ordinances, etc.)
2. Contractual parties
3. Duration of the general contract (as a rule, four years)
4. Output groups with
    • operative objectives
    • target groups, output customers
    • access to the outputs
    • outputs for third parties
5. Special provisions (divergent/supplementary)
    • personnel
    • compulsory outputs (profit carried forward)
    • commercial outputs
      (turnover limits for commercial activities)
    • investments and use of facilities
    • terms and conditions of payment
    • contributions to and from third parties (subsidies)
    • insurance policies
6. Competencies and reservations of competence
    • monitoring of private firms
    • subcontracts
7. Quality assurance measures
8. Modifications to and dissolution of the contract

Annual contract
1. List providing an overview of outputs according to
   product groups with volume, proceeds and costs (net)
2. Contractual amount
3. Annual objectives for special projects

Figure 6.8   Grid for a contract or performance agreement.

expected from other suppliers, a new invitation to tender will be envisaged. This requires, of course, that award agencies have a good overview of the current market. If this is not the case, then periodical invitations to tender must be conducted nonetheless.

This course of action can also be observed in New Zealand, where particularly in the health sector, some experience has been gained with agreements. If in terms of effort and expenditure, it is inconceivable to repeatedly invite tenders for all the outputs (in New Zealand, every GP's surgery has a contract), then the areas where competitive tendering is necessary can be selected. In this case, the responsibility for this selection lies with the ministry.

Divergences from Performance Agreements

It is postulated that for the duration of a contract, politics does not interfere with the way in which the contract is performed, whereas the administration produces the stipulated outputs. Reality will sometimes fall short of this ideal picture: divergences are possible on either side in that either the politicians' expectations change or the administration does not produce the stipulated outputs or produces them poorly. These possibilities will be dealt with in the next few sections (better performance is only a problem if funds should be saved instead).

Change in the Range of Stipulated Outputs

The postulated restraint on politics with regard to involvement in operative matters causes many politicians to fear that they will no longer be able to exert any influence on the output range during the year. Since sociopolitical changes also occur during the year, however, it must be possible for politics to modify individual outputs stipulated in a contract during the year, too, if need be. These conclusions were also reached in the Netherlands, where in connection with the Tilburg case study it was noted that contract management is by no means an instrument used to elbow politics out of the administration. It is expected, however, that political interventions will take place in close coordination and after a discussion of possible consequences with the unit director, and that it is therefore important to define an order of priorities (KGSt, 1992, p. 146).

The satisfaction of this postulation gives rise to a situation whereby the politicians' change requirements are taken into account but a *unilateral* modification of a contract is precluded. Every change to the output range must be examined for its financial consequences, and financial resources must be adapted accordingly. Here again, there is a close logical connection between outputs and budget.

From a practical angle, politicians would have to be called upon not to change any stipulated objectives unnecessarily during the duration of the contract. It may be necessary, however, for individual administrative measures to be adapted in order for an objective still to be attained despite changes to the environment that have occurred at short notice. Such adaptations must be carried out unbureaucratically, in bilateral discussions between the contractual partners, and be communicated to parliament in the annual report.

Non-Performance or Poor Performance of an Agreement

The other party to the contract, the provider, can also cause divergences from the agreement by failing to perform it or by not performing it well. A problem situation arises when the agreed output is not produced or is poorly produced.

A flexible configuration of a contract is possible even though it is likely to prove troublesome to one-line budgeting. Here, the actors will have to adapt to the new situation. Nonetheless, a cut in the one-line budget as a consequence of an output volume that is smaller than stipulated in the contract is unlikely to cause major problems. A real problem arises, however, if volume variances have to be blamed on the administrative unit itself, i.e., if promised outputs are not delivered or are delivered in poor quality.

This case calls for possibilities of improvement or sanction. Since according to many legal experts, a contract between administrative units does not constitute a formal contract in spite of the actual meaning of the term but is more likely to be an agreement with which both parties are *courteous* enough to comply, the question of sanctions remains open. What is conceivable, in particular, are sanctions against the head of the administrative unit. As the official who is responsible for the outputs of his unit, he has to expect sanctions if he does not produce the agreed outputs.

In certain countries it has been suggested on occasion that the budgets of the administrative units concerned should be cut by way of *sanction*. In view of the improvements that the model aims at, however, the consequences of such a course of action are somewhat questionable: would a budget cut result in improved outputs the following year?

The same problem arises if, when the outputs are not delivered or not delivered properly, the budgets are extended in order to enable the unit to produce better outputs. This raises the question as to whether—to speak in banking terms—good money should be thrown after bad or, to put it differently: if more funds are made available, will this not even increase inefficiency?

The answer to this is patently obvious: it is an indispensable management task of the awarding agency to explore the causes for the deviation and to take the correct measures in each individual case. Generalised, quasi-automatic rules will not yield the desired success. This addresses an important constraint that has general applicability: *OPM cannot replace sound management (political decisions)* (cf. also KGSt, 1992, p. 148).

Qualifications Required for Contract Management

The necessity of having to conclude quite detailed contracts for practically all the outputs of public administration leads to a situation whereby the awarding agencies are becoming home to specialists who are capable of drawing up such contracts. As a rule, this competence does not exist in the various units at present. In the health sector, for instance, specialist (medical) competence is often solely the province of the hospitals. This head start with regard to information and knowledge is bound to make it extremely difficult for awarding agencies such as a ministry to exercise central control of even the quantity structures through agreements with hospitals. In order to be able to counter the hospitals' factual *superiority*, the awarding agency responsible for the health outputs will require personnel with a grounding in medicine and management who are capable of

- concluding the performance agreement (contracts), and
- assessing contract performance with respect to quality and quantity according to purely economic criteria.

Because it is extremely difficult in such a complex and rapidly changing environment, in particular, to have all the necessary specialist knowledge available in a central unit while still keeping the costs of contract management at a reasonable level, it must also be conceivable for administrations to work with *external specialists* (for example in the field of quality assessment). This type of quality management would have the additional advantage that international comparisons could lead to a similar effect to that which is aimed at by benchmarking: the discovery and dissemination of *best practice*.

Discuss

 What would the OPM control process look like in an administration in terms of a specific output? Try to develop such a process, and then discuss its consequences for performance precepts and measurement.

 What advantages and disadvantages does control through performance agreements have over traditional control through regulations?

Q Many elements of OPM are already used successfully in individual cases. Give examples of such existing control elements of OPM in your own environment.

Q Why is OPM (but not only OPM) governed by the principle, "No one-line budget without a performance agreement"?

Q OPM is criticised, among other things, for basing its control mechanisms on political objectives. Political scientists, in particular, raise the objection that clear-cut political objectives cannot realistically be expected. What is your opinion about this objection?

Further Readings

Bouckert, G., Halligan, J. (2008). *Managing performance, international comparisons.* London: Routledge.

de Bruijn, H. (2002). *Managing performance in the public sector.* London: Routledge.

Hatry, H. P. (1999). *Performance measurement: Getting results.* Washington DC: Urban Institute Press.

van Dooren, W. (2008). *Performance information in the public sector: How it is used.* New York: Palgrave Macmillian.

United States General Accountability Office (GAO). (2005). *Managing for Results. Enhancing Agencies Use of Performance Information for Decision Making.* Washington, D.C.: GAO.

7

The Reinforcement of Leadership Responsibility through One-Line Budgets and Management

One essential concern of Outcome-Oriented Public Management is the reinforcement of the public managers' leadership responsibility. "Let the managers manage" has been one of OPM's best-known slogans from the start. Similarly, OPM seeks possibilities of extending the public managers' scope of action and discretion without, however, relinquishing democratic control. This happens with a dual package of measures:

Firstly, the managers' discretionary scope of action in the operative field is extended by the replacement of detailed (line-itemised) budgets with one-line budgets.

Secondly, the resulting control gap is compensated for by the establishment of modern management accounting, which besides financial data also takes into account output and outcome data.

Outcome-Oriented Public Management, pages 127–147
Copyright © 2010 by Information Age Publishing
127

Both measures will be described in detail and commented upon in this chapter.

Demands Made on Financial Management

One-Line Budgeting

One of the most outstanding features of OPM is the change to financial control in public management. The abandonment of input-oriented control through line-itemised budgets leads to a number of adaptations in the area of financial management, with the focus being on the so-called one-line budget. A one-line budget is characterised by the fact that the only legally binding element it stipulates is net expenditure per output category or organisational unit (Hood, 1991).[1]

The *advantages* of this system for public management can be summarised as follows:

- an increase in managerial flexibility;
- greater motivation and responsibility on the part of personnel;
- a reduction in government monopolies when there is competition;
- an efficient fulfilment of functions;
- an encouragement to think in terms of costs;
- an objectification of the conflicts of interest between output buyers (top-level management/awarding agency) and output funders (parliament/council).

However, these advantages are countered by *problems:*

- At the political level, in particular, a change of thinking is necessary to ensure that the new distribution of roles can work successfully.
- Legislation will have to be amended; what is certain is that some areas of the law are directly affected, such as budget law, personnel law and organisation law.
- More elaborate control mechanisms are needed to monitor compliance with contracts.

A conversion to the new model requires the executive's full support even if it is attacked by reform opponents.

---

1 Americans tend to prefer the term *lump-sum budgets* (Thompson & Jones, 1986). In either case, what is meant must be defined precisely since there are great differences between practical applications with the same name.

One-line budgeting and performance control are systematically related in OPM. An introduction of one-line budgets on their own without a simultaneous improvement in performance control is irresponsible in the longer term. This is why the following rule applies: *no one-line budget without a performance agreement.* This combination finds application in all the control instruments of OPM, primarily in the integrated tasks and finance plan and in performance budgets.

___

Definition 7.1:   One-line budget

In a *one-line budget,* certain functional areas or organisational units are allocated the resources for the fulfilment of their tasks in the form of a net amount. This means that administrative units can spend more money than has been budgeted, provided that they fund this expenditure through additional revenue. Moreover, resources are no longer earmarked according to types of expenditures, which results in a delegation of the responsibility for resources. The allocation of a one-line budget is linked to the conclusion of a performance agreement. This establishes a connection between the finance side and the output side, i.e., between politically stipulated performance targets and the resources available for them.

One-line budgeting is intended to shift a majority of the budgeting principles that are applicable today from input to output orientation, which is often interpreted as a deviation from or even the abandonment of prevailing principles (for a comparison between traditional and new budgeting procedures, cf. Bertelsmann Stiftung & Saarländisches Ministerium des Inneren, 1997, p. 24). In fact this is no more than a *reorientation* of the perspective:

- *Substantive budget commitment*:[2] this generates a prohibition of moving a credit line from one item to another. In as far as it is *input-oriented,* this principle is abandoned in one-line budgets because the relinquishment of specification means that there is no detailed structure of items. A new qualitative commitment, however, emerges in that the *contract amount* is linked to *output groups.* It would be in perfect conformity with the system to prohibit a transfer of credit lines between output groups.

___

2   In this connection, reference is often made to the *principle of specification* or *speciality.* This principle covers the three pillars of qualitative, quantitative and temporal commitment, which are discussed here (Saile, 1995, pp. 33ff.).

- ▪ *Quantitative budget commitment*: this must also be considered in a differentiated way—it is not relinquished without any substitution. However, commitment is no longer based on detailed budget items but on the contract amount, which is naturally more global in nature. The contract sum, however, is strictly binding on the provider as long as the agreed output range has not been modified. Here, too, supplementary credit lines will have to be applied for if the planned amount is not sufficient.
- ▪ *Temporal budget commitment*: the prohibition of carrying remainders of budgeted amounts/credit lines forward to the following year is lifted in order to quash the existing incentives to exploit the budget before the end of the year (*December fever*). For such carry forwards to be permissible, however, the agreed outputs must have been produced in the course of the year. The extent of such carry forwards varies: whether the funds may be carried forward in total or whether the polity skims off part of them depends on individual arrangements and has a tangible impact on the administrative unit's incentive situation.
- ▪ *Prohibition of netting* this prohibition is lifted to the extent that it is no longer the gross items reports in the budget that are legally binding but only the net funds earmarked for individual output groups. The output provider may thus have greater expenses than budgeted, provided they are financed through additional revenue. As an accounting principle, the gross reporting of all items still enjoys *unlimited validity*. The recognised principles of commercial accounting are not affected by one-line budgeting.
- ▪ *Annual budgets*: in connection with the conclusion of general contracts, top-level administration and the awarding agencies will have to consider whether they want to continue to budget annually. In future, finance and performance plans will have to be accorded greater significance, whereas annual control through budgets should become correspondingly less important.

One-line budgets conceived of in such terms are not as revolutionary as they might seem. A similar approach is pursued, for instance, if a credit line for a project (such as the renovation of a school roof) is granted net, i.e., without an itemisation of individual types of expenditure and less any contributions to be expected from other polities. Subsidies to third parties that produce outputs on behalf of the polity are basically also one-line budgets. However, what is lacking in this case are the performance agreements that are regularly necessary for output-oriented control.

The Internal Providers' One-Line Budgets

If the one-line budgeting for administrative units is carried out consistently, then this must mean that internal outputs are now budgeted with the output buyers and are charged internally when the output has been bought. Provided that this is a zero-sum game, the providers' one-line budgets will increase with the volume of outputs that are charged internally (decentralisation of the responsibility for resources). The internal providers' budgets will decrease to the same extent. In an extreme case, this can lead to a situation whereby an internal provider no longer has a budget of its own since the internal sale of outputs makes it totally self-financing (cf. Chapter 7, Cost Accounting, pp. 135ff.).

Although the political debate should primarily pivot round the output side, interministerial services will continue to be of significance since they have a crucial impact on output costs. It is erroneous to believe that the sole representation of the outputs' "full costs" is sufficient for political control. Internal providers may be able to report balanced accounts, but the latter should still be analysed with regard to the efficiency and effectiveness of their output production.

It may be necessary to issue certain guidelines for interministerial services so that the whole structure does not come apart at the seams. In the internal providers' performance agreement, for example, it should be stipulated that internally charged prices will have to be fixed in advance in order to prevent inefficiencies from being transferred to the line offices at the end of the year.

Experience with one-line budgeting in Germany reveals that positive effects clearly outweigh negative ones. A research team from Speyer headed by Klages (Klages et al., 1998) evaluated budgeting approaches in municipal schools and confirmed the positive results; however, they also discovered weak points in respect of output orientation.

Calculation of the Contract Amount

It was not only the calculation of the prices of individual outputs that was tested in OPM projects, but also the calculation of the contract amount as a whole. Rieder (2004) rightly called for the introduction of planned cost calculations in order to be able to make the effects of deviations from volumes transparent. Such deviations can also occur quite naturally, without any blame resting with providers: a state school, for instance, is as unable to control the number of new entrants as the road maintenance department the number of snowy days per year. Yet both factors can cause substantial changes to costs. The solution would therefore have to consist in a variable contract amount that is calculated

    a. in purely variable terms (i.e., per output) or
    b. mixed with a fixed component.

Thus in variant (b), a fixed stand-by price would be paid.

This second case is typically applicable if an output causes so-called step-fixed costs. An example may serve to illustrate this: the class ceiling at a school has been set at 25 pupils. Pupil number 26 thus triggers off the establishment of an additional class, which leads to higher fixed costs in one single step: additional teachers, rooms, etc. Or it is the simple offer of a service that results in higher costs that are independent of the service volume: the fact that a school is even run, for example, causes very high fixed costs.

For such cases, the so-called *taximeter model* has been developed (Figure 7.1), which distributes a basic grant, provided there is an offer at all. In addition to this, a variable amount is credited per output unit, calculated in such a way that a minimum utilisation becomes necessary to be able to fund the entire organisation. As a rule, no "reserve" is planned, so planned utili-

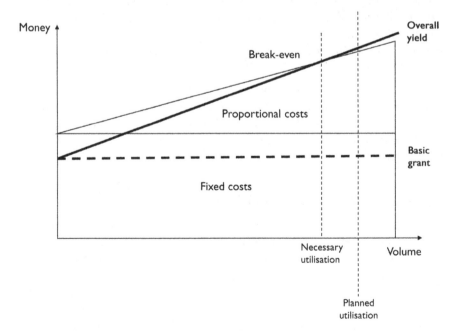

Figure 7.1 Taximeter model of contract amount calculation.

sation comes to be situated above the necessary utilisation, which means that the unit can make a small profit if the output is produced efficiently and if utilisation is optimal.

Many administrative units produce outputs which are fully or partially funded through contributions from other polities. When the contract is being concluded, the question arises as to whether these payments are part of the contract amount. If they are included in the contract, the risk of their reception is transferred to the provider. This creates an incentive to initiate compensation payments by satisfying the criteria of entitlement to them. This is in the interest of the polity concerned and in conformity with the model, provided that the compensation payments can indeed be influenced by the output provider itself. Compensation payments which are wholly or partially determined by agreements between the polities or unilaterally by another polity should not be included in the contract amount. This (ultimately political) risk is the polity's own, and the satisfaction of the compensation criteria constitutes the substance of the contract with the output provider. Thus the way in which the contract sum, and particularly the payment flows that it involves, is calculated, determines the risks for the output buyers and providers.

Financial and Management Accounting

As soon as an administration manager is no longer able to personally monitor all the activities that are carried out in his organisation, he requires information for management purposes. Ulrich (1990, p. 15) described the management functions of *checking, deciding* and *launching* as a circular procedure as early as the 1960s in the St. Gallen Management Model, and these basic functions have not changed in the least. However, *checking* in German is *kontrollieren,* and that verb is often confused with the English verb *control,* which also has the connotation of "checking," but mainly means as much as "to keep under control." Ever since the 1990s, however, actors in the German-speaking areas have increasingly used the term *controlling* for what in the English language is called management accounting.

Definition 7.2: Management accounting

Management accounting takes places when managers and management accountants cooperate. Management accounting is the entire process of goal setting, planning and control with regard to finances and outputs. Management accounting consists of activities such as decision-making, defining, specifying, controlling and regulating. Consequently, managers must engage in management accounting since they have to make decisions concerning the objectives to be attained, to fix the level of these objectives and to draw up the plan as such; and they are responsible for the result that is actually achieved (International Group of Controlling, 1999, p. 34).

The control process model presented in Chapter 6 makes these circular processes of planning/goal setting and implementation monitoring by stipulating a comparison between planned and actual values at each level. Only when the objectives have been defined for each level and the actual values have been registered, can it be discovered where what deviations occur and where public managers have to scrutinise the matter in more detail.

The control process was primarily developed for individual output processes. Conversely, models of political evaluation target overall social relationships and assume that outcomes can only be achieved through changes in individual people's behaviour (impacts). This evaluation would therefore place these elements in a different order.

Accountancy

Today, the accounts of the public sectors are largely geared to the observation of finance flows and of the past. They can be ascribed to *financial accounting*. If public administration is to be managed in an outcomeoriented way, then this perspective must be supplemented by an internal and management-oriented view. Existing accounting systems are combined with a cost/output oriented accounting and information system in order to improve the information basis for top-level administration.

Accrual Accounting as the Basis

In parallel with OPM, many public administrations have also adopted that form of accounting which is customary in the private sector, namely accrual accounting. In Switzerland, an accrual accounting system was developed for the cantons and municipalities in the 1970s, which by now has been introduced virtually throughout the country. After years of debate about the issue of accrual accounting vs cameralistics, Lüder (1996) developed a municipal accounting system based on accrual accounting that has the potential for widespread introduction.

Definition 7.3:   Accrual accounting and cash accounting
Cash accounting is an accounting concept that reports finance flows when they occur as actual (and occasionally fictitious) payments.

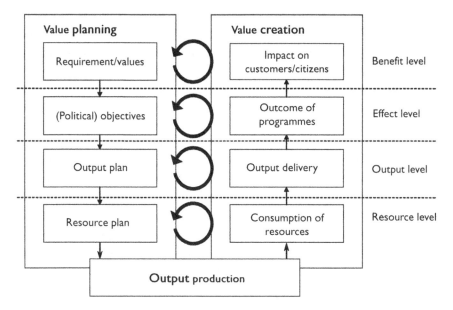

Figure 7.2 The OPM control process as a management accounting grid.

> *Accrual accounting* is an accounting concept that reports finance flows at the time of the generation of claims and liabilities, i.e., partially before or after money actually flows.

If, however, a new type of public management intends to primarily promote outcome orientation, then a concentration on finances alone will fall short of requirements. It is for this reason that in practical projects we conducted in Switzerland, four levels of a management-oriented accounting and information system were developed that can be located in the heuristic model of the control process in the politico-administrative system (cf. Figure 7.2). This separation cannot be smoothly implemented in practice; the levels often overlap with the result that costs, outputs, outcomes and/or benefit accounting merge into each other. By way of a simplified representation, however, the concept is capable of illustrating the major elements of the new accounting system. Every account can (and should) be configured as both a planned and an actual account.

***

Cost Accounting

Cost accounting is situated on the *middle level* of the control process. It reports the costs of resource utilisation incurred by every cost type and cost centre, and how these costs are distributed. It has chiefly been designed for internal management purposes but is not least employed by many practitioners to determine the foundations for internal prices and for the comparison of indices (for details, cf. Flury, 2002, pp. 204ff.).

To date, cost accounts have only been partially standardised. A harmonisation of cost units, in particular, would have the advantage that comparability between different polities would be enhanced—even though pure cost comparisons will never result in propositions that are valid in their own right. An attempt in Switzerland to arrive at a harmonised definition of cost units for cantons and municipalities failed, however, since the distribution of tasks between, and the fulfilment of tasks in, the various polities proved to be too different.

So far, cost accounts have been used in areas which at least aim to introduce the user-pays principle to the greatest possible extent, i.e., to make outputs self-financing. They were therefore primarily an instrument to legitimise the level of charges, i.e., an aid for the general procurement of revenues (Budäus, 1995, p. 29). However, the instrument of cost accounting can be employed throughout public administration; in that case it is not the legitimation of revenues but the optimisation of efficient and effective output production that will be its main purpose. Thus cost accounting becomes an important element among the management instruments used in public administration (for more details, cf. Brede, 2001, pp. 199ff.).

A decision-oriented cost/output accounting system should be in a position to convey knowledge about fixed, step-fixed and proportional, direct and indirect, as well as influenceable and non-influenceable costs (Rieder, 2004). This is of importance to political control, in particular: if a political body cuts expenditure on the basis of average cost calculations, the administration may in certain circumstances no longer be able to produce the required outputs since its fixed costs cannot be cut in proportion to its outputs.

Moreover, actual cost accounting must be complemented by *planned cost accounting* so that both cost variances (given the planned volume) and volume variances (given planned costs per unit) can be recorded and analysed (cf. the recommendations expressed by Flury, 2002, pp. 340f.). This, however, requires output accounts to be kept.

A further step could be constituted by the additional introduction of activities based on costing which define the distribution keys for common costs in new ways. These activities no longer serve to determine the costs of an output through traditional distribution keys but through the allocation of activity costs, which are defined as cost drivers. This allocation of not directly assignable activities is also effected through a classification system (Zimmermann, 1993, pp. 177ff.).

Cost accounts are primarily management instruments for the administration. In relation to politics, the information they yield is processed and communicated in the form of indicators (mainly efficiency indicators). Experience with OPM projects demonstrates that as a rule, political bodies are incapable of properly evaluating cost per output information in its entire complexity. For this reason, a full publication of cost accounts is not advisable.

Internal Recoveries

To obtain management-relevant data for individual administrative units, it must be ascertained with the help of cost accounting which internal charges should be debited to the outputs. It is clear that the costs incurred by the administrative unit itself are passed on to the outputs—but what about the outputs that the ministry produces for the administrative unit? What about the expenditure caused by the political bodies, the executive and parliament? The answers to these questions can be inferred from the purpose of the cost/output accounting that is pursued under OPM:

 a. creating transparency,
 b. fostering cost awareness,
 c. making data available for the make-or-buy decision.

If variant (c) is prioritised, then this decision means that all the costs that are not incurred if the output is produced by a third party will have to be passed on to the output. These are the classic proportional costs of production, albeit in a broad sense of the term. Conversely, the costs that are incurred anyway, independently of this choice—for instance in the ministries and in political bodies—do not fall into this category.

The call for transparency (a) entails the accounts providing information both about the costs incurred by the administration itself and by outputs bought in. This would mean separating the administrative unit's own costs from costs that are recovered internally. In addition, there is probably also a political demand for a comprehensive view of costs (the so-called "*full costs*"), which would include the ministries' outputs.

Cost awareness (b), however, can only be fostered if the administrative unit is made accountable for the controllable costs. Expenditure incurred by the ministries without any influence on the part of the administrative unit must therefore be reported separately. What must be called for in this

Level I:	Costs incurred, and proceeds realised, by the administrative unit itself
Level II:	plus costs incurred and proceeds realised by other administrative units (e.g. interministerial offices) which can be influenced by the output buyer,
Level III:	plus costs and proceeds that cannot be influenced by the administrative unit but have been caused by it,
Level IV:	plus costs that cannot be influenced and are not caused by the administrative unit, such as the costs of the political system. These, however, are merely of statistical value.

Figure 7.3 Responsibility-based multi-level statement of account of an administrative unit.

instance is a decision-oriented *individual cost accounting* system for administrative units. These various requirements lead to a system of a multi-level statement of accounts that takes into consideration, and highlights, different levels of responsibility on the part of the administrative unit's manager (Figure 7.3). This responsibility-based concept of cost accounting creates transparency in order to hold different administrative units accountable for the costs they cause.

Cost accounting on its own is incapable of furnishing essential management information unless it is employed to make historical, horizontal and vertical comparisons. Cost types and cost centres, however, are unsuitable as reference objects since they hardly serve to compare like with like. A valid comparison will only result from a standard definition of cost units. For this reason, it is necessary to proceed above and beyond the pure resource perspective and envisage another level: the output level.

Accounting for Outputs

At the second level of the control process, the administration's outputs are agreed in terms of products, and the production of these outputs is measured. The instrument for this is called accounting for outputs, which is part of the overall performance measurement system of the administration. Output-related information substantially improves transparency for politicians.

Output accounting reports the administration's immediate production volume, usually in purely quantitative terms. Often outputs are already reported today that could be combined into groups in the sense of OPM.

Many data that are gathered from business checks, however, are incapable of this. Output accounting closes this gap and tries to measure the outputs at least in quantitative terms throughout the administration and to evaluate these data systematically.

Thanks to the link of cost and output accounting it can be worked out, for example, what costs a product service causes in comparison with other services—a piece of information that politics lacked before. It is rightly asserted, then, that *outcome-oriented* control is more effective and radical than *input-oriented* control.

Accounting for Outcomes

Outcome accounting reports the outcomes of administrative action, i.e., of the programmes, and relates them to the political goals that they served to pursue. It provides information about the entirety of the outcomes that were triggered off by the programmes (including unintended side effects).

The prerequisite for meaningful information in the context of outcome accounting is the existence of *clear and measurable objectives*. If objectives are defined in a methodically inadequate manner, effectiveness cannot be measured at the level of outcomes. For these reasons, the introduction of outcome accounts often starts with an examination of the objectives and, in many cases, an improvement in deficient definitions of objectives. This process has a dimension that is shaped by politics and the culture of the administration and will therefore be somewhat time-consuming.

Where outcomes cannot be measured with the help of indicators, the *methods* of outcome accounting are often related to evaluations. These, in turn, make great demands on the evaluators' specialist knowledge and cause substantial financial outlays. The administration will therefore usually base its work on a system of indicators that are capable of furnishing pointers to changes or prevailing conditions.

Accounting for Impact

The assessment of the benefit of a measure for the addressed target group is the most complex task in this management accounting model. It expresses the effect of administrative action as it is subjectively apprehended by the addressees (and is therefore called an *impact*). Customer requirements, whose measurement is often as blurred as that of the impact itself, serve as the reference value. Data are frequently gathered with quantitative procedures such as observations, customer panels, complaint analysis and similar methods. The closer to customers a polity works, the easier it is to ascertain these benefits.

Indices for Public Management

A more outcome-oriented consideration of public administration leads to new requirements with regard to information, which financial accounting can only partially satisfy. Management *indices of the financial position* focus on

- completely reporting all the expenditure, both that of one's own administrative unit and of other administrative units,
- reporting the revenues of the administrative unit and allocating them to the outputs,
- calculating the actual costs of the outputs.

Moreover, an index system must be capable of processing information from the output, outcome and impact levels in an updated manner and of presenting it in condensed form. When it comes to establishing the relevant index or indicator accounts, the control process again stands us in good stead (Figure 7.4).

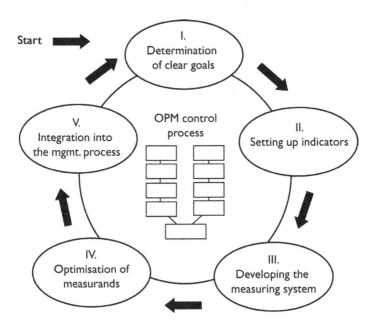

Figure 7.4 Establishment of an indicator system for public management. *Source*: Schedler and Weibler (1996, p. 16).

The first step in the establishment of an indicator or index system for management purposes consists in the determination of clear objectives. The result of this specification process is a catalogue with operationalised, i.e., measurable objectives to be pursued by the administration. In a next step, indicators are set up that are capable of reflecting goal attainment. Then the measurement of these indicators is organised, and the collected data are entered in the system in analogy with financial accounting. On the strength of experience with indicators, the measurands are optimised so that they can be integrated into the management process as the last and most important measure. This entire process is repeated on a regular basis; its initialisation will take up a great deal of time, but adaptations can be carried out more quickly.

Various models are known from management theory that are helpful for the establishment of index systems. However, the question must always be asked as to the purpose for which these models were developed. Business excellence models such as that of the European Foundation for Quality Management (EFQM) are only suitable for management purposes with reservations since they were created for a different purpose. On the quest for concentrated information that would be relevant to strategic management, Kaplan and Norton (1997) developed the *balanced scorecard* (see Figure 7.5). With this instrument, the relevant objectives are formulated for four areas in strategy meetings of top-level administration with the executive. To measure their attainment, indicators are defined for each objective. The most important task here is not to exceed a certain number of indicators so as to avoid an information tsunami, similarly to the way this is done in modern aircraft cockpits.

The balanced scorecard (BSC) is not completely new. It is one of a number of attempts to improve performance measurement in the private sector. "Performance measurement" in this sense of the term aims to base strategic management decisions not only on the customary indices from financial accounting but, above and beyond this, to pervade the enterprise's performance domain with an information system (for more details, cf. Klingebiel, 2001). Public managers are given a balanced set of information that includes non-financial areas of responsibility in which they must be active with their managerial decisions. In this respect, the BSC steers a similar course to Outcome-Oriented Public Management. It is impressive, however, owing to some principles which should also be taken over into the indicator systems used in OPM, namely:

- concentration on the information that is really crucial for addressees, and the active involvement of addressees in the substantial structure of the BSC;

- the inclusion of information about the past and about future developments;
- the inclusion of information about the organisation itself and about the relevant environment; and
- the inclusion of information about finances, outputs and outcomes.

It is becoming increasingly clearer that such management information is part of OPM's most important potential. Where the administration cannot manage to furnish meaningful information about outputs and outcomes, politicians will not be persuaded to turn their backs on input control.

Meanwhile, the BSC is also being used successfully in various public polities. Ösze (2000), for instance, illustrates on the basis of the tax administration of Switzerland's Canton of Berne how a multi-level use of the BSC as a strategic management and management accounting instrument

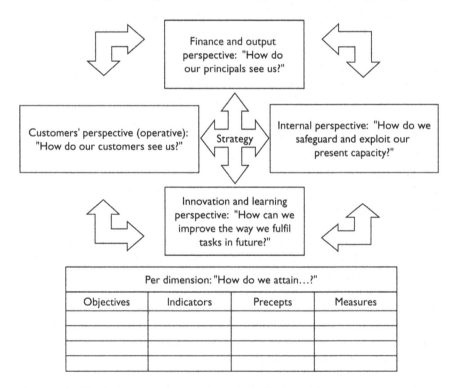

Figure 7.5 The balanced scorecard for public administrations. *Source*: in analogy with Kaplan and Norton (1997).

would be feasible. As a rule, however, this will require adaptations to the fundamental structure, which is something the "founders" of the BSC actually recommend (cf. Kaplan & Norton, 1997). In simplified terms, it can be said that the *financial perspective* has to be extended. It is the mirror-image of the success of the enterprise in the "feeding system" of the private sector, the market. For a public institution, however, this feeding system is usually not the market but politics in the guise of the principal (cf. Chapter 3, pp. 49ff.). For this reason it is indispensable for the survival of a public institution that the fulfilment of tasks is turned into the central topic of this perspective. In the mindset of OPM, this becomes the outcome, output and financial input perspective or, put differently, the task perspective. The question, "How do our shareholders see us?" is replaced by, "How do our (political) principals see us?"

Comprehensive Management Accounting

This far-reaching and simultaneously heterogeneous information must be processed for practical purposes, i.e., so as to be suitable for its addressees. Only when it has been integrated into the management process and is really exploited for management decisions does it finally make sense. Its collection, assessment, maintenance and archiving is a complex exercise: keeping such information systems up to date and maintaining them does not only cost a fair amount of money but takes up many working hours. In public administration, which is characterised by particularly information-intensive services, it will in future be everyone's permanent task to correctly feed information into the relevant receptacles so that it can later be retrieved by other administrative units (which may be completely detached from the workstation into which it was originally fed).

Such systems are developed, introduced and maintained by specialists who do not, however, primarily set their sights on the technology, but on management. In modern administration, this task is taken on by management accounting services, which are the administration's in-house management consultants.

The more strongly an administration is decentralised, the more important the establishment of effective management accounting becomes. Budäus (1995) rightly lamented the missing integration of those areas which had been effectively decentralised even without OPM. Here, management accounting must ensure the coordination of management tasks at the various control levels.

Reporting in Cockpit Systems

The more information is available, the more difficult the selection of the relevant management data becomes. The internet illustrates that we are technologically capable of accessing a multitudinous amount of data online but that, as human beings with a limited capacity and limited time, we are overtaxed unless we set up certain selection mechanisms for ourselves.

The same happens in public management and in politics when all the information that has been made available comes flooding in: information overload often results in a rejection of everything that is new, or else in an inadequate filtering-out of information which, as such, would be important. Management accountants who are responsible for the establishment of the reporting system must therefore ask themselves which parts of the information they have to supply are relevant for that specific management level.

When it comes to the establishment of the reporting system, it is important that some distinctions are made:

- Will the information be made available in its *raw form* or will it be *processed?* If the latter is the case, will this be a graphic evaluation or an additional interpretation with a commentary?
- Will the information be placed on a user's desktop, as it were (*push information*), or will it be prepared for retrieval from a database (*pull information*)?
- What information will be gathered and processed *routinely*, and what information will relate to *projects* that will be completed at some stage?
- How can it be ensured that any information that is no longer required will no longer be supplied?

So-called *data warehouses* offer processed management information which users can retrieve according to their requirements. Our experience—with political bodies in particular—shows that this has a lot of potential but is also treated with a great deal of reluctance. Moreover, it must be said that information that is relevant to management need not necessarily be relevant to politicians, too. A management accounting report full of operative indices is pointless for many politicians and will always remain just that. For this reason, Mastronardi (1998, p. 105) is among those who rightly postulate the creation of "political indicators," i.e., a possibility for politics to request information from the administration which from the administration's point of view may not even be of any interest. This partly removes the responsibility for adequate control information from the administration to the recipients of the information: the politicians.

In practice, so-called cockpit systems have been successful which turn a monitor into a kind of car dashboard or, as the term says, the cockpit of an aircraft. Presenting information without any figures, visualised and reduced to the six or seven most important indices per area, such cockpits offer a valuable aid for public administration. Technically, a possibility can be created to access a specific figure or a commentary, or maybe further, more detailed representations, by means of a double click on a certain graph.

Just as a driver does not only drive on the basis of his dashboard instruments but determines the direction through an independent system, so the information provided by the cockpit alone will not be sufficient for politicians to be able to make their political decisions. Thus it is necessary, but not enough for good management. However, the cockpit provides the important piece of information as to whether the administration is on the right course or whether corrective measures are required.

Hoch (1995) emphasises that the number one success factor for the operation of an information system is personified responsibility. This does not only refer to the responsibility for the information system as such; rather, this statement must be understood in a wider sense than was originally

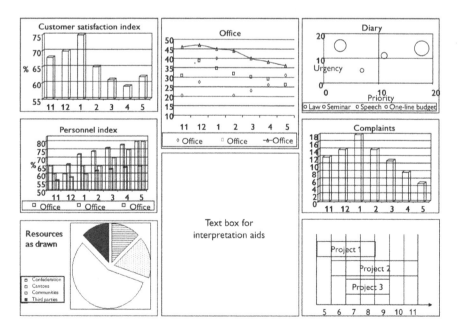

Figure 7.6 Example of a cockpit for public management.

intended, at least in its explicit context: if it is not clear who is generally responsible for which processes inside the administration, it is also not clear who requires which pieces of management information.

Discuss

Q The one-line budget as one of the core elements of OPM is vehemently criticised by its opponents. They argue that it causes democratic control over administrative expenditure to be lost. What is your opinion about this argument?

Q Recent developments in Europe point in the direction of reinforcing the medium-term view of political control (4-5 years). What reasons can be behind this? Who would profit from medium-term control? What would speak against it?

Q Cost accounting is often described as an absolutely essential foundation of OPM. How much OPM can also be introduced without cost accounting? Of what benefit is cost accounting in traditional, bureaucratic structures?

Q How would you arrange a cockpit for the political leadership of a city with 100,000 inhabitants? Search the internet for good examples.

Q Many administrations seek their salvation in customer and citizen surveys when it comes to measuring impacts. What possibilities do such surveys offer, and what are their limitations?

Further Readings

Hood, C. (2004). *Controlling modern government: variety, commonality and change.* Cheltenham: Elgar.

Wildavsky, A. (1974). *The Politics of the Budgetary Process.* Toronto: Little Brown Company.

Ridder, H.G., Bruns, H.J., Spier, F. (2005). Analysis of Public Management Change Processes: The Case of Local Government Accounting Reforms in Germany. *Public Administration, 83*(2), 443–471.

Ruben, I., Kelly, J. (2005). Budget and Accounting Reforms. In *Oxford Handbook of Public Management* (pp. 561–590). Oxford: Oxford University Press.

8

Competition and Market Mechanisms

One outstanding postulate of OPM is the application of market mechanisms in public administration. This is based on the basic tenet that in general terms, the market is better suited to generating an efficient and effective production of goods and services than regulations. The introduction and establishment of competition and market mechanisms are intended to supplement measures concerning administrative structures, such as the separation of roles, performance agreements, etc., with an increase in the efficiency, effectiveness and flexibility of public service provision, as well as an improvement in the monitoring mechanisms and in transparency. Competition is not an aim of OPM but an instrument whose integrative effect should "energise" the OPM model (Reichard, 1997a, p. 651).

Competition in Public Administration

Managed Competition

In many European countries, a classic model of government control and welfare-state supply by administrative units and non-profit organisa-

Outcome-Oriented Public Management, pages 149–167
Copyright © 2010 by Information Age Publishing
All rights of reproduction in any form reserved.

tions predominated until the early 1980s. Competition and the market did not have any great significance in this model of public administration; indeed, theories only dealt with them in the private sector for a long time. A very polar image prevailed between government control, on the one hand, and the private market, on the other hand. The idea of introducing competition into public administration was only discussed under the headings of *privatisation* and *downsizing*. Since, however, public institutions mostly produce goods that are not subject to a complete market (market failure) or were removed from the distributive function of the market for political reasons (e.g., education), the privatisation debate has always been highly ideological and the object of a great deal of criticism.

In OPM, competition is regarded as a mechanism for the enhancement of efficiency, which through the use of so-called "market mechanisms" can also be exploited in the context of public service provision. Competition orientation (cf. Chapter 3, Competition Orientation, pp. 64ff.) does not aim to shift the production of services previously provided by the government into the private market; rather, it aims to make the state's provision of services competition-oriented (cf. Chapter 1, The Concept of the Guarantor State, pp. 24ff.). Various mechanisms are used to generate what is known as *managed competition*.

Definition 8.1: Market mechanisms
Market mechanisms are employed to make use of the advantages of competition without relinquishing the advantages of government responsibility for the relevant tasks. With the help of market mechanisms, public administration creates market structures for goods and services for which no private market exists or for which the free private market leads to suboptimal and politically undesirable results. A whole number of mechanisms are available for this purpose, such as output comparison, competitive tendering and contracting out, with the optimal variant being chosen from individual case to case.

Competition orientation in OPM is thus not a question of private vs government service provision, but primarily a question of providing such services in competitive or non-competitive structures and arrangements. The cornerstone of this orientation is the insight that it is not a matter of which sector the service provider belongs to but the question as to whether the service provision is exposed to competition (Boyne, 1998; Savas, 2000; Shleifer, 1998). Since real competition, i.e., competition between several private and public providers, does not exist or is not desirable for many public services (market failure), market mechanisms are employed to introduce individual elements of competition.

Government Institutions as Market Participants

If various administrative units are to be placed in competitive relationships among each other and with other, non-governmental organisations, then it must first be ensured that all the competitors enjoy "*level playing fields.*" Failing that, there is a danger that competition will be distorted by the public institutions' special position:

- Public institutions can exploit their special position and are capable of achieving a considerable *competitive edge* over private suppliers, for instance, as a practical monopolist or as a consequence of cross-subsidisation from the law-enforcement domain of administration to its commercial counterpart.
- Public institutions' special position can place them at a considerable *disadvantage* in comparison with private suppliers owing to the fact, say, that they are subject to public law.

An important prerequisite for a comparison between different service providers is the creation of cost and output transparency in the administration. The introduction of cost accounting should provide a clear picture of the actual cost of public output provision. In administrative competition mechanisms inside the administration, reference values based on input-oriented financial data are not meaningful, since as a rule it cannot be ascertained which outputs were provided with which resources—which means that one reference value is missing.

Numerous objections have been lodged, and difficulties listed, with regard to the convincing pricing and costing of public output provision (Walsh, 1995, pp. 91ff.). Broadly speaking, this concerns general problems caused by the allocation of indirect costs such as very high investment costs, high overheads/administrative costs, etc., which typically also occur in the production of public administration but are not specific to it. As a condition for the effective introduction of competition mechanisms, it will suffice to calculate the costs of output provision in such a way that they contain no hidden cross-subsidies.

Competition Mechanisms in Public Administration

In practice, a wide variety of instruments have evolved with whose help competition mechanisms are introduced into public administration. The competitive intensity of these instruments varies and ranges from competition on the market to the introduction of competitive structures inside the public sector and to mechanisms that strengthen competition orientation simply through the idea of "competing with others" and through the introduction of pricing mechanisms without any changes being made to the existing monopoly structure of the public provider.

Non-Market Competition

Many outputs provided by public administration do not have any parallel products in the private sector. It is therefore impossible for public administration to acquire the ability to change and adapt by means of confrontation with the private sector. These tasks are among the core activities of government and will continue to draw on a large part of budgetary resources in the future. For this reason, instruments must be put in place in these areas that serve to provide incentives for improved and efficient performance without having recourse to direct competition with several suppliers.

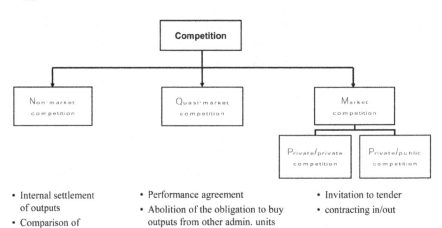

Figure 8.1 Forms of competition in public administration. *Source*: Wegener (1997, p. 83).

The forms of non-market competition are not tantamount to a real market. Incentives to discover and remedy inefficiencies are created here through *additional transparency* and *comparisons* of the units involved.

Internal Settlement of Outputs

Charging outputs to other administrative units aims to increase officials' cost awareness. Outputs provided by the department of planning and building inspection for the maintenance of administrative buildings, by the finance authority for interest payable, write-downs on properties, material deliveries, mutual consultations and a long list of further internal outputs are basically charged to those units which order and buy them. The introduction of such settlements is backed by a view from incentive theory: only those who have to feel the pinch of their own consumption decisions in their own (limited) budgets will have an economic incentive to streamline their consumption into efficiency and effectiveness. This is why OPM postulates the introduction of internal output settlements concerning those internal output purchases that can be influenced (cf. also Chapter 7, Financial and Management Accounting, pp. 133ff.).

The registration and correct allocation of costs is a first important step towards cost transparency but still does not constitute a guarantee of efficiency. In particular, there is no incentive to cut costs when they can be charged to others in full. This incentive must therefore be created, for instance, by an obligation to discuss cost settlements in the course of budget negotiations or by admitting external suppliers as a procurement alternative. The consequence will and should be increased pressure on internal providers, since administrative units will start to think in terms of costs and benefits. This will even be enhanced once economic behaviour in the context of one-line budgeting results in advantages for the administration.[1]

Competitive Testing

A further variant of non-market competition is the pure comparison of data between similarly situated institutions. In this context, we speak of a

---

1 When, for instance, Laux (1994, p. 174) voices the criticism that there would be a great danger of different administrative units having permanent altercations concerning the pricing of outputs and that the whole thing would degenerate into a form of keeping busy or that it would open the door to manipulation, it should be borne in mind that it is exactly this pricing of internal outputs that will be a component of the new budgeting process. It is the intention behind the model to trigger off this discussion in order to bring the provider/customer relationship in internal relations into a clearer focus, too.

comparison of organisations or more generally of competitive testing. This process, which can also be regarded as the first step in a benchmarking process, leads to insights that help the leadership to ask the right questions and to clarify matters. Although there still is no proper market, such comparisons will create a pressure which detects inefficient organisations and allows for concerted improvements.

For the political leadership and the administration alike, comparisons of organisations result in new insights because such comparisons help them conduct targeted investigations. Traditional across-the-board administrative analyses should be complemented by methods of organisational comparison. It must be emphasised, however, that pure comparisons are not sufficient for an assessment. The fact that one district is more expensive than another does not mean to say by far that it is worse. Such evaluations must always be interpreted in depth.

In Germany, a number of comparisons have established themselves in recent years. The starting shot was fired as early as 1990 by the Bertelsmann Foundation with its project on the foundations of efficient local administration in which numerous output comparisons were made with regard to various municipal tasks (Adamaschek, 1997, p. 14). Another project launched in 1996 by KGSt (an association of local authorities which are active in modernizing their administrations), in which no less than four per cent of all West German municipalities had participated by 2001, is also very well known (Kuhlmann, 2004).

Competitions for prizes are a further possibility, where municipalities or administrative units are selected and adjudicated by a jury. Participation in or qualification for such competitions alone may already be an incentive for innovations and improvements within the administration. Some of these competitions, such as the Carl Bertelsmann Prize, are accompanied by considerable publicity and promise a reputation enhancement and a favourable media presence for the winners. Thus the cities that won the Bertelsmann Prize in 1993, Phoenix, Arizona/USA and Christchurch/New Zealand, have become internationally renowned case studies whose reform models have earned them a great deal of recognition both in the literature and in practice.

Benchmarking

Since benchmarking consists of two essential elements, it can be used as an instrument for two things which are both of great significance for public administration:

a. In the private-sector applications that have been put to use so far, it is primarily the aspect of *learning* that is emphasised. Thus benchmarking is part of the quality management conducted by individual institutions (in this case, administrative units).
b. The aspect of comparison becomes important when inefficiencies should be discovered without the help of the market. In this respect, benchmarking contains a competitive component.

This comparative process is part of a more comprehensive concept that is intended to systematically promote *the learning organisation*. In management theory, the term "benchmarking" denotes a method of how a firm can compare itself with other, similarly situated enterprises. It employs comparisons to determine the best competitor for each individual constituent of corporate activities. This competitor should then be used as an example of how the task under observation can be fulfilled with the greatest degree of efficiency and with the highest quality.

The introduction of benchmarking is meant to complement references to the past with references to the present. Comparisons are not only conducted in-house but also with others. It is at this point that the notion of *quality standards* must be introduced. Quality standards allow for consistent quality management, which should in turn lead to improved outputs in the administration. The overriding idea is: *learning from others, learning from the market.*

Quasi-Market Competition

In a quasi-market competition, the conditions under which competition is intended to take place are created by competition surrogates without any recourse to the private sector. Like non-market forms of competition, quasi-market forms of competition can be found in all areas that do not admit of any direct competition between public and private providers, or in areas that have not yet been subjected to competition.

The Delegation of Responsibility, and Contracts

The instrument of the performance agreement, which has already been explained in detail, coupled with the delegation of responsibility demanded by OPM, represents one form of quasi-market competition. For one thing, the contract-like agreement gives rise to checks on quality and requirements, which also occurs in the market. For another, genuine competitive relationships can be observed in the provision of internal services. In the personnel sector, for instance, decentralisation creates competition between interministerial units and specialist units in that it is up to the specialist units to provide the outputs themselves or to "buy" them from the personnel department.

Competition within a Polity

In sizeable polities, tasks are often fulfilled by various operations with different catchment areas. This leads to a situation whereby individually, such operations occupy a virtual monopoly position in their respective regions and often erect political safeguards against change. Examples of operations with different catchment areas include schools, hospitals, forestries and many others.

A market and competition, then, can be created between such operations if the borders of their catchment areas are abandoned. In this way, excessive capacities—of whose existence there is clear evidence today—can be reduced if a catchment area is extended, provided that the transaction costs of this geographical extension admit of this. It can then be expected that geographical reforms will take place in an unspectacular manner; this, however, will require constructive involvement on the part of local and regional politicians.

In internally competitive situations, a market can be created by cancelling any possible arrangements between the suppliers. This means that, for example, the training department of unit X also offers courses to participants from unit Y and funds these through internal settlements. In principle, the same is conceivable for legal departments, organisation and IT departments and similar staff functions that are not completely tied to one single specialist area.

This would give rise to a type of specialisation that takes its bearings more from subject matter than from specialised organisational units. Some problems confront all the specialist units alike; the creation of such an internal market could thus allow for a fruitful specialisation without any formally organised central staff units having to be established.

Market Competition

Market competition makes use of public invitations to tender to find competent business partners who provide the services directly to customers. Competition may occur either among private suppliers only or between public and private suppliers. The second form, in particular, represents an outstanding innovation of modern reform movements.

Competitive Tendering

Competitive tendering is conducive to the search for a competent business partner who is in a position to supply a certain output range in the desired form and time at the most favourably priced terms and conditions. Depending on the form of the invitation to tender, either private suppliers only or private and public suppliers are asked to submit their offers. Tendering processes that involve private suppliers only have long been known in the award of public construction contracts. The Swiss Canton of Berne, for instance, uses the following criteria to find the most favourably priced offers in such tendering procedures: lead time, quality, price, cost effectiveness, operating costs, customer service, functionality, aesthetic appeal, creativity, ecological requirements and technical value (*Submissionsverordnung des Kanton Bern* Art. 6a lit. b). Only tendering procedures that admit both public and private suppliers constitute an innovation within the meaning of OPM for the promotion of the competitive idea in the administration.

The most prominent example of this form of competition mechanism was the *Compulsory Competitive Tendering* (CCT) that was widely introduced through the Local Government Acts under the Thatcher government in the UK. The provisions of these acts stipulate that in the areas they specify, tenders *must* be invited. After the offers have been received, the costs of the outputs provided by the administration are compared with those of all the interested private suppliers. The award goes to the supplier with the most favourably priced offer (Gerstelberger, Grimmer, & Kneissler, 1998, p. 284). Today, the overall success of this project is appraised in rather critical terms, and the nationwide project has been scrapped. Nonetheless, the conclusion may be drawn that in selected areas in which competitive goods are provided, CCT resulted in substantial increases in productivity. The weak point of the British programme was more likely to have been found in the style of its introduction and in its radical application to all areas of local government activities (Naschold, 1995, p. 35).

Contracting Out

The terms "contracting out" or "outsourcing" denote the situation whereby subsequent to a tendering process, the contract is awarded to a non-government supplier. The contracting out of government tasks is the last step in a whole number of instruments that result in increased competition for the provision of an output without placing the responsibility for these outputs in the hands of third parties, i.e., private suppliers or other polities. Thus outsourcing is not about the privatisation of government tasks but about the *make-or-buy* decision (cf. Chapter 8, Public–Private Partnerships, pp. 159ff.). Contracts for tasks are not awarded to non-government providers because the state shirks its responsibility for them but because it is expected that competition will result in cheaper or higher-quality provision or in order to examine the administration's own efficiency and to enable transfers of know-how.

Often, contracting out does indeed create actual competition in that it is not only one single provider that is allowed to supply the output but that several providers offer the same output. Thus in Phoenix, Arizona, waste disposal is the responsibility of a public supplier in half of the city's districts and of various private waste-disposal firms in the other half. In Christchurch (New Zealand) planning permissions are not only granted by the planning permission authorities but also by various licence construction engineering firms. This procedure creates actual competition beyond the tendering stage, and the administration retains know-how and capacities to prevent the establishment of private monopolies or the sudden loss of a supplier (so-called emergency capacities).

In management theory, make-or-buy decisions are often associated with *outsourcing*. The distinction between contracting out and outsourcing is not always clear-cut; even in practice, the terms are used with different meanings and as synonyms. For the purposes of this publication, the following demarcation is used (cf. Figure 8.2): if the administration buys outputs *for its own use*, we speak of outsourcing (e.g., IT outputs); if outputs are supplied to customers *directly and without any further processing*, we speak of contracting out.

The one big difference between contracting out and outsourcing can be found in quality assurance. In outsourcing, the administration itself is

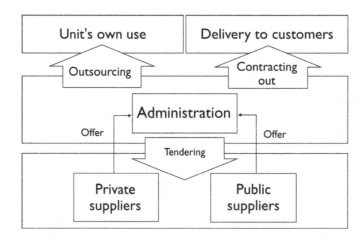

Figure 8.2 The state as output buyer.

the recipient of the outputs and thus has direct control of the quality and quantity of services. In contracting out, as the output is delivered directly to the citizens, the administration needs to find indirect ways of quality control—which are costly and bear the risk of excessive delays.

Applications of the different forms of competition vary greatly in national modernisation movements. Where the USA, the UK and New Zealand are strongly committed to market competition instruments, this element has not exactly been prevalent in Continental Europe. The reason for this may well be found in the strict separation of public and private law, which the Anglo-Saxon legal system does not have to the same extent (cf. Chapter 9, Legal Systems—The Functions and Configurations of Law, pp. 170ff.), but also in cultural differences. These legal circumstances make the inclusion of private output providers more difficult. In Continental Europe, then, competition orientation is primarily introduced by means of quasi-competition (Reichard, 1997; Kuhlmann & Bogumil, 2006; Pollitt & Bouckaert, 2004; Steiner, 2005).

Public–Private Partnerships

The inclusion of private suppliers in the fulfilment of public tasks has also increasingly been discussed under the heading of public–private partnerships (PPPs). Despite the great deal of attention that has been paid to this approach, there is no generally valid and clearly differentiating definition of this term. Thus the EU Commission states in its Green Paper on PPPs:

> The term public–private partnership ("PPP") is not defined at Community level. In general, the term refers to forms of cooperation between public authorities and the world of business which aim to ensure the funding, construction, renovation, management or maintenance of an infrastructure or the provision of a service. (Commission of the European Municipalities, 2004)

Thus PPP is a collective term for various forms of cooperation between public units and the private sector. In contrast to the market mechanisms described in the previous pages, a PPP is not a concrete instrument or a specified mechanism; rather, it is an approach to solving problems, often in a broad sense of the term (Bolz, 2005). The demarcation and application of the term is often made contingent on the existence of several constructive features and not on specific procedures; this applies to Continental Europe, in particular. Besides (1) the fulfilment of a public task and (2) cooperation between at least one government actor and one non-government, private actor, the essential characteristics of PPPs are usually considered to be (3) longer-term, process-oriented cooperation, (4) the provision of outputs in accordance with economic criteria, (5) joint responsibility borne by private and government actors, and (6) the need for harmonisation in the course of time (for instance as regards the resources used and risk allocation) (Bolz, 2005; Wissenschaftlicher Beirat der Gesellschaft für öffentliche Wirtschaft, 2004). The focus is on the attainment of *converging objectives*. In this goal attainment, *synergy effects* can be put to use. The *identity of the partners* and their responsibilities remain unchanged (Budäus & Grüning, 1996, p. 281).

There have been various approaches to systematising PPPs. Thus PPPs are divided up according to their structures into types such as organisational or contractual PPPs, or according to their tasks into infrastructural, service-provision or management PPPs, or even according to their purposes into procurement or task-fulfilment PPPs. The wide variety of types points to the wide variety of forms that PPPs can assume. At the same time, there are certain overlaps and partially blurred borderlines with other approaches and instruments for involving private actors in public output provision, such as outsourcing, contracting out or the partial or complete privatisation of organisations. Thus organisational PPPs refer to mixed-economy enterprises, which in turn represent a form of partial privatisation of an organisation. However, not every mixed-economy enterprise is a PPP; to become a PPP, mixed-economy enterprises have to serve the equilibrium of public and private objectives and satisfy the specific PPP requirements. Equally, a contracting-out relationship between private and public actors may qualify as a PPP if the contract on which it is based stipulates a long-term relationship between partners. A contracting-out relationship with clearly specified outputs and compensations, plannable contract durations and a buyer/seller attitude relationship between the parties, however, lacks important PPP features. Thus the borderline between the various competition elements and PPPs remains blurred and equivocal in many cases. In both approaches, the objective is a shift towards an enabling administration (Chapter 4, The Model of the Enabling Authority, pp. 85ff.), the involvement of private suppliers in public output provision, the reduction of the state's output depth and the exploitation of efficiency advantages (Savas, 2000).

Cooperation models between public and private actors which are described as PPPs can be found in a wide variety of tasks such as the promotion of trade and industry, structural policy, urban development, utilities, waste disposal, culture, infrastructure, etc. PPPs are intended to combine the strong points of private institutions with those of public institutions. Through partnerships, public and private actors are able to realise substantial synergy effects, which are created, in particular, through the fact that the partnership's specific goals could not be equally well attained without the partners. It is possible, for example, for the public partner to bring its planning and regulation authority into play whilst the private partner takes on management and funding functions. Many PPPs are designed to last until the completion of a project or infrastructure, thus extending to different stages and periods where outputs, costs and risks cannot be unequivocally settled when the contract is signed. Efficiency advantages can be generated when each partner bears the risk he is best suited to managing. A clear and expedient allocation of risks, i.e., an assessment and distribution of risks, constitutes a central driver and success factor of PPPs. The possibilities of mutual rights and obligations are highly diverse and depend on individual negotiations and formulations (Budäus & Grüning, 1997, pp. 55f.).

On the part of the public sector, PPPs are often seen as opportunities for easing the financial burden and for generating efficiency gains. However, other synergy effects such as the faster realisation of projects, flexibility and the exploitation of private know-how are also considered to be important arguments in favour of PPPs (Stainback, 1999, p. 1). Private partners expect PPPs to yield better chances of success through increased planning and funding security, the proximity to public decision-makers that is conducive to implementation, but also the development of new markets (Stünck & Heinze, 2005).

In German-speaking administrations, PPPs still have the potential for modern and efficient public management. Nonetheless, the risks that such partnerships may cause for the public sector must not be forgotten. Thus long-term mutual ties imply certain risks for both partners and reduce their future scope for action. There is also a risk that PPPs will fall into a "complexity trap" since very extensive and interlaced contracts, uncertainties and long contract duration periods make particular demands on systematic contract management and the control of PPPs. At the same time, private and public partners have diverging interests and decision-making strategies, which additionally impair the controllability of PPPs. So far, the public sector has faced a particular risk in that it has little experience of the negotiations and configurations of such partnerships (Budäus & Grüning, 1997, pp. 58ff.; Stünck & Heinze, 2005).

PPPs are at present enjoying a considerable amount of keen attention in politics and the administration. They are often regarded as solutions to and ways out of financial bottlenecks for the preservation, renovation and procurement of public infrastructures and outputs. It would be a great and highly dangerous misunderstanding, however, to conceive of PPPs as mere funding instruments. PPPs are alternative forms of organisation and provision that make great demands on, and involve great risks for, the partners with regard to control and management.

Performance Depth in the Public Sector

Institutional Options

The forms of competition orientation described above cannot be introduced to all areas of public administration to the same extent. Generally it can be said that any forms of market competition are more difficult to apply in law-enforcement administration than in service-provision administration. It is important, however, that entire clusters of tasks are not excluded from considerations regarding competition from the very start; rather, individual links in process chains must be tested for their competitive suitability, in law enforcement as well as in service provision (Proeller, 2002).

The forms of competitively oriented output provision outlined above also represent various institutional possibilities of public output provision. The question as to the institutional form of task fulfilment—i.e., by public or private institutions, non-profit organisations or even private individuals—again and again confronts administrations with the decision as to what institutional framework would be most suitable for which public tasks in what situations. This so-called *constitutional choice* is determined by the *institutional competence* of the various institutional arrangements. Each form of institutional organisation has certain properties that are better or worse suited to the output provision of a certain public function.

When it comes to tasks that require social commitment, a non-profit organisation is likely to be more suitable than a profit-oriented enterprise. The better the institutional competencies are in harmony with the requirements of the task, the easier the administration will find its contract management.

It is vital that those institutional arrangements can be found whose institutional competence best supports the provision of the specific output. The differences between the organisation forms are mostly located in the differing *objectives* and prevalent *external control*. The *form of funding*, too, can have a significant impact on the choice of institutional arrangements (Reichard, 1998, p. 131).

The institutional choice still does not say anything about the intensity of cooperation. The time frame can also be considered for further differentiation. The distance between the two corner points, "individual order" and "material privatisation," can be envisaged as an intellectual continuum on which interim stages such as the conclusion of a general contract, licensing and functional privatisation are situated.

Performance Depth Analysis

The scientific discussion of performance depth policy is largely based on findings of institutional economics, i.e., the transaction cost approach, agency theory, property rights theory and contract theory. In the German-speaking area, the concept of performance depth policy as developed by Naschold et al. (1996) occupies a predominant position in the theoretical analysis of optimal performance depth and institutional choice.

In this concept, optimal performance depth is subjected to a three-level assessment process: first, the *strategic relevance* of the output is examined, then the *specificity* of the factors to be vectored in, and finally the *efficiency* of output provision in the administration. On the basis of this analysis, the business field recommendations relating to the most suitable form of provision are deduced, as illustrated in Figure 8.3. Tasks of high strategic relevance and high specificity are part of the core area of government tasks and tend to be fulfilled by the administration itself for reasons of transaction costs. Outputs of low specificity and of strategic irrelevance tend to be bought in. For outputs of low specificity and high strategic relevance,

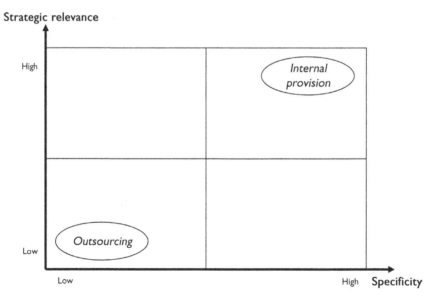

Figure 8.3 Performance depth portfolio. *Source*: in analogy with Naschold et al. (1996, p. 76).

or for outputs of low strategic relevance and high specificity, in-between forms of provision can be used, such as competition between public and private suppliers, long-term contractual relations or standardisation and regulation by law. The more efficient the output provision by the administration itself is, in comparison with output provision by external suppliers, the more likely the output will be provided internally owing to considerations of transaction costs.

The strategic relevance of a public output is determined by whether this output is relevant for the long-term guarantee of a *political programme*. Strategic relevance is important with regard to the make-or-buy decisions since the political programme and the outputs related to it must remain *politically controllable*. For all the strategically relevant outputs, a form of provision must be chosen that can be politically controlled. Traditionally, this is subject to a certain "hierarchical myth" according to which hierarchical control works more reliably in-house than control by third parties (Reichard, 1998, p. 143). Phenomena such as "hierarchical failure" indicate, however, that the efficiency of hierarchical structures is often overestimated and that consequently, the transaction costs of market and cooperation relations are overestimated, too. More recent trends in management therefore posit that outcome-oriented contract management can be expected to result in as effective a form of control as hierarchy. Since tasks and processes in this area are usually complex and not what is customarily encountered in the market, a contract relationship will have to be fairly long-term if both parties want to safeguard their interests (cf. also below).

The term "specificity" denotes the exclusive orientation and availability of resources for a certain output. High specificity carries a great risk of *sunk costs*[2] and thus increases the need for mutual ties in cooperative ventures (which results in long-term cooperation relations in field A). High specificity usually leads to an expansion of the administrative unit's own capacity and structures. A performance depth analysis should therefore not be limited to establishing a certain degree of specificity but should aim at despecification wherever this make sense and is possible. An increased use of information and communication technology and the concomitant standardisation may cause such a reduction in specificity. Outputs of low specificity and strategic irrelevance such as cleaning work can be bought on the market with relatively few problems. Contract relations are labelled "short-term" because no labour- and cost-intensive preparation and selection work has to be done.

---

2   The term "sunk costs" describes expenses and investments for certain tasks that are "lost" when a task is relinquished.

The efficiency analysis pivots on issues concerning minimum overall costs, which in essence are made up of production, procurement and transaction costs.

Our own research (Proeller, 2002) makes clear that the question of performance depth—particularly in law-enforcement administration—can certainly be viewed in a differentiated light. It is wrong to assume on principle that law-enforcement administration can simply not be outsourced. It is equally wrong, however, to negate the special requirements of law-enforcement administration. If acts of law enforcement are divided up into their component (operational) processes, these can be assessed individually with a set of interdisciplinary criteria, where the legal limits become more important in proportion to the severity of the administration's interference in citizens' rights. The fundamentals of process management make an important contribution in this respect.

Task Review and Relinquishment

In the last few decades, government tasks have been expanded continuously. A performance depth analysis must therefore also ask the question as to whether all these tasks are still being accorded such a high priority that they must be numbered among the state's tasks. The accompanying expansion of the apparatus of the state, as well as the general conditions—financial and otherwise—call for a *regular examination of the activities listed in the government's catalogue of tasks*. The method of a task review is applied to identify government tasks which no longer need to be provided by the state. Such tasks must be removed from government by means of *privatisation*. What tasks this concerns is a political decision that must not be made on the strength of management criteria alone.

This method was developed in the 1970s in order to curb the constant increase in government and its functions (cf. KGSt, 1989), with a fundamental distinction being made between reviewing the purpose of a task and reviewing the process of how it is fulfilled.

To preserve the character of the welfare state, a *qualitative task review* must be conducted, which does not simply aim to reduce the state to its core functions such as jurisdiction and internal and external security. In contrast to a quantitative approach, a qualitative task review does not call for privatisation as an end in itself but only demands it if it is possible without jeopardising the needs of people in a welfare state (Sachverständigenrat "Schlanker Staat," 1997, p. 49).

Tasks reviews and OPM are in a harmonious relationship with each other:

- The transparency of outputs and outcomes established by OPM—also in relation to the administration's efficiency and effectiveness—allows for well-founded task reviews to be conducted.
- A critical review of the necessity of government activities should precede any reform process as a matter of principle.

Discuss

Q The concept of *managed competition* is criticised in many quarters. What arguments can be raised against the concept from the points of view of the various disciplines (management, law, political science and economics)?

Q The call for market competition in OPM converges with international developments (for instance, in connection with WTO provisions) according to which tenders must be invited for all public jobs. At the same time, we note that private principals often award their contracts within a predefined group, i.e., do not invite tenders to the same extent. There must be reasons for this. How do you rate the call for consistent tendering in the public sector? What are the pros and cons of contracts being awarded within existing network structures?

Q Market mechanisms are established to enable the fresh winds of competition to blow through administrative units. How do you think public administration as a system will react to this "disturbance"?

Q Task review was developed as a method years ago but has been successfully implemented in only a few cases so far. What are the pros and cons of its being put to better use in OPM?

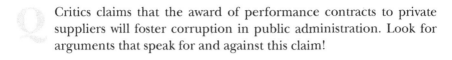 Critics claims that the award of performance contracts to private suppliers will foster corruption in public administration. Look for arguments that speak for and against this claim!

Further Readings

Akintoye, A. (2003). *Public-private partnerships: managing risks and opportunities.* Oxford: Blackwell Science.

Deakin, N., Walsh, K. (1996). The enabling state: the role of markets and contracts. *Public Administration, 74*(1), 33–48.

Domberger, S., Jensen, P. (1997). Contracting out by the public sector: theory, evidence and prospects. *Oxford Review of Economic Policy, 13*(4), 67–79.

Donahue, J. (1989). *The privatization decision.* New York: Basic Books.

Bovaird, T. (2004). Public–private partnerships: from contested concepts to Prevalent practice. *International Review of Administrative Sciences 70,* 199.

9

The Relationship between OPM and the Law

When we speak of controlling the administration in the constitutional states of Continental Europe, we quickly and inevitably encounter legal aspects and questions. The influence and interactions between the law and OPM are many-layered and complex. An analysis can tackle this problem at various levels. Thus a distinction must first be made as to the control philosophy and government tradition to which the legal system must be ascribed. Then, a legal system has specific principles and conventions from which state action must take its bearings. These are often not explicitly laid down in the constitution or the statute book. In Switzerland, for example, we speak of *principles of governance. Not least, law appears in the form of material and formal statutes and justiciable principles of procedure with whose help the administration and its activities can be controlled and monitored.*

Outcome-Oriented Public Management, pages 169–178
Copyright © 2010 by Information Age Publishing
All rights of reproduction in any form reserved.

Legal Systems—The Functions and Configurations of Law

It is customary to distinguish between legal systems by asking whether they must be assigned to the tradition of Roman law, as in the countries of Continental Europe, or to the tradition of common law, as in the UK. With a view to the state and public administration, the state in the tradition of Roman law is regarded as an object in its own right. This perspective is made clear by the German usage, according to which *der Staat* legislates, "the state" employs people and *state* officials, and people pay taxes to "the state"— the state has its own identity, is equipped with specific competencies, and acts through its organs such as parliament, the executive and administrative units (Dyson, 1980; Johnson, 2000; Wollmann, 2000). In the common law tradition the state does not possess this identity of its own. Rather, reference is made in such systems to individual institutions such as *the crown, parliament* and *the local council* or—in general terms, to the *government.* This, too, is reflected in linguistic usage, not least by the fact that the term "state" has a different meaning and application from the German *Staat* (Johnson, 2000). Whereas the common law system does not postulate different spheres of law for government and society, the Roman legal system makes a fundamental distinction between *public* and *private law.*

In close connection with this, a distinction is made according to whether the control systems of a given state follow the "philosophy" and "culture" of a *constitutional state* or of *public interest* (Pollitt & Bouckaert, 2004). In the tradition of the constitutional state, the state is viewed as the integrating force in society, which is different from society in both institutional and legal terms, and is situated "above" society. This is accompanied by the strict bond between state and administrative action and its legal foundations, which in turn constitute the central instrument employed to control and monitor public administration. Besides, there is an independent system of administrative courts, which work separately from civil and criminal courts. The preparation, issuance and implementation of laws is regarded as the core function of the state and public administration. Thus it does not come as a surprise that in countries that are considered typical exponents of this tradition, such as Germany, training in law is accorded a great deal of value, and many junior and senior civil servants are lawyers by profession (indeed, reference is often made to "lawyers' monopolies"). In the public interest tradition, however, government has a more strongly institutional role to play in the satisfaction of society's needs. The state is often regarded as a necessary evil. Here, too, the law plays an important part as a control mechanism; however, it is not so much to the forefront of executive and administrative action. Accordingly, specialist legal knowledge is of much less significance to civil servants, who are often generalists (Proeller & Schedler, 2005). Internationally speaking, different countries represent different variants of these traditions. Thus it can be said of the German-speaking area that although all three countries must be ascribed to the tradition of the constitutional state, this tradition is less strongly pronounced in Switzerland than in Germany and Austria, which are regarded as typical exponents of it.

Pollitt and Bouckaert (2004, p. 53) revealed in their internationally comparative study of NPM reforms that countries that adhere more strongly to the tradition of the constitutional state are less likely to conduct radical reforms and tend to conduct their reforms more slowly and incrementally. The reason for this, they say, is that on the one hand, most changes in such countries involve the amendment of legislation. Thus it is most astonishing to note, from a German (or Austrian or Swiss) constitutional perspective, that the British *agency programme* was sufficient to move a large majority of civil servants out of the ministries into new organisations within ten years without any new law having to be enacted. On the other hand, Pollitt and Bouckaert also perceive a cultural component, according to which a shift to a management perspective is more difficult in a system of specialists than in a system of generalists. Similarly, Ridley (2000, p. 134) comes to the conclusion that it is probably easier to turn civil servants into managers in the UK because they do not conceive of themselves as representatives and agents of a superordinate state and common good. Moreover, Wollmann (2000, 2001) considers the separation of state and society to be an important reason why private management techniques were almost ignored by German administration in the past. Compliance with legal precepts is accorded absolute priority over efficiency and effectiveness.

The legal traditions and systems described above are deep-rooted mechanisms and value structures that refer to the overall (self-)conception of the state and its members. Demands for change, such as are made by OPM, come up against and indeed often clash with these traditions. At the same time, they are in keeping with the zeitgeist and therefore attract attention. It must also be stated here that NPM originated in the Anglo-Saxon area before it reached the German-speaking countries. The differing legal cultures indicate that the modernisation of administration follows different development patterns in constitutional systems and raises other problems than in public interest countries. NPM models in a constitutional context, like the *Neues Steuerungsmodell* (New Control Model) or Outcome-oriented Public Management, have taken those contextual specifics on board and must, for instance, comply with the requirement of legal regulation. It becomes equally clear, however, that the thrust and objectives of NPM represent a lengthy and profound challenge in a constitutional tradition.

Principles of Governance—Requirements and Guidelines for Administrative Action

In contrast to the private sector, public administration may only act when and where it is legitimated by law to do so (principle of constitutionality). The public legal system is characterised by a hierarchy of norms that range from the constitution itself through laws to individual administrative acts. All these serve as the basis for the demands made on the organisation of administration. In addition, every legal system has developed specific principles and conventions from which state action must take its bearings. These are often not explicitly laid down in the constitution or in the statute book. According to Mastronardi (1997, p. 61), their purpose is to hold together the diversity of government objectives and tasks through normative requirements to be satisfied by the organisation of administration. In Switzerland, we speak of guiding *principles of governance*. These are: constitutional state (*Rechtsstaat*) and democracy, nation state (*Nationalstaat*) and federal state (*Bundesstaat*), and provider state (*Leistungsstaat*) and economic state (*Wirtschaftsstaat*) (Mastronardi, 1996, 1998):

- *Constitutional state* and *democracy* provide the basis for the classic organisation of administration with its hierarchies and delimited responsibilities, as well as leadership through structures, procedures and resources. The principle of constitutionality ties state power to the law and to the constitution. It calls for a framework of (guaranteed) procedures and clearly demarcated responsibilities, which establishes a well-defined system of competencies. The democratic principle aims at a democratic legitimation of government action. Administrative action is indirectly democratically legitimated through the delegation of competencies, structures of responsibility and by the commitment to the law.
- The *principle of the nation state* formulates the principle of national sovereignty and national unity, which confers the highest power in the land to the Confederation. The *principle of the federal state* regulates the division of competencies between the Confederation and the cantons, with the subsidiarity principle being applied in favour of the cantons.
- The *principles of the provider* and *economic state* emphasise the output and outcome orientation of public administration, its fitness for purpose and its conformity with objectives. In the field of organisation law, these principles result in the demand for efficiency, effectiveness and economy.

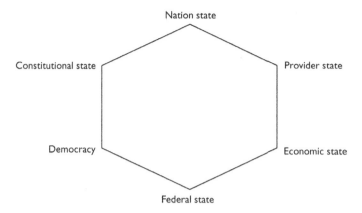

Figure 9.1 The hexagon of the principles of governance. *Source*: Mastronardi (1998).

These guiding principles, particularly the principles of constitutionality and democracy and the principles of the provider and economic state, are situated in a field of tension and lead to conflicting goals, which is expressed in Figure 9.1 by the arrangement of these maxims around a hexagon. This tense relationship makes it necessary for these principles to be weighed up against each other. In the field of administrative structures, for instance, this weighing-up process is revealed when, on the one hand, the hierarchical sectoral structure of the administration constitutes the main form of administrative organisation. In this way, the constitutional and democratic demands for procedures, hierarchies and delimited competencies are asserted. On the other hand, however, there are also project organisations in traditional administration which have more in common with the objectives of the productive and economic state.

The demands made by OPM are based on a higher degree of outcome orientation away from the perspective of the principles of governance in the direction of the maxim of the provider and economic state. OPM invokes constitutional principles as much as conventional administration. It does not aim to replace the constitutional state and democracy in favour of an efficient provider state, but it aims to challenge the frequently perceived general prioritisation of the constitutional state and democracy. OPM wants to strengthen the principle of the provider and economic state wherever this is appropriate. With its many demands, OPM challenges the organisation of administration as we know it now, and aims to introduce new organisation and management mechanisms, thus launching a debate on a (re-) assessment of the various guiding maxims. This is related to the question of the political legitimation of the administration, which is increasingly called upon to supplement political and juridical legitimation at a factual, pragmatic and economic level.

Besides, it is not in the interest of OPM either to weaken the constitutional state and democracy as cornerstones and characteristics of the political system. To the contrary: it is pointed out again and again in discussions about OPM that a working democratic constitutional state is an indispensable prerequisite and general condition for OPM (cf. Chapter 2, The Problems to be Solved in Administration Are Efficiency and Effectiveness, Not Legality or Legitimation, pp. 43ff.). In keeping with this, Schick (1998) expressly appeals to developing countries not to carry out any NPM reforms because the control mechanisms of NPM are very strongly based on reliable and formal implementation and control mechanisms. As long as these achievements of a dependable democratic constitutional state are not in place, the application of NPM mechanisms carries a very substantial risk of abuse.

Requirements Under Administrative Law—Selected Issues and Fields of Tension

OPM can have far-reaching consequences for legislation. These effects have been the subject of intense debates all over the German-speaking area (cf. for instance Lienhard, 2005; Kettiger, 2000, as well as the contributions by Mastronardi (St. Gallen), and Zimmerli & Lienhard (Berne) for Switzerland; Neisser & Hammerschmid, 1998 for Austria, various contributions by Schmidt-Aßmann (Heidelberg) and Hoffmann-Riem (Hamburg), but also by Schuppert, who teaches in Erfurt, for Germany). Bolz and Lienhard (2001, pp. 2ff.) rightly call for the pilot projects that have been run so far to be converted into a stable form, for instance by enshrining the cornerstones of OPM in legal norms.

Obstacles in the way of OPM measures result when reforms clash with specific provisions and regulations of administrative law. Besides concrete legal provisions as stipulated by, say, financial law and budget law or by service law, justiciable constitutional and procedural principles must be taken into consideration. These include civil rights and liberties, equality before the law, the separation of powers, the principle of legality, the obligation to serve the public interest, the principle of proportionality and the principle of trust. Selected areas where the ideas of OPM and requirements under administrative law clash will be briefly dealt with below.

Outcome and Output Orientation versus the Principle of Legality

An outcome- and output-oriented control of administration requires a stronger alignment of administrative action with objectives, results and outcomes. To emphasise this orientation in law enforcement, too, OPM wants legal control to be more informed by objectives and fundamental regulations. Existing legal norms usually provide specific codes of conduct according to the "if ... then ..." pattern. In the literature, this demand is generally discussed as the transition from conditional ("if ... then ...") programming to final (objective-related or results-related) programming (Luhmann, 1993, pp. 195ff.).

From the perspective of the principle of legality, control through legal propositions covers a democratic and constitutional function (cf. Chapter 9, Principles of Governance—Requirements and Guidelines for Administrative Action, pp. 172ff. about the constitutional state and democracy). In both respects, conditional programming is often indispensable and cannot, or can only partly, be replaced by final regulation in conjunction with OPM control mechanisms. From a democratic perspective, there are doubts about the extent to which the reduced precision of the laws can be compensated for by the non-legal instruments of outcome control. From the perspective of the constitutional state, it is particularly the predictability and uniformity of individual decisions that are criticised, especially when legal norms regulate the rights and obligations of private individuals. Audits by judicial organs also encounter new problems if a law does not have clear-cut provisions (Müller, 1995, p. 16).

A decrease in the density of regulations and an increase in final programming must be judged differently depending on where this takes place. According to the rulings of the Austrian Constitutional Court, final programming in public administration is already compatible with the requirements of a constitutional state (Hartmann & Pesendorfer, 1998, p. 342). By the same token, final regulations can be found in certain legal fields, for instance in construction, planning and environmental law (Hill, 1998a, p. 69). Wherever legal norms primarily provide private individuals with constitutional guarantees such as legal security and legal equality, however, detailed regulation through legislation is a necessity, which is not cast into doubt by OPM, either. For this reason, conditional programming and detailed legislation will persist under OPM even though OPM aspires to extend the application of final programming. Under OPM, parliament will still reserve the right to issue detailed and conditional rules in individual cases if this is politically desirable and necessary as a sanction vis-à-vis the administration (Mastronardi, 1998, p. 85). Parliament cannot be limited to the issuance of final norms but only encouraged to *limit itself in this respect.*

Decentralised Leadership Structures versus Organisation Law

In constitutional and democratic terms, the primary purpose of organisation law is to regulate the conduct of the executive and the administration. If we assume that administrative structures or the assignment of certain tasks to certain units exert an influence on politics, then these issues are consequently subject to political regulation. Thus public administration should not be able to carry out actions internally, either, that have not been legitimated by parliament.

Under OPM, decentralised administrative units are created which are granted a higher degree of autonomy. This does not only extend the competencies of the executive and top-level administration, but also enlarges the scope of the individual subordinate administrative units.

From a juridical point of view, an increase in the autonomy of administrative units makes it more difficult to enforce responsibilities (Häfelin & Müller, 1998, p. 263). It is feared that loosening up strict hierarchies will impede the allocation of responsibilities for political and administrative failures to the actual culprits.

By way of compensation, OPM offers performance agreements, contracts and management accounting. Since basically, organisational regulations do not interfere with the rights and obligations of private individuals, such a transformation of the organisation of administration should be within the realm of the possible. In the areas where organisational issues are of great political significance, as in the relationship between legislative and executive, detailed regulations will continue to be necessary. Modern developments point in the direction of increased organisational autonomy—irrespective of, but in keeping with, OPM. In Switzerland, too, the responsibility for organisation has been assigned to the executive in almost all polities by now with the result that the executive is able to exercise its function as the administration's governing organ.

One-Line Budgeting versus Financial and Budget Law

One-line budgeting infringes various principles of budget law (cf. Chapter 7, One-Line Budgeting, pp. 128ff.). The original control instruments and mechanisms of parliament are severely limited. In return, however, OPM offers parliament new instruments and possibilities of influence which promise more effective and outcome-oriented leadership (Bertelsmann-Stiftung & Saarländisches Ministerium des Inneren, 1997, p. 25). These are, in particular, indicators, standards and other indices, which enable parliament to monitor the performance agreements on a continuing basis.

Budgeting and accounting reforms at a municipal level have progressed furthest in Germany. The legal foundations for municipal budget law are laid down by the *Länder* for their municipalities, which leads to differences in the implementation and direction of reforms. Generally, it can be said that so far, budgeting, costing and product catalogues have not been integrated into a standardised overall system, which means that extended cameralistics has held its ground in analogy with the state level. Some *Länder* aim to introduce product-related budgeting on the basis of accrual accounting, and pilot and transitional stages are underway. The necessary amendments to legislation are being drawn up (Budäus, 2004, p. 83). In Switzerland, the cantons and their municipalities have their own budget laws and financial sovereignty. Here, the new control instruments must frequently be tested with experimenting and exemption clauses. After the pilot stages have been concluded, the relevant laws are then amended accordingly, as has been the case in the Cantons of Zurich, Berne, Solothurn and Aargau (cf. the relevant legislation of the various cantons). Also, Art. 38(a) of the Federal Budget Act (*Finanzhaushaltsgesetz*) has created a generally formulated legal foundation for control exercised through one-line budgets, which permits a special accounting arrangement for administrative areas that are managed with performance agreements, with deviations from the accounting principles being provided for.

Discuss

 The *public-interest* tradition and constitutionality are represented by two different philosophies and cultures. Where do you see specific differences for the conception and implementation of OPM?

 It has been said that OPM can only work on the basis of a working and democratic constitutional state. What consequences would this generally have for newly industrialising countries?

Q OPM requires some legislation to be amended. In your opinion, is this conducive or prejudicial to the introduction of OPM?

Q How do you rate OPM's typical demand for increased final control in the public sector?

Q In places, OPM calls for the replacement of hierarchical structures by more flexible forms of organisation ("tents instead of palaces"). Where are the limits to such changes?

Q What effects does OPM have on democratic processes and the distribution of power when the instruments of political control are changed as intended by OPM?

Further Readings

Drewry, G. (1985). Public Lawyers and Public Administrators: Prospects for an Alliance. *Public Administration 64*, 173–88.

Freedland, M. (1994). Government by Contract and Public Law. *Public Law, 86*, 86–104.

Taggart, M. (1997). Public Service Law and the New Public Management. In *The province of Administrative Law*. Oxford: Hart Publishing.

Bertelli, A. M. (2005). Law and Public Administration. In *Oxford Handbook of Public Management*. Oxford: Oxford University Press.

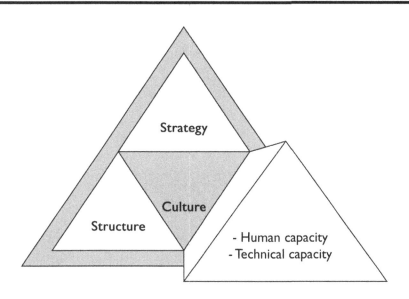

10

Human Resources Capacity

Personnel management is likely to be the most vehemently criticised, but also the most fiercely disputed area of public management. Interestingly, however, international research on the effects of administrative reforms on personnel management is rather sparse (Donahue et al., 2000).

In personnel management, the cultural differences between the various countries are particularly conspicuous. In some countries, civil servants have traditionally been (and still are) awarded life-long tenure as public officials (*Beamte*) on their appointment; it could be said that they are "commissioned" very much like military officers, and like them are able to rise in rank while never losing their status. By contrast, other countries such as Switzerland are more open: all civil servants have always been appointed for a certain period of time (as a rule, four years); and in the 1990s a trend set in to abolish the status of a public official completely and to employ newcomers to the administration with contracts under public law that differ from private-law employment contracts in only a few elements (Richli, 1996, pp. 118ff.). This—albeit short—practical experience shows that the abolition of the status of a public official had formal rather than factual ef-

Outcome-Oriented Public Management, pages 181–194
Copyright © 2010 by Information Age Publishing
All rights of reproduction in any form reserved.

fects since the differences between public officials and government employees hardly existed any longer in many cantons. In this respect, the abolition of the official status in Switzerland is primarily symbolic, but as such is of great value.

The situation in countries like Germany and Austria must be judged differently. In these countries, both officials and employees enjoy privileges that make their working conditions distinctly different from those prevalent in the private sector. Increased flexibility in personnel management, not least greater mobility and performance orientation, would definitely be in the spirit of OPM.

The call for modern personnel management had already been a talking point before the emergence of OPM. It would therefore be wrong to credit all the progress in personnel management to OPM. Our practical experience shows that the modernisation of personnel management is also possible and necessary independently from OPM. It is part of an extensively understood OPM, which offers a conceptual framework into which modern personnel management can be integrated. Thom and Ritz (2000) criticise the traditional personnel management of government institutions for not being able to satisfy the requirements of modern personnel management. A lack of achievement motivation, no development and training opportunities, deficient incentive and reward structures, but often also restricted personnel selection are issues that the reforms of public administration have to tackle. These problems can only be solved if a city's or a country's personnel department provides the relevant conceptual foundations. The implementation of possible solutions, however, is a management task that cannot be delegated. This shows that the demands made on senior staff increase substantially through OPM.

Personnel Policy

Personnel policy determines a polity's basic direction with regard to its most important resource. The crucial question here is often not whether personnel should be deployed but what they should be deployed for and how. Personnel policy is directly affected by OPM. An increase in management scope means, among other things, that the most important personnel management functions are delegated to the individual units. This also leads to the abolition of centrally dictated staff appointment plans, which in the traditional system occupy a relatively important function in connection with cost-cutting measures. It is therefore foreseeable that it will be difficult for politics to relinquish this system.

The direction to be taken by personnel policy has been established in several countries in that the status of public officials has been abolished. Although this is not directly related to OPM, it is in line with its fundamental stance of introducing a higher degree of flexibility into personnel management. Ultimately, this is about repealing obsolete protective provisions in favour of a modern social partnership ("guaranteed work rather than a guaranteed job"). Gerstlberger et al. (1999, pp. 27ff.) rightly emphasise the fact that the social partners are not sufficiently involved in many reforms and that the actors who are, often lack the necessary qualifications.

The opening-up of the entire system that OPM aims at will entail a change in the "typical" careers of civil servants. It is bound to be reflected in the training of public managers, which takes very different forms in Germany, Austria and Switzerland. Whereas in Switzerland, no specialised administrative traineeship is required for a career in administration, which means that administrations automatically also employ newcomers from the outside, the German and Austrian systems of specialist training appear rigid and closed (cf. the various contributions in Schedler & Reichard, 1998). An opening of personnel policy is a direct consequence of the introduction of OPM. Various international examples illustrate, however, that this is inevitably accompanied by worse working conditions for civil servants: in New Zealand, for instance, an ethical standard for the state in its capacity as an employer was only formulated in connection with the NPM reforms.

If nothing changes for the personnel, OPM will fail to achieve an important goal. They are in danger of falling into a "futility trap" (Gerstlberger et al., 1999, p. 28), with nothing left in the end save resignation and the question: "What has all the fuss been about then?" The higher degree of autonomy and responsibility must become palpable for administrative staff. New employee surveys have revealed that many changes have not yet trickled down to the grassroots, and this is where increased efforts will have to be made in the future.

OPM's Demands on Managerial Behaviour

Bureaucracy is a good-tempered system. It corrects human conduct through a balance that is inherent in the system, for it was established in order to objectify its decisions and to remove them from human influences. A good boss's sustainable positive effect is just as negligible as a bad boss's negative effect. Procedures are prescribed and monitored. Those who stick to the rules are in the right. Those who avoid failures survive, for failures can be blamed on the political masters, which in turn has repercussions. Staff are led through directives, and information may be found on the notice-board, if at all. Civil servants are sparing with praise, and criticism is rather unusual—particularly bottom-up.

This portrait of bureaucracy is certainly exaggerated but it shows that a bureaucratic system permits all this more or less without sanction. A survey conducted by Klages (1989) and a research team on leadership and work motivation in municipal administrations revealed that a quarter of interviewees experience their superiors as autocrats who do not bother about either the fulfilment of their tasks or about the personal concerns of their staff, while another 11 per cent attest their superiors' excellent specialist knowledge but complain about their lack of concern for the needs of their staff.

OPM does not provide an automatic cure for such grievances but sanctions poor leadership more severely while rewarding good leadership. The reason for this is the managers' wider scope of action and personal responsibility. Those who are able to put these newly created opportunities to good use will be more successful than in a traditional bureaucracy. Those who do not, will fall by the wayside.

In an ideal case, the leadership environment undergoes great changes owing to OPM in that it is no longer primarily the legal procedures that are specified and monitored, but the objectives of the administration. Virtanen describes this as follows: "This changes the traditional professional pride of normative commitment to that of strategic commitment." (Virtanen, 2000, p. 341). Successes will then not be scored by the senior civil servants

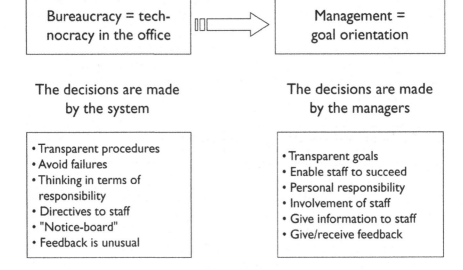

Figure 10.1 New demands made on managers under OPM.

defending their own patch but by leaders who conceive of themselves as coaches and strive to enable their staff to be successful. In OPM, successes are scored by those senior staff who are pleased when their staff are successful. Communicating objectives to staff is of particular importance since otherwise they lack the basis to succeed under their own steam. One of the most important functions of superiors is constant critical, but supportive feedback. Only those who know where they are will be able to improve themselves.

Nonetheless it must be borne in mind that even *public managers*, i.e., the leaders in the system of OPM, are part and parcel of a political environment that makes its rightful demands on the administration. As Röber (1996, p. 188) puts it: "What is needed is a new type of managerial bureaucrat who respects the primacy of elected politicians and also has a respected role as a political bureaucrat."

Leading through Target Agreements

A comparison of European administrations reveals that daily interactions within the administrations of individual countries, i.e., the administrative culture, evince great differences. These manifest themselves in the way in which the politico-administrative system works internally, i.e., in how the system's individual members communicate with each other, but also in the way in which it responds to disruptions from the outside. In a comparative study, Jann (1983, pp. 519ff.) detected that a distinction can be made between three different basic types of culture:

- *Regulation culture*: control is primarily effected through rules and norms. Interactions between the various instances, but also between the people working in the system, are determined by this regulation. An example of this form of control is a detailed organisational rulebook for the administration.
- *Contact culture*: control is primarily effected through arrangements and negotiation, i.e., through direct contact between those involved. Examples of this form of control are citizens' fora, in which, for example, the people resident in property adjacent to a park have a direct say in that park's design by the municipal authorities.
- *Negotiation culture*: control is primarily effected by all kinds of agreements, i.e., contracts, targets, personal agreements, etc. Examples of this form of control are performance agreements used by OPM.

Although such pure forms cannot be found in practice, systems still lean towards one type or another. Jann describes contact culture as typical of Sweden, negotiation culture as typical of the UK, and regulation culture as typical of Germany. This tallies with the great significance of specialised public law in German-speaking countries, which is unlikely to be found in such a distinctive form in any other geographical area.

Since the fundamental philosophy and many instruments of OPM originated in the Anglo-American area, OPM consequently contains elements that do not derive from regulation culture but from negotiation culture (contract culture), control through performance agreements (contracts) being a case in point. The same culture, however, can also be recognised at an individual level—and it spread as early as the 1970s. The still topical leadership model of Management by Objectives" (MbO) was developed at that time and is now used in practice as an authoritarian variant (top-down target setting) and a cooperative variant (Target Agreement) (Wunderer & Grunwald, 1980, pp. 305ff.). The Swiss government (Schweizerischer Bundesrat, 1974, p. 38) adopted MbO as an effective method of cooperative management in its guidelines for the management of federal administration at the time.

A cooperative form of MbO extends to both cultural elements besides regulation: in the contractual process and in the course of the concomitant interim discussions, the focus is on the element of contract, where the establishment and specification of objectives, and particularly the monitoring of their attainment, is an element of negotiation. Thus a certain shift of the focal point from regulation to control by contact and negotiation has been taking place since the early 1970s (cf. Figure 10.2). In addition, further de-

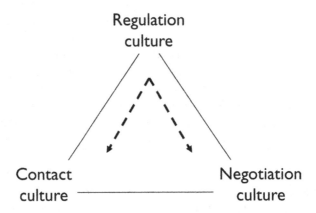

Figure 10.2   Shift of the control focus in the three types of culture according to Jann.

velopments such as service provision in networks or public-private partnerships, make clear that there is a move away from the contracting culture of the early NPM models towards a contact mode of control, such as in later OPM or in "public governance" approaches.

From the point of view of staff motivation, it becomes apparent that the relinquishment of "management by precepts and individual instructions" leads to a higher degree of autonomy for individual members of staff. As a rule, this results in an increase in motivation, which in turn has a favourable effect on the working climate. However, this is offset by greater demands being made on members of staff, who are expected to assume personal responsibility. Ultimately, this may increase the pressure exerted on individual members of staff to perform, which in certain cases is perfectly desirable.

Elements of Modern Personnel Management

If a concept of modern personnel management has to be developed for public administration, this does not have to be invented from scratch. A great deal has already been written about this, and the relevant publications transpose private-sector experience into the public sector (cf. for instance Thom & Ritz, 2000). However, this is exactly what Brown (2004) criticises, namely that these models were originally developed in completely different contexts. Even so, he does not deny that the more general models have a certain relevance, particularly against the background of NPM, for according to Brown, this leads to the relinquishment of pure personnel management in favour of the establishment of a personnel management that takes over many elements from the private sector.

Below, we will have recourse to a simple concept which has, however, been tried and tested in practice: Hilb's (1997) concept of integrated personnel management (see Figure 10.3). This concept pivots on the organisation's strategy for which a personnel management should be developed or revised. All the measures of personnel management have to be aligned with this strategy if personnel management is to make a contribution towards the organisation's success. This means that in a first step, it must always be the strategy (or the vision) of the administrative unit that must be defined.

The elements of the selection, development, reward and assessment of staff must be aligned with these strategy goals. This results in the following course of action:

1. Clarification of the vision of the administrative unit and definition of strategic objectives (in analogy with those aims which must also defined for a balanced scorecard).

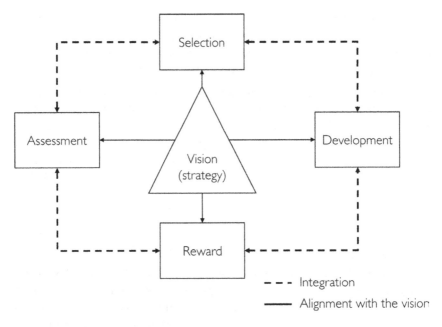

Figure 10.3 Elements of integrated personnel management. *Source*: according to Hilb (1997).

2. Deduction of requirements that the staff of the administrative unit will have to meet. These requirements can be used to deduce criteria for the selection of new staff. Moreover, staff performance reviews should be in tune with these requirements, etc. This leads to the next step:

3. Structuration of the personnel management functions: this step serves to align all the elements of personnel management with the organisation's requirements consistently and without contra-diction.

4. Examination of integration and consistency: once the elements of personnel management have been developed, the entire concept has to be checked for consistency and integration with a healthy degree of "detachment," with the help of questions like: Are there any elements that clash? Are there any strategic goals that are not reflected in the elements? Have criteria been used that are not in tune with the organisation's vision?

5. Evaluation of success: finally, any form of personnel management must be checked for success. Again, the basic question is this: Is this kind of personnel management capable of retaining the staff who meet the requirements of the organisation?

No matter how simple these things seem to be, the most fundamental rules are often violated in practice. In particular, the precept of consistency is not easy to implement in practice. An example may serve to illustrate this:

The new vision of a school contains a sentence to the effect that the teacher team must be strengthened and that successes should be achieved together. For the selection of new teachers, this means that the ability to work in a team must be accorded a higher priority and must be taken into consideration. The actual ability to work in a team, and teamwork as such, must be given weight in performance reviews. Additional training sessions must focus on teamwork, and provided that a performance-related reward system has been envisaged, team performance must be taken into account in it—it would make little sense if only individual performance were assessed and rewarded.

Staff Selection in OPM

In accordance with the guiding principles of OPM, the selection of new staff focuses on the performance principle, which is a foundation for the merit system—in contrast to the spoils system, which would base staff selections on political connections. The challenge for both line managers and personnel experts thus consists in finding the most suitable person for a job in terms of capability and commitment, and of encouraging him or her to take up the job. In this respect, the applicant's original education and training (for example, an academic degree) is only one piece in an extensive jigsaw puzzle that must be completed for each individual candidate.

The methods of staff selection used in the public sector hardly differ any longer from those employed by the private sector. The central point is neutrality in assessment. The responsibility for selection must always remain with the line, i.e., the managers who will work together with the applicant later on are responsible for the decision concerning selection. Having a post filled by people who are not directly involved—for instance, by politicians who want to smuggle in people from their political networks—must be consistently opposed by OPM, even though it may still be customary in public administration.

The selection of senior staff must be carried out with particular care, for it is only through committed managers that an administration can be established that will act in an efficient, effective, legal and legitimated manner. In this context, recourse is increasingly made to so-called assessment centres (Mauch, 2005), where applicants are observed by a group of experts in various context like

- written exercises;
- group situations, decisions and exercises;
- role play, interviews, presentations;
- self-descriptions by applicants.

The behaviour patterns that have been observed will then be compared with the job profile that has resulted from the vision of personnel policy.

More modern methods can also be employed for recruitment under OPM. Mauch (2005) mentions e-recruiting, for example, where applicants are able to fill in a test sheet through the internet to ascertain their suitability for the advertised job even before they submit their application. Traditional procedures such as standardised interviews (Hilb, 1997) or trainee programmes are also suitable for performance orientation to be foregrounded in the selection process.

Performance Reviews in OPM

Fair and honest performance reviews constitute the basis for further measures in personnel management. No reward system can exist without clear assessment criteria, and no development concept can be established without finding out where individual members of staff actually stand. However, the conduct of expedient performance reviews requires

- that managers cultivate performance reviews as an active leadership tool rather than ticking them off as a bureaucratic duty; and
- that managers are given the scope to carry out the reviews honestly, i.e., that they are also able to state that a certain staff member's performance has been poor. Any kind of entrenched right of complaint by, say, personnel associations against unwelcome assessments of individual members of staff must therefore be consistently opposed from the point of view of performance orientation under OPM.

For performance reviews, too, there is a sufficient number of literature sources and of concepts that can be used in public administration. Many modern administrations no longer limit themselves to such reviews being conducted by direct superiors but involve further reference persons. If, for instance, working groups are assessed by their direct customers, as was organised by Koci (2005) in a Swiss social insurance institution, then a further reference level can be opened. In many organisations, assessments or comparisons can also be conducted horizontally, for example by colleagues or with similar administrative units. Finally, there should also always be feed-back from staff to superiors, as well as self-assessment by members of staff. If all this is in place, we can speak of a 360-degree review. OPM with the in-struments of customer surveys and benchmarking, in particular, furnishes important cornerstones that did not exist in traditional administration.

Staff Reward in OPM

OPM calls for an increased output and outcome orientation of control in the politico-administrative system. It therefore stands to reason that the same fundamental attitude must also be brought to bear on the design of the incentive structures in public institutions.

Definition 10.1: Incentives
Incentives are monetary and non-monetary "payments" or promises with which the conduct expected from staff members cannot be enforced but can be made more attractive by bonuses (or less attrac-tive if disincentives are used). Staff members are still formally free to decide whether or not they want to change in response to the (dis) incentives on offer.

Incentive systems aim to reduce the discrepancy between the objectives of the administration and individual requirements. In an ideal case, it should be possible for personal needs to be satisfied in the attainment of administrative objectives. However, Sprenger (1992) rightly warns that incentives should not be instrumentalised to bring about a certain kind of behaviour through ma-nipulation that disregards staff members' legitimate requirements. Rather, OPM tries to identify and analyse existing incentive structures, to reinforce the positive ones and to eliminate the negative ones.

Every system contains incentives which reward a certain type of conduct while punishing people for another. In the bureaucratic model, a lack of awareness of these circumstances has led to a situation whereby it creates in-centives that entice people to act in an inefficient rather than a performance-oriented way. The rewards go to those who create no problems. No problems are created by people who do not attract any attention and always stick to the rules. In a bureaucracy, the "administrative machine" works thanks to the inconspicuous cogs in the system rather than in spite of them.

OPM acknowledges the important role played by incentives for public administration to work efficiently and effectively and employs them for the attainment of its goals. There is, however, an awareness of the fact that incentives such as high bonuses may create dysfunctional pressure on civil servants to go for figures rather than for real results. Performance-oriented remuneration can be introduced along with OPM as it is an element that is in conformity with the system as long as it emphasises the acknowledgement of good performance rather than large monetary incentives. It is not imperative, however: OPM can also work without performance-linked remuneration, provided that other incentives promise the same or even a better effect. Thus it becomes clear that the specific design of incentive systems in public institutions cannot be imposed in a standardised form from the centre but must always be adapted to individual situations.

The configuration of a reward system must always pivot on the outcome that should be achieved. If OPM demands that the administration should work in a more customer-friendly and unbureaucratic manner, top-level administrators must take into consideration the incentives with which they can encourage the members of their organisation to behave accordingly.

Personnel and Organisation Development

The above demands made on the staff and management in the public sector cannot be fulfilled with the skills and knowledge that are necessary for work in bureaucratic administrations. New tasks require new skills (capacities) and new structures. It is therefore indispensable for the implementation of OPM that both the personnel and the organisation are enabled to deal with the new model. Successful projects place great weight on personnel development, as is illustrated by the example of the City of Saarbrücken, where the subject matter of (continued) training was defined as follows (Hoffmann et al., 1996, pp. 56ff.):

- continual management training (e.g., improvement of leadership behaviour, know-how and skills; use of management tools),
- advancement of high potentials,
- "citizens as customers" (e.g., case-work in a dialogue with citizens, letter-writing and telephone skills, complaints management),
- establishment of key qualifications (e.g., communicative, methodical, technical and innovative competencies),
- support of special concerns (e.g., gender equality concerns),
- methods and guidelines in personnel management (e.g., capacity assessment, establishment of requirements, training schedules, etc.).

Taking personnel development seriously is tantamount to reorientation: personnel are no longer merely regarded as a cost factor but become a "strategic success potential" for the administration. Individual staff members' readiness to undergo development is taken into account in personnel management; not every member of staff is interested in professional advancement to the same extent. However, personnel development is not simply career planning and promotion; rather, it is also the conscious cultivation of people who want to do a good job in the administration regardless of whether they aim for a career or not.

In more strongly personnel-oriented administration, personnel development also means the creation of individualised development paths in order to provide members of staff with the possibilities of determining their careers for themselves. A central point remains the consideration of orientation patterns that are specific to individuals: creativity, specialist competence, social competence, etc. lead to completely different profiles of ideal people/work relationships that can only be filtered out by constant interaction with staff, such as takes place in performance appraisal interviews.

Discuss

 OPM aims to bring about new leadership patterns in superiors in public administration. How can new leadership conduct be promoted?

OPM is often associated with performance-linked rewards. In this publication, we hold the view that this is not a fundamental requirement of OPM. What are the opportunities and risks of performance-related rewards?

In an international comparison, trade unions have decidedly varying attitudes towards OPM. Put yourself in the place of a trade unionist: what position would you occupy in response to OPM?

With what means does OPM try to prepare personnel, i.e., the most important factor in the provision of administrative outputs, for their task? Do you know any practical examples that are in line, or out of step, with the OPM approach?

Further Readings

Brown, K. (2004). Human resource management in the public sector. *Public Management Review, 6*(3), 303–309.

van Wart, M. (2008). *Administrative leadership in the public sector.* Armonk: M. E. Sharpe.

Demmke, C. (2004). European Civil Service between tradition and reform, Mastricht. *European Institute of Public Administratino.*

Horton, S., Farnham, D., Hondeghem, A. (Eds). (2002). *Competency management in the public sector, European variations on a theme.* Amsterdam: IOS.

11

Technical Capacity

Information Technology

The use of modern information and communication technology (ICT) in public administration has become a matter of course in Europe by now. Especially in the large divisions of law-enforcement administration, such as tax administration, social administration, inventory management and public finances, its application is widespread and has led to substantial improvements in the last few decades. The possible scopes of application of ICT, however, vary a great deal; particularly the potential of networked ICT is only partially used in public administration. It is often assumed that the acquisition of hardware and software would be sufficient for the administration to be made more efficient and more effective. This, though, is a fallacy: several studies conducted both in the private and in the public sectors reveal that the provision of the infrastructure alone will not suffice. Fountain (2001, pp. 10ff.) therefore distinguishes between existing technology and enacted technology. Enacted technology is only that part of a technology that is actively used in the organisation and has become part and parcel of its working life. For an organisation to reach this point, however, it must not

Outcome-Oriented Public Management, pages 195–206
Copyright © 2010 by Information Age Publishing
195

only make the technology as such available but must also change its own processes and its members' actions.

ICT capacities have had a considerable impact on the strategy of organisations in recent decades. Many changes are based on new possibilities offered by ICT. OPM, too, requires a certain ICT standard. Whether the impulses for modernisation stemmed from the technology rather than from a reform movement such as NPM is often difficult to assess in retrospect. Generally, it may well be said that this involved well-known concerns whose implementation only became possible through ICT. OPM requires a high level of data processing capacity for the measurement of results, in particular. This would not be possible without the potential of modern ICT, whose alternative configurations usually only evolve in practice (Grimmer, 1995, p. 169).

As a rule, any fruitful use of ICT is contingent on a redesign of processing processes. In this context, reference is also made to process optimisation or *business process reengineering*. Such measures are very much in line with the changes called for by OPM. Besides process optimisation, the support of processes among citizens may also serve to attain a modern form of the *empowerment of the citizens* (Heeks, 1999, p. 17): thanks to their use of the internet, they are capable of participating in the decision-making and implementation processes. With the idea of the guarantor state, the citizenry should be encouraged to get involved for the benefit of the common good and participate in the production of goods as *"pro-sumers."* However, this can also be criticised as "passing the buck" of state bureaucracy on to citizens and the economy (Reinermann, 1995a, p. 392).

Application Levels of Information Technology

The rapid development of ICT in the last few decades has resulted in great changes to the possibilities and forms of application in both private enterprises and public administration. To place the various levels that can be passed through in ICT application and the concomitant organisational transformation in a system, the following distinction will be helpful (Scott Morton, 1991, quoted from Bellamy & Taylor, 1998, pp. 38ff.):

▪ Automation
At this level of ICT utilisation, computers are seen as a production technology rather than as an information technology. The focus is on reducing the costs of existing processes by means of automation, i.e., on making existing data processing activities more efficient. It is *existing* processes that are made more effi-

cient without being linked up with other processes or subjected
to a critical review.

▪ Informatisation
At this level, ICTs are used to process information and thus to
make *new information* available. Examples of this range from the
evaluation of service recipient profiles to an official in a *one-stop
shop* who has access to the databases of various administrative
units. OPM requires the administration to become informatised,
or causes such informatisation, in many areas. Owing to results
orientation, contract management and the delegation of responsibilities, all the parties need information about the required
outputs, contract fulfilment, relations between outcomes and
outputs, etc. Only informatisation can make all this available
within a reasonable time frame and at reasonable costs.

▪ Transformation
This level of ICT application is fundamentally different from the
other two. Whereas automation and informatisation are based
on existing forms of organisation, the level of transformation
involves a *total reconstruction of previous structures and processes* according to the possibilities offered by ICT. This reconstruction
takes its bearings from the outputs provided to customers. The
logic behind this radical demand argues that the hierarchy and
division of labour encountered in bureaucratic organisations
were appropriate forms of organising complex and large-scale
activities in the industrial age. Modern ICT, however, enables
information to be available at all levels. Thus it allows for the
removal of vertical hierarchies and their replacement with a linkage and integration of activities within and beyond the organisation. Moreover, ICT enables specialist knowledge to be utilised
better and irrespective of locations, which in turn determines the
definition of the critical organisation and catchment area size.

OPM aims at transformation. A reengineering venture of such a scale,
however, is confronted with various obstacles in public administration. For
one thing, there are certain legal barriers regarding organisation and processes; for another, the problem arises—as it does in the private sector—as
to the suitability of various activities for reengineering. Generally, therefore, restructuring in the area of policy-making is likely to be less easy to
conduct than in the field of specific output provision. Reengineering projects in various areas of public administration enabled the achievement of
astonishing results with regard to efficiency improvements and customer

orientation. The City of Kerpen, for example, reduced the processing time of planning applications from 111 days to 10 days through restructuring (Hill, 1997b, p. 59).

Target Groups and Interfaces

Publications dealing with the significance of ICT both in the public and private sectors primarily highlight its ability to enhance customer orientation. In this context, customers must be conceived of as process-oriented; depending on the task in hand, they are citizens, council members, companies or even other administrative units.

Within government, ICT can be used to support processes between administrative units of the same polity, or different polities, and between politics and the administration. In the Bangemann Report, the question as to what implications ICT would have in the European environment was even discussed at the level of the EU (Bangemann, 1995). Within the administration itself, it will be the interlinkage of data inventories and informatisation that will lead to increases in efficiency in the very near future. At the interface between politics and top-level administration, decision-making quality can be boosted by a convincing presentation of information that is relevant to management.

Electronic Government

In analogy with the terms of "e-business" and "e-commerce," the term "electronic government" was coined for the above-mentioned government applications of modern ICT. The concepts that are associated with this term have meanwhile become as diverse as the possibilities of ICT application in general, and consequently it has degenerated into a shell that means all things to all men. In this book, a concept of e-government is used that is interaction-oriented and covers the entire politico-administrative system.

Definition 11.1: Electronic government

Electronic government is a form of state organisation that integrates the interactions and interrelations between the government and citizens, private enterprises, customers and public institutions through the application of modern information and communication technologies (Schedler, Summermatter, & Schmidt, 2003, p. 6).

Electronic government conceived of in this way can be employed in various applications in the different fields of state activity. The following categorisation does not constitute an exhaustive and generally valid break-down; rather, it is intended to be a conceptual structuring aid (Bertot, 1998-99, p. 28; Bertelsmann Stiftung, 1998, pp. 17f.):

- ▪ "Display window":
  The internet is used as a publication platform with whose help information can be disseminated. In lieu of, or parallel with, official journals, the publication of, for example, legislation, public and official announcements, reports, etc., can be effected through the internet. This category also covers information provided by individual authorities online, for instance about documents to be submitted or official channels to be observed, opening hours, information sheets etc. (informational function).
- ▪ Virtual administration:
  With this output group, the administration provides its custom-ers with a 24/7 service. Customers are given access to the services provided by the administration around the clock and usually irrespective of place, time or persons. Electronic applications for passports and licences of all kinds are cases in point (transac-tional function).
- ▪ Interactive services:
  In this category, complete administrative acts are conducted. In Arizona, for instance, driving licences can be renewed online. In contrast with the output group of virtual administration, the en-tire process is carried out electronically, and no personal interac-tion between customers and the administration is required for a process to be brought to a conclusion, i.e., in the case of Arizona, customers do not have to collect their renewed driving licences in person. The administration itself makes use of the possibilities of electronic commerce and invoices its outstanding fees through electronic payment transactions (interactive function).
- ▪ Promotion of democratic processes:
  Democratic processes can be reinforced by means of electronic fora, discussion groups, surveys and ballots. Direct e-mail contact with top-level administrators or politicians is often also listed as an instrument (participative function). It must be borne in mind, however, that this technology on its own does not trigger any reforms; rather, it is the citizens' open-mindedness that is a sine qua non. Thus the Public Exchange Network, a public electronic conference and postal system of the City of Santa Monica, basical-ly failed because it was mainly only organised stakeholder groups

that utilised the direct communication channels and because the city's representatives were completely harassed by various groups. The post was therefore presorted, and the dialogue was discontinued (Kraemer, 1995, p. 187). The same category also covers the determination of public opinion in a state by means of, for instance, the national government's consultation process with the sub-national level.

E-government can be considered the new *Leitbild of administrative IT*, with the new concepts being created on the basis of the existing, partially already far advanced developments in public administration. What, however, does e-government do differently in comparison with previous administrative IT? In essence, two things: firstly, technology now allows for adaptable applications that were not known in this form before. Customer-oriented solutions can be set up and, in particular, maintained, away from the centre, wherever services are provided. Then, the so-called *content management*, i.e., the management of data on the internet, is executed by the officials themselves. The previous "bottleneck" of central IT units has dwindled in importance, which means that the implementing units' individual initiative hardly faces any obstacles any longer. Those who want to be customer-oriented now have the necessary technical support but at the same time require a new type of training.

Secondly, general conditions inside public administration have been completely different since the discussion of an increasingly customer- and outcome-oriented approach. A simplification of processes, responsiveness to customers' wishes, transparency and openness have become a matter of course in many quarters. In a manner of speaking, OPM paved the way for successful e-government. The customer orientation of OPM, for example, finds its technical implementation in applications of customer relationship management (Proeller & Zwahlen, 2003) that support an extensive and as individual a customer service as possible by means of IT. It has become apparent that administrative units which already work with OPM are also further advanced with regard to CRM than others.

Development of a Conceptual Frame for e-Government

The interaction-oriented basic model used in this publication structures and describes the make-up of comprehensive e-government. External interaction partners of e-government can be the politicians, parliament and the courts, citizens and groups as decision-makers in the democratic process. Enterprises appear as suppliers or cooperation partners, citizens and groups as customers or recipients of services provided by the administration. Other external administrative units are in regular contact with their own organisational unit. But internal interactions, i.e., interactions that only take place within an administrative unit, are given a new shape by e-government applications and are integrated into an overall system.

To establish the derivation of the model, it is first necessary to distinguish between areas that cover the entire spectrum of administrative action. Schedler (2001, p. 38) makes use of the "political decision-making and production process" to structure the model, and calls its individual elements *"decision—production—provision."* The structuring patterns for these areas are furnished by the interactions which take place there and which can be supported by e-government applications. Thus a great number of e-government applications are assigned to every single area. This assignment results in the core elements of comprehensive e-government.

In this way, four core elements can be derived for e-government, namely *Electronic Democracy and Participation* (eDP), *Electronic Production Networks* (ePN), *Electronic Public Services* (ePS) and—by way of an interlinking internal element—*Electronic Internal Collaboration* (eIC).

The element of eDP—Electronic Democracy and Participation—denotes the electronic mapping and support of democratically legitimated decision-making procedures, as well as their preparation. Interaction partners are citizens and groups as shapers of political opinion and decision-makers, on the one hand, and the political organs that are democratically legitimated by the citizens' approval, on the other hand. The administration supports the operative implementation of democratic processes. In addition, the electronic support of interactions between politicians, parliament and the administration is also attributed to eDP. This covers examples like the parliamentary enquiries addressed to certain administrative units.

ePN—Electronic Production Networks—describes the electronic support of cooperation between public and private institutions, as well as among public institutions themselves for the purpose of joint output production. In particular, this refers to electronic production networks for the fulfilment of public tasks. Private enterprises appear as suppliers to, and cooperation partners of, public administration. In cooperation between administrative units, this concerns the horizontal and vertical interlinkage of the administration, i.e., the establishment of a network inside and between various government levels. This network is particularly relevant when the fulfilment of public tasks requires the involvement of more than one area and level of the state.

ePS—Electronic Public Services—or rather, the electronic provision of public services, is usually something that still takes place on the internet today; however, mobile forms of communication such as mobile phones or DPAs are conceivable future applications. Even now, such mobile users are occasionally referred to as m-government (for "mobile government"). Service recipients can be private individuals or groups such as enterprises or interest groups.

The three elements described so far, which cover interaction between the administration and the outside world, are complemented by the element of eIC—Electronic Internal Collaboration—which covers the administration's internal processes and communication procedures. Here, electronic support includes e-mail systems and the internet, as well as numerous intranet applications. In an integrated system, many working processes are modelled as electronic process control, i.e., workflows.

One of the core activities of public administration is the processing of dossiers, i.e., individual cases, which was previously done with the help of hard-copy files. An optimisation of Internal Electronic Collaboration now requires files to be processed by means of what is known as digital file management (Hristova & Schedler, 2005) or records management (Myburgh, 2005). Files that are processed digitally can also be archived in an electronic form. All this is part of the eIC element, i.e., a function to be fulfilled by the internal organisation of public management.

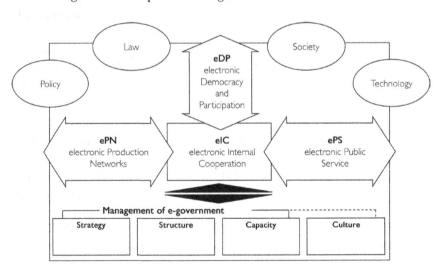

Figure 11.1 Comprehensive e-government model. *Source*: Schedler, Summermatter and Schmidt (2003).

		Core elements			
		eDP	ePN	ePS	eIC
Interaction partners	Private individual	Citizen Politician Voter Lobbyist		Customer/ service recipient	
	Enterprise	Sponsor Stakeholder	Supplier Partner	Customer/ service recipient	
	NGOs/ NPOs	Stakeholder	Partner	Customer/ service recipient	
	Parliament	Legislator Decision-maker			
	Judiciary	Judge			
	Other admin. units		Supplier Partner	Customer/ service recipient	
	In-house				Supplier Partner Customer

Figure 11.2 Roles of the interaction partners in the four core elements. *Source*: Schedler, Summermatter and Schmidt (2003).

Contrary to the *relationship concepts* (B2G, C2G, etc.) that are often encountered at an international level, we assume that one and the same individual is able to take on different *roles* in contact with government, which are strongly informed by varying quality standards.

"A to B" relations are often not sufficiently significant, nor are they very fruitful for either practical implementation or scientific research. After all, what is of the essence for the functionality of e-government are not the actors but the roles they play when they are in contact with the state. The above table provides an overview of the interaction partners of the administration and their roles in the four core elements of e-government.

Each of these elements has its own peculiarities with regard to its implementation and to the value-creation potentials that may be realised by the state. However, they only constitute a basic model of e-government through their interplay, which is why an extensive e-government system can only be introduced into public administration if all four elements are taken into account.

Obstacles in the Way of e-Government

Irrespective of the constant progress of technological possibilities, there are some fundamental general conditions whose significance increases along with the integrative nature of modern ICT. In practice, such general conditions result in limits to be imposed on the technologically conceivable possibilities of application.

Data Protection

Data protection is intended to protect private individuals against infringements of their personality rights or other interests in connection with person-related information. Citizens are entitled to a guarantee that in the wake of the necessary standardisation of data for efficient e-government, no data combinations are created which impair their personal freedom and integrity. Data protection becomes particularly relevant when an administration offers services across the borders of individual administrative units. For such services to be provided, the data inventories of the various administrative units would be interlinked and be made mutually accessible. It is also conceivable that one-stop shops would want to collect all the centrally stored information about service recipients from all the administrative units concerned in order to have the data at their fingertips.

Without going into national data protection laws in any more detail, it can be said in general that the state is obliged to ensure that administrative units are only able to access such data as they require for their specific output production. Any unintended dissemination of personal data must be avoided. For this reason, data protection frequently requires a complex system of access authorisation for the optimisation of processes that are shared by two or more administrative units. If external partners are involved in the production of outputs, then these requirements become even more stringent.

Data Security

Data security focuses on the protection of actual data and systems. In principle, this is about the prevention of unauthorised access to and abuse of data. In the public domain, very high security standards are called for on account of the special sensitivity of the data. This issue has attracted a sudden upsurge in attention ever since 11 September 2001, particularly in the USA, since the internet as a vital system for both the public and the private sector is also exposed to possible terrorist attacks.

Besides unauthorised access by hackers, for example, this area covers user identification and authentication criteria, particularly of a legal nature. The significance of reliable user identification need not be explained in detail at this juncture. However, the public sector is confronted with the problem that there are clear-cut legal provisions regarding the form of official decisions such as injunctions, for which electronic solutions are often not sufficient. Moreover—like in the private sector—there is the problem of the legal validity and binding nature of digital signatures. Germany was one of the first countries to enact rules concerning the requirements to be satisfied by digital signatures; however, these rules do not yet govern the legal acceptance of such signatures in legal relations.

Digital Divide

Digital divide is the term that denotes the unequal distribution of internet access among a country's various population strata (OECD, 2001). Surveys conducted in different countries clearly indicate that this disparity also leads to unequal access to administrative outputs and—if such possibilities are in place—to the exercise of political rights through the internet. In the USA it is known, for example, that white people tend to have better access to the Internet than African Americans; the same applies to rich and poor people, and to the urban and the rural population, respectively. Particularly when administrative outputs should be addressed to the socially weaker members of our society, the digital divide is therefore of great significance.

It is also of great significance for the entire domain of Electronic Democracy and Participation, where it is especially important for equal access to be ensured. To counter this problem, existing communication channels are therefore often kept open, which leads to redoubled costs—a weakening of the financial performance of e-government. Conversely, the element of Electronic Production Networks would appear to present no problems in this respect since it may be assumed that professional partners in our economic area have the internet access this requires.

Discuss

 How does *electronic government differ from the normal informatisation of an administrative organisation?*

 Various authors are of the opinion that although financial pressure explains why the administration moves, it does not explain why it moves in precisely this direction (OPM). Rather, they say, this is a consequence of technological progress. What do you think about this argument?

Q What functions do the individual elements of the e-government model described in these pages fulfil, and what benefit do they create for the administration and for society?

Q What is the difference between electronic banking and electronic government? What particular requirements must the state satisfy with its electronic services?

Q How relevant is the digital divide for developed countries such as Germany, Austria and Switzerland?

Further Readings

Hood, C., Margetts, H. Z. (2007). *The tools of government in the digital age*. Basingstoke: Palgrave Macmillan.

Schedler, K., Summermatter, L., Schmidt, B. (2004). *Managing the electronic government: from vision to practice*. Grennwich, CT: Information Age.

Mayer-Schönberger, V., Lazer, D. (2007). *Governance and information technology: from electronic government to information government*. Cambridge: MIT Press.

Margetts, H. (2003). Electronic Government: A Revolution in Public Administration? In *Handbook of Public Administration*. San Francisco: Jossey-Bass.

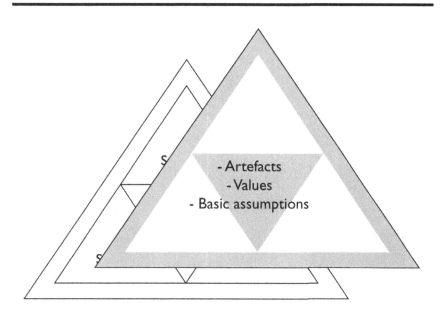

12

The Administrative Culture of OPM

In German-speaking countries, administrative reform is never merely a reform of structures, a formulation of new strategies or the development of new potentials. Even though these three elements are necessary, they are not sufficient for a genuine change in public administration. A large part of OPM aims to establish a new culture in public institutions. The culture of public administration is therefore the fourth element to be dealt with in the heuristic organisation model on which our publication is based.

The fact that public administration cultivates its own culture, which is different from that of a market-based medium-sized enterprise, can be seen straight away. The question arises, however, as to what extent culture is shaped by the typical situation and environment of public administration. At this juncture, it is of particular interest to see whether there is a typical OPM culture and what characteristics it has.

Outcome-Oriented Public Management, pages 209–218
Copyright © 2010 by Information Age Publishing
All rights of reproduction in any form reserved.

What is Administrative Culture?

In simplified terms, administrative culture can be described as the entirety of life and experience within the administration. It is characterised by informal aspects, actual events and experiences of daily life among officials and their contacts outside the administration. This culture is thus perceived both inside and outside the administration, and it is always interpreted subjectively in inter-relational identity processes within groups of civil servants. It is by definition not set down in writing or in any other terms; rather, it evolves out of the way people deal with each other.

Every organisation *has* its own culture and, as a rule, an additional number of subcultures. The more differentiated an organisation and/or functional structure, the greater the possibility of its being proportionately more diverse. In government structures with a wide range of tasks, this must be expected from the start. At the same time, every organisation is also a culture in that it is shaped by shared values and basic assumptions.

Reforms directed at the purely structural level are not rare in public administration. Although the significance of cultural change is often emphasised, genuine "cultural work" is hardly ever done, and many projects are not allocated sufficient funds for this important task. In Table 12.1, we list a few examples to demonstrate how far structural changes and real experience can drift apart if administrative culture follows entrenched routines.

As the first example shows, even if one-line budgets are formally introduced to extend the latitude of administrative managers, the widespread culture of mistrust creates a tendency to annihilate the new freedoms through excessive checks by "headquarters." The other examples point in a similar direction. Of course there are also positive cases in which a de-

TABLE 12.1 Examples of Structural and Cultural Elements

Structural level	Level of administrative culture
• Decentralisation of responsibilities	• Experienced perception of decentralised responsibility by managers • "Overcompensation" for decentralisation through increased checks and reporting by headquarters
• Introduction of one-line budgeting	• Information input precepts for budgeting by the treasurers
• Involvement of customers, for instance in surveys, panels, etc.	• Lack of trust in customers' judgement with regard to administrative outputs

liberate change of cultural course resulted in an effective change to the administration.

Differing cultures can be perceived if the same norm (in the form of a law, for example) is interpreted and applied in completely different ways. If, for instance, a planning authority with an authoritarian culture treats a planning application in a somewhat passive, impersonal and defensive way, a service-oriented culture would actively welcome such an application, and feasible solutions would be sought in personal meetings, although the legal structure would still be precisely the same. In one Swiss canton, planning authority staff were even called upon by their minister to contact potential principals proactively in order to ensure that their applications would be drawn up according to requirements and in good time. This example shows that contrary to many arguments, public administration has a wide scope for customer-oriented conduct—even today.

Many authors (such as van Wart, 1998) writing about organisational culture refer to Edgar Schein (1985), who developed a three-level model for the cultural elements of an organisation which covers both the explicit and implicit cultural elements of an organisation:

- basic assumptions about how the work functions shape an organisation's conception of itself: views of humanity, an understanding of nature, a good political organisation, etc;
- values expressed by staff determine the organisation's course of action: how the world, an organisation or politics functions or should function;
- artefacts and symbols are the visible parts of organisational culture; they are expressive of its implicit levels.

In our view, the most important proposition of this model relates to the observability of cultural dimensions. While outsiders are able to discern the artefacts and symbols as cultural elements that an organisation *has*, they are only the tip of the iceberg, as it were. The driving factors of administrative culture reside in the basic assumptions and values that *are part* of the organisation. However, they can hardly be made "measurable." Basic assumptions are implicit ideas of how an organisation should be structured as a system (for example, administrative staff subordinate themselves to the politicians' precepts: the primacy of politics). How this must be effected in concrete terms is part of the organisation's value system: should the administration leave all the decisions to politics, or should politicians only set strategic courses?

Artefacts	formal	Structure	Capacity	Strategy
	informal			
Values				
Basic premises				

Figure 12.1 Adapted culture model. *Source*: in analogy with Schein (1995, p. 17).

If Schein's model is viewed from the perspective of our heuristic organisation model, a further level can be inserted. A survey conducted at the University of St.Gallen in 1998 revealed that artefacts can be subdivided into formal and informal observable elements of the administration, with the three formal areas of strategy, structure and capacity having their counterparts in informal actual experience. The formal requirement of a specific communication process (such as the principle of "proper channels") as a structural element of the organisation is reflected in informal reality, which is characterised by, for example, direct communications exchanged by information teams.

The Significance of Administrative Culture

Many administrative outputs are *personal services*. This means that the output provision process takes place at an individual level characterised by direct interaction between output provider and service recipient. Individual public officials are on their own; interaction with customers cannot be influenced or monitored by a central office (cf. Bieger, 1998, p. 207). Public administration thus differs from a manufacturing plant whose products can be consumed without any relationship with the manufacturer in person.

Wherever hierarchical or physical product or production monitoring processes cannot be of any effect, an organisation depends on the good conduct of its members. For this reason the informal, cultural component assumes a particularly great significance for the quality of the overall system. This applies in the main to a large part of public administration. It is not without reason, then, that many authors point out that a change in administrative culture is one of the major objectives of administrative reform.

After the reunification of Germany, public administration was also unified. Public officials from the old and new federal *Länder* were meant to work together virtually from one moment to the next. Reichard and Schröter (1993) investigated the role conception and working styles, as well as the professional and general political values of senior administrative staff in Berlin. They also looked into the question as to the significance which differences had for the process of the integration of the two personnel bodies and thus for the efficiency and effectiveness of administrative work as a whole. Reichard and Schröter did not predict any major problems for acculturation but were of the opinion that the integration process—i.e., the internalisation of the new code of values and attitudes by public officials— would take a lengthy period of time.

Administrative culture, or the concrete conduct prevalent in administrative organisations, is often considered to be responsible for inefficiencies in output provision (Barzelay, 1992). Bureaucratic organisational cultures, states Koci (2005) with additional references to further authors, are frequently associated with a high degree of resistance to change.

How Does OPM Change Administrative Culture?

The litmus test for the cultural effectiveness of reforms in accordance with the OPM model includes an examination of changes that actually take place as a consequence of the introduction of OPM. There is relatively little reliable material about this, at least in Continental Europe. The findings outlined below derive from explorative interviews with people involved at all hierarchical levels in Swiss public administrative units that were subjected to OPM reforms. They are intended to outline how as early as 1995-1999, effective changes took place in a relatively short time.

Little or No Awareness of Administrative Culture

The most important discovery that emerges irrespective of the above-mentioned criteria, is the fact that the soft factors of change go unheeded: there is only little awareness of the significance of cultural dimensions in a reform project. Measures taken by the administration itself to support the reform process in this respect are lacking in many projects. Although administrative culture is talked about to a greater or lesser extent in most projects, a clear idea of what administrative culture is and what relevance it has to change is largely lacking. Even the professional offices within the administration, such as a personnel or an organisation office, still appear to have little sensitivity to and training in this field, or else they are unable to make their presence felt in this respect. Often, activity homing in on administrative culture only involves staff satisfaction surveys without any further specification.

This lack of awareness of administrative culture has the practical consequence that dissonances between formal interventions and cultural realities go unrecognised and become pitfalls for processes of change. Nagel and Müller (1999) describe a change project in which administrative managers were granted all the freedom for action and development virtually without any transition period—and they did not know what to do with this freedom. The bureaucratic, rule-controlled administrative culture was not prepared for this open-ended situation of change; only when clear change and learning rules were introduced could progress be achieved in the change process.

This results in the paradoxical situation whereby the debureaucratisation of a bureaucracy only appears to succeed with the help of bureaucratic approaches. In Switzerland, it was a voting public consisting entirely of men who had to decide to introduce the franchise for women, i.e., the new system had to be introduced by means of the old. The same evidently also applies to changes in bureaucracy. The first steps of change require a bureaucratic foundation, which must then be gradually reduced. Formal change must therefore always be embedded in a cultural sensitivity that takes into account possibly the toughest factors of change: the cultural mechanisms that reject implants that are extrinsic to it.

Customer Orientation was Enhanced

In a very new area of public administration, namely customer orientation, a distinct change in administrative culture was palpable. Almost all interviewees had taken over the new OPM terminology and spoke of customers, products and customer requirements. Customer surveys conducted in parallel with our investigation also revealed that customers, too, experienced distinct changes. This allows for the conclusion that customer orientation was enhanced through OPM.

In more detailed workshops, it also emerged that the motivation behind a customer orientation that is experienced similarly on the outside, may vary a great deal. Whereas in some units it was a genuine service mentality that led to customer-oriented action, other units gave in to customers' wishes relatively quickly because it appeared to be the easiest thing to do. One interviewee said: "If the customer then complains and I then have to correct everything, I'll only have more work to do."

On the strength of the interviews it can also be assumed that OPM is not the actual cause of customer orientation but only creates an ideal framework for the legitimation of a change in conduct that has long been desired. If this is the case, then it must be expected that the bureaucratic socialisation of fresh new entrants is less bureaucratic under an OPM regime and that therefore the human potential, and particularly the selection mechanisms that are used in this field, will increase in significance.

Legality Does Not Impose a Limit on Customer Orientation

Customer orientation is the object of vehement criticism in some of the literature because it is said to contravene the overriding concept of equality before the law. For this reason, it is particularly interesting to examine the view held by practitioners, who must be able to deal with this seeming contradiction in daily working life. All the evidence that we were able to gather from interviews and workshops would indicate that in practice this issue is experienced as something academic and theoretical, but not as practically relevant. The supposed contradiction between a legalist and a customer-oriented view is not experienced as an obstacle to the practical implementation of OPM but as an extension of the concept.

Bureaucrats Do Not Experience Themselves as Bureaucratic

Many interviewees pointed out that in general, a majority of administrative units worked very bureaucratically. Relations inside the administration are therefore frequently bureaucratic in nature. However, the interviewees only rarely experience themselves as bureaucratic although they accuse their colleagues of being over-bureaucratic most of the time. Thus public administration creates an internal bureaucratic image from which civil servants distance themselves by identifying with their own administrative units and by not considering themselves to be bureaucratic.

The Middle Management is Ignored

A closer look at the dimension of leadership patterns, both in the interviews and in the subsequent workshops, made clear that not only the nature, but also the strength of leadership is of cultural importance. Thus the question must be asked as to how strongly the presence of leadership is perceived in public administration. At the same time, it is interesting to know what management level is perceived as how strong; this is connected with the degree of centralisation within the unit.

Here, the results are rather surprising. In all the units that were surveyed, it became apparent that a centralist leadership culture was predominant. In other words: staff experienced their direct superiors as not very strongly present in terms of leadership, whereas the head of the administrative unit played a defining part. When "the boss" was mentioned, it was practically always the head of the administrative unit; in some cases, it was the political superior, i.e., the minister; but never the group leader or head of department.

This fact can be interpreted to the effect that the level of middle management of an administrative unit is today primarily occupied by the best members of staff rather than group or department managers. It must therefore be assumed that correspondingly few management functions are really exercised at this level. What would have to be examined is the self-assessment of officials in middle management: do they primarily conceive of themselves as managers or as members of staff? This question is of considerable significance for OPM, since an implementation of the slogan, "let the managers manage", means that there must be reliable managers in the first place. On the basis of existing findings, it is to be feared that the management potential that is necessary for OPM does not exist in the administrative units—for the practical change process this means, in turn, that special efforts must be made with the middle management of administrative units if the introduction of OPM is to be successful.

Political Culture

In a democratic system, public administration cannot and must not take place in isolation from politics. This has the consequence that changes in administrative culture cannot be effected without consideration of the political culture.

The issue of political culture is the subject of a wide range of publications, albeit hardly ever in connection with OPM. Berg-Schlosser and Schissler (1987) describe the combining of two notions with such different connotations as "politics" and "culture" into a term of political science as fraught with problems. In an OPM context, then, political culture is perceived more from the perspective of approaches derived from management and organisational psychology. Moreover, the concept of "political culture" is primarily understood as a descriptive model in the present context, which is intended to describe a change in conduct on the part of politicians.

A political culture that is "in conformity with OPM" is characterised by the following points, which have been indicated time and again in this publication:

- cooperation of the political institutions (parliament—executive—ministries) on the basis of results agreements rather than regulation;
- consideration of citizens/customers as a relevant factor in the output provision process, with a simultaneous opening towards influence from "non-political" surrounding systems;
- voluntary restraint of politics in operative matters that the administration can handle itself;
- systematic and thus regular occupation of politicians with strategic decisions, and introduction of a type of political understanding of management accounting.

Needless to say, this is only a narrow excerpt from the entire spectrum of political culture, which also covers relations with stakeholders, political parties and other levels of government. To elucidate the issue of the relationship between OPM and political culture, however, this should suffice—albeit more as a pithy pointer than as a finding, which reflects the scarcity of existing research in this field.

Thalmann (1999), a former mayor of the Swiss town of Uster, which has undergone a number of reforms, recommends that municipal councillors should adhere to the seven golden rules that characterise political culture in OPM:

1. Stay in open dialogue.
2. Become personally involved.
3. Let others participate.
4. Follow up ideas.
5. Regard failures as opportunities.
6. Cooperate in a judicious manner.
7. Think strategically.

His own reform project proved a success, so these rules appear to have stood him in good stead.

Discuss

The model proposed here tackles the issue of administrative culture in instrumental terms: culture is intended to be changed with the help of three areas of intervention. What do you think about this approach?

Q   Many authors hold the view the OPM is primarily contingent upon cultural change. Can an administrative culture be changed without involving politics? How, specifically, would you proceed to do this?

Q   What problems do you perceive in the fact that the middle management is practically ignored in the administration? How would you counter this?

Q   Bureaucrats do not experience themselves as bureaucratic. How can you explain this fact against the background of your own experience?

Q   The issue of political culture is often only perceived as a lack of culture. How can this be explained? What contribution has OPM made to remedy this situation?

Further Readings

Schein, E. H. (1992) *Organisational culture and leadership*. San Francisco: Jossey-Bass.

Schröter, E. (2000) Culture's consequences? In search of cultural explanations of British and German public sector reform. In *Comparing public sector reform in Britain and Germany: Key traditions and trends of modernization* (pp. 198–211). Aldershot.

Schedler, K., Proeller, I. (Eds). (2007). *Cultural aspects of public management reform*. New York: JAI Press.

PART **VI**

Reflections on the Model

13

The Model of Outcome-Oriented Public Management under Scrutiny

The objective of this concluding chapter is to look back at the model of Outcome-oriented Public Management in a constructive and critical light. The previous chapters aimed to depict OPM as a model in as neutral terms as possible. The questions raised at the end of every chapter were intended to stimulate a debate on what had been presented in the preceding pages. Quite deliberately, however, little was said about the practical effects of what OPM involves.

Below, we would like to provide stimuli for reflection on OPM by homing in on, and giving an account of, a few selected criticisms. Like every reform model intended to trigger genuine changes, OPM has always been and still is the target of fierce attacks, from various perspectives:

- *Criticism motivated by professional concerns* often asserts that OPM is used by the guild of economists and managers to raise their own

Outcome-Oriented Public Management, pages 221–232
Copyright © 2010 by Information Age Publishing
221

logic above that of the professions concerned with a specific task area, and that this results in a kind of "economic imperialism" in public management. Doctors' criticism, for instance, asserts that in the health sector, human beings are the most important factor, not cost/benefit considerations. Teachers say that pupils are not customers and cannot be measured by the same yardstick.

▪ *Criticism motivated by control theory* highlights the deficits of OPM that can be perceived in comparison with the control power of the traditional model. Harringer (2000), as an example of a sceptical city treasurer in Switzerland, doubts the functionality of the one-line budget because it leaves too many unanswered questions with regard to the influence of politics. The loss of control capacity by the state which results from the decentralisation and privatisation of output provision is also pilloried.

▪ *Criticism motivated by power theory* results from deliberate or factual shifts in the influence of various groups. Finger (2002), for instance, predicts that at various stages of the introduction of OPM, different actors will gain advantages in the political system, which in turn will provoke resistance on the part of the other actors. Indeed, one must admit that the greatest interest politicians show in the reform concerns the balance of power and its change.

▪ *Criticism motivated by systems theory* casts doubt on the politico-administrative system's ability and willingness to play the model of OPM in such a way as it has been conceived of in theory. On the basis of his own painful experience with the practical application of policy analysis, Knoepfel (1995) pointed out early on that several assumptions that OPM makes about how the politico-administrative system works were erroneous and would therefore result in failure.

Any assessment of OPM must be based on data that are as objective as possible. This means that OPM must be evaluated as a reform. In Continental Europe, there is still no distinctive culture of project evaluation, yet neutral evaluations do exist. In the meantime, academia has also produced a sufficient number of independent studies so students can get an idea of the success of OPM.

How Can the Implementation of OPM be Judged?

Target/Performance Comparison: Does the Reform Attain Its Own Objectives?

OPM-style reforms have meanwhile become 25 years old (15 years in the German-speaking area). It is therefore time to reflect no longer merely on the communication of the model, but on the practical effects the introduction of OPM has had in practice. By now, good overviews are available for the German-speaking area; for Germany, for example, there is the festschrift for Christoph Reichard (Jann et al., 2006), but also more specific studies such as the overview of performance measurement and comparison in politics and public administration (Kuhlmann et al., 2004) or a manual of administrative reform by Blanke et al. (2005). A summary of ten years of administrative reforms in book form is also available for Switzerland (Lienhard et al., 2005). All these publications contain descriptions of practical examples combined with conceptual considerations and suggestions for further developments. They make clear that OPM has been successful in changing many bureaucrats' minds, and in introducing management as an indispensable function of top civil servants. However, they also reveal that there are some practical obstacles that still need to be surmounted, such as the improvement of performance measures for political control.

In an international study of public management reforms that received wide attention, Pollitt and Bouckaert (2004) proceeded more systematically. They examined the "trajectories" of the public management reforms and divided them up into "what" trajectories and "how" trajectories (Table 13.1).

On the basis of this division of reform movements into types, the two authors demonstrate what changes had to be expected from the reform concepts and where evidence of change could indeed be furnished. OPM

TABLE 13.1   Reform Trajectories According to Pollitt and Bouckaert

"What" trajectories	"How" trajectories
• Finances: budgeting, accounting, auditing • Personnel: recruitment, staffing, rewards, job security, etc. • Organisation: specialisation, coordination, decentralisation • Performance measurement systems: objects, organisation, utilisation	• Top-down vs bottom-up • Legal dimensions • Distribution of tasks: new assignments

at an international level resembles many other reform projects in that there is often a yawning chasm between rhetoric and practice. Success reports by official authorities can frequently not be confirmed to the same extent by independent and critical researchers. Assessing the *effects of Outcome-oriented Public Management* is therefore necessary, albeit not easy (Ritz, 2003).

Pollitt and Bouckaert try to find indicators of whether evidence of changes in the areas addressed can actually be furnished and whether these changes correspond to the reform objectives. This is indeed the case in many countries, for instance with regard to the financial effects of reforms. However, there is always the problem of blurred causalities: although major changes can be evidenced with respect to the selected input indicators over the years, it remains largely unclear whether these changes must be attributed to public management reforms alone. The causal nexus between reform measures and observable effects in the system is often not as clear-cut as the proponents of reforms would wish. Nonetheless, studies reveal that OPM certainly does have positive effects on the administration and its control (Rieder & Lehmann, 2002).

Comparison with Other Reform Efforts

In work of so far unparalleled breadth, Siegel (2006) examined empirical studies of reforms in the US federal administration from 1945 to 2000 and analysed these reforms from the point of view of public administration. His aim was to identify and classify reform problems and deficits—which enables us here to compare his findings with problems and deficits encountered in the introduction of OPM. Even if the temporal, spatial and political context of the reforms examined by Siegel (2006) differs from the OPM context in Continental Europe, remarkable similarities can still be observed.

Siegel differentiates between three stages of reform: firstly, the formulation of and decision concerning the reform strategy; secondly, the implementation of the reform; and thirdly, the reform results.

In the formulation and planning of the reform strategy, Siegel recognises the following problems with regard to the question as to how the process should be designed (i.e., the "how" of the reform):

- the existence of inconsistent reform objectives;
- a lack of public and/or parliamentary support;
- resistance by powerful interest groups;
- inadequate support from top-level administration;
- the difficulty of quantifying reform objectives.

In terms of substance (i.e., the "what" of the reform), the following points lead to problems or deficits of the reform:

- the fundamental assumption of a synoptic and deductive rationality as opposed to the incremental rationality of "muddling through," as Wildawsky (1974) describes it for budgeting processes;
- the difficulty of defining measurable and monitorable objectives in the politico-administrative system, which casts doubt on any control exercised in the spirit of management rationality;
- the underestimation of the problem of creating a sound information basis—a problem that would appear to become less pressing with the development of more recent information and communication technology;
- the underestimation of the ambiguity of information, particularly against the background of the fact that different actors with different perspectives interpret such information differently;
- a limited readiness in administration and politics to be made accountable for results on which the actors themselves can only exert scant influence.

In the implementation of the reforms, Siegel (2006) finds a number of points that are also perfectly typical of change projects in the private sector:

- lack of time as a central implementation problem,
- resistance in the organisation concerned,
- failure of the authority entrusted with the implementation,
- lack of resources for implementation,
- unclear management structures for implementation,
- unclear definition and demarcation of competencies,
- inappropriate advice from outside,
- change in the political balance of power during implementation.

Finally, the studies of US-American reform projects analysed by Siegel demonstrate that when problems and deficits became evident in the assessment of reform results, they concerned roughly the following points:

- the reform result was considered to be unsatisfactory in relation to costs;
- new management instruments were introduced but ignored, manipulated and "outfoxed" until they became useless;
- occurrence of unintended consequences;

- reforms can jeopardise an authority's ability to provide outputs;
- institutional incentive structures could not be changed sufficiently;
- insufficient availability of measured data on conclusion of the reform.

Siegel does not mean to say, however, that the various reforms were not crowned with success time and again. Rather, he points out that although every reform had its positive effects, the (ambitious) objectives of a reform were often not attained.

In comparison with its predecessors in the history of public management reforms, OPM thus does not stand in isolation by any means. The problems and deficits outlined above are no strangers to OPM projects, which often fail precisely because of these points. Basically, it must be said that it is likely that OPM only has a chance of durable success if it is introduced in such a manner as to involve the politico-administrative system as comprehensively as possible in terms of its *subject-matter* while taking into account the complexity of the public sector in processual terms.

NPM Put Up for Discussion

The death of New Public Management has been announced off and on for many years—prematurely, as it happens, since NPM still occupies the scientific community as much as practitioners. In February 2004, an administrative scandal was exposed in Canada, in the wake of which the examining official said: "New Public Management has been completely discredited, thank God!"—a remark that led to a detailed internet dispute that was summarised by Jones (2004). This dispute ended with a clear result: internationally, NPM has so many layers that there will always be reasons for contradictions. Jones et al. (2001) plead that the term NPM should be eschewed in any academic treatises. Those, like ourselves, who do not want to go that far are well advised to make clear what elements of NPM are discussed and analysed in what context—thus OPM as the specific adaptation of NPM for the German-speaking area has been developed for practical purposes and has been described in this book.

Below, we would like to encourage readers to subject OPM as described in this publication to a critical discussion. Selected propositions will be presented without going into any conclusive detail.

Debating Point 1: Changes in the Personnel Situation

From the point of view of the personnel situation, the break-up of administrative structures and the decentralisation of responsibilities have not been exclusively advantageous. Brown, for example, criticises an erosion of employment conditions and of the possibilities of career development (Brown, 2004), which are a consequence of an extensive reduction of state institutions and of contracting out. Pollitt and Bouckaert (2000), too, regard this as a great weakness of current public management reforms in an international context: there is a dichotomy between the promised modernisation of personnel management (which is intended to increase employee motivation) and the fact that outsourcing and privatisation impair job security to an unprecedented extent.

In the German-speaking area, however, changes in the personnel situation have been moderate overall. Austria and Germany still retain their life-long tenureship model for civil servants, at least at the national level. In Switzerland, where the special status of a public official has been abolished, hardly any observable changes have been reported.

Debating Point 2: The Haziness of the Term, "New Public Management"

There is still disagreement about what "New Public Management" actually is—this is the quintessence from the above-mentioned discourse. Some hold the view that it is a kind of toolbox that can be used very differently in different specific contexts. Others speak of a political philosophy. Others again call it a tool. Pollitt states that it is wrong in any case to simplify things by only seeing the two poles of bureaucracy and NPM since further models have evolved in practice which deserve labels of their own.

Indeed, it is a problem of NPM that almost any kind of reform finds some shelter under its umbrella. This entails the danger that nonsense can also be peddled as NPM or as Outcome-oriented Public Management—which does not only put a strain on the term but actually discredits it.

Debating Point 3: New Public Management Weakens the Working Order of the State

In this debate, Tim Tenbensel points out that the pioneering reforms in New Zealand in the 1990s rang in a period that is less attractive since up to a point, it has meant normalisation and the restoration of orderly conditions. Tenbensel writes that the two most important problems of NPM are the fragmentation of the public sector (and the consequent big coordination problems) and a lack of state capacity. In the latter context, Milward and Provan (2003) speak of a "hollow state." In their view, contracting out has eroded the state and its institutions to such an extent that they are no longer capable of providing appropriate solutions to new problems.

The quintessence of such arguments: an efficient state must have its own skills and capacities to react adequately to new requirements.

_____

Debating Point 4: New Public Management as a "One Size Fits All"

After New Public Management was so successful in New Zealand in the 1990s, international organisations such as the OECD (PUMA Group) and the World Bank praised it as a model that could be used almost universally in all countries. In fact, the terminology was often taken over without reflection although it was difficult to find suitable terms for some concepts in a variety of languages. In Chinese, for instance, there is no linguistic differentiation between "administration" and "management"; the same term is used for both. Garcia (for Spanish) and Pacheco (for Portuguese) report in the IPMN discourse (Jones, 2004), that there are no terms corresponding to the English "accountability" in their respective languages, which is all the more important as accountability plays an absolutely central part in the original model of NPM.

This results in a situation whereby the meaning of a concept is either distorted by bad translations or the English term is used in other languages, which necessitates continuous explanation efforts. Such terms frequently become so elastic that they can be used differently in different contexts or that the range of their connotations can be extended even further. Such a broad definition of NPM will not finally clarify the analysis but cause confusion. According to this argument, the concept of NPM would have to be reduced to an unequivocal definition again—which in fact can only happen in a specific context such as a city, a state or a nation.

_____

Debating Point 5: New Public Management and Power

Although OPM as described in this book provides politicians with instruments that enable them to exert an effective influence on the activities of the administration, many of them feel that their possibilities are limited (Brun, 2003). Although the OPM concept enables them to exercise control through output targets and performance indicators, they often fail to understand the complex relationship behind the indicators, or the administration supplies them with information that has no political relevance. Moreover, OPM focuses too much on questions of management and too little on political issues. All this results in politicians losing interest in the subjects that are relevant to OPM—which means that they yield the floor to the administration.

Debating Point 6: The Technocracy of NPM

Gregory (2001) argues—primarily with regard to the NPM reforms in New Zealand—that NPM is excessively focused on restructuring the public sector and that it has transformed a complex, vibrant and dynamic reality of government processes into an artificial world of dualities in which notions like "output," "outcome," "buyer" and "provider" have to be crammed. The price of this simplification is the neglect of non-quantifiable and more holistic elements that used to characterise New Zealand's administrative culture on a basis of trust. Similar reservations are also expressed by others, for instance by the sociologist Christoph Mäder (2000), who even speaks of a "moral crusade" which NPM with its new technocracy was waging against other professions.

Debating Point 7: Outcome Orientation and Outcome Measurement

Right from the start, the central concern of OPM as it was developed in Switzerland was the outcome orientation of public management. Other countries, such as New Zealand and Germany, only gradually started to focus on outcomes and first concentrated largely on the level of outputs. However, outcome orientation is a concern which according to a recent study (Proeller, 2006) still hovers between vision and utopia. Genuine outcome control and measurement is still rare and only possible with difficulties, whereas an increased alignment of output control with the desired outcomes can be observed (Rieder & Lehmann, 2002).

OPM's Dilemma of the Supervisors and the Supervised

Like NPM worldwide, OPM conveys two contradictory messages that can be traced back to their differing theoretical sources. What Aucoin (1990) analysed early on has also led to lasting confusion in Switzerland. In another publication (Schedler, 2005), we pointed to a very important but neglected phenomenon of OPM implementation: the dilemma between the supervisors and the supervised.

The main theoretical cornerstones of OPM are modern Management Theory and New Institutional Economics, and in the case of the latter especially Public Choice Theory and the Agency Theory (Aucoin, 1990; Hood, 1991; Thom & Ritz, 2000). Modern Management Theory provided OPM with a new management philosophy that focused on delegation, a clear definition of tasks, decision-making latitude and intrinsic motivation ("Let the managers manage"). In simplified terms, it can be compared with McGregor's (1960) Theory Y. The fundamental message that derived from this was trust in the administration's willingness to perform efficiently, provided the proper general conditions could be created. The reforms were intended to enable "good people trapped in bad systems" (Gore, 1993) to perform better.

Conversely, Public Choice Theory and the Principal/Agent Theory are based on the idea of *homo œconomicus*, who attempts to maximise his own (material) benefit. The different constellations of interest between the principal, i.e., the executive, and the agent, i.e., the administration, combined with the information advantage enjoyed by the administration, give rise to the moral hazard of deceiving the principal. To prevent this, the Agency Theory recommends the introduction of monitoring instruments and specific incentive mechanisms. In OPM, this recommendation is reflected in the instruments of performance measurement and monitoring, as well as in performance-linked rewards.

Both messages can be found in the relevant publications about OPM. The introductory chapters of this textbook also deal with OPM's view of humanity, placing it clearly in Modern Management Theory. In some of the following chapters, however, this same book also describes in some detail how the monitoring instruments that are typical of OPM should be developed and introduced. On its own, this would not be tragic if the target group of the OPM message possessed a certain homogeneity.

Here, however, another peculiarity appears which again is not new but was dealt with in more detail in a different context: in the public budgeting debate in the USA. Wildavsky (1974) distinguishes between spenders and guardians, i.e., between those who spend money and those who retain it. In the OPM environment, it would appear more appropriate to speak of the supervisors and the supervised. Typically, the supervised are the line managers, who have to fulfil tasks in their various areas and thus depend on being given a certain amount of leeway. The supervisors, however, typically sit at the control levers of administrative control, i.e., in interministerial units such as the financial administration or the personnel office, or else in those staffs of the ministries whose job it is to coordinate and/or supervise administrative units.

The literally ambiguous message of OPM now reaches two groups whose perception has been shaped by their respective programming. The supervised feel strengthened in their concerns by the elements of Modern Management Theory and tend to blank out the monitoring instruments that are of less advantage to them. The supervisors, in turn, find the new monitoring possibilities offered by OPM attractive: now, they are not only able to monitor whether credit lines are adhered to, but they can also check on output provision. They welcome OPM because from their point of view it allows for more, and for more precise, checks.

From the angles of their respective (focused) perceptions, the two groups construct a partial picture of OPM that they regard as complete, for it satisfies their requirements. These contradictions then manifest themselves in meetings in which the two groups come together. They frequently reproach each other for not having understood what OPM is or should be. The supervised accuse the supervisors of behaving like spiders in the centre of the web and of wanting to keep all the threads in their hands. The supervisors, in turn, point out that it is not acceptable for all the possible freedoms enjoyed by the line managers to result in a situation whereby the administration as a whole can no longer be managed and controlled. Both groups invoke the same model, often even on the basis of the same book.

It may be said that there is a tendency for OPM projects to be more likely to fail if the tug of war between the two administrative groups is won too clearly by the supervisors, for in such a case, there is a danger that the motivation in the line units is lost when all the monitoring possibilities offered by OPM are exhausted. Extensive reporting is a classic object of criticism that can increasingly be heard in Switzerland and may be deemed a cultural artefact for the "sovereignty" of the supervisors in the reform process. In such cases, outcome orientation frequently mutates into an excessively bureaucratic check on costs and outputs.

It seems that the conflict is unlikely to be solved, and the public management literature has had little to offer to date. Although in Switzerland, Nagel and Müller (Nagel & Müller, 1999; Nagel, 2001) have demonstrated the significance of appropriate cultural development, the response so far evinced by practitioners is still insufficiently clear as far as we know. One important theoretical approach may well be found in the literature on organisational behaviour. Here, the Structuration Theory (Giddens & Turner, 1990) could well furnish fruitful results that focus investigations on communication between individuals and the perception of communication by individuals in an organisation. The fundamental question is: how must communication processes be designed to enable the supervisors and the supervised to address their latent conflict in a constructive framework and to enhance mutual sensitivity?

Discuss

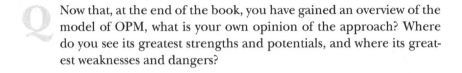

Now that, at the end of the book, you have gained an overview of the model of OPM, what is your own opinion of the approach? Where do you see its greatest strengths and potentials, and where its greatest weaknesses and dangers?

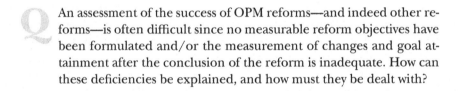

An assessment of the success of OPM reforms—and indeed other reforms—is often difficult since no measurable reform objectives have been formulated and/or the measurement of changes and goal attainment after the conclusion of the reform is inadequate. How can these deficiencies be explained, and how must they be dealt with?

Further Readings

Barzelay, M. (2001). *The new public management: improving research and policy dialogue*. Berkeley: University of California Press.

Christensen, T. (2001). *New Public Management: the transformation of ideas and practice*. Aldershot.

Pollitt, C., Bouckaert, G. (2004). *Public Management Reform: a comparative analysis* (2nd ed.). Oxford: Oxford University Press.

English–German Glossary

accrual accounting	betriebswirtschaftliche Buchhaltung / doppelte Buchhaltung
administrative unit	Amt
constitutional state, *Rechtsstaat*	Rechtsstaat
Control Model	Steuerungsmodell
cost and output transparency	Kosten- und Leistungstransparenz
economic state	Wirtschaftsstaat
guarantor state	Gewährleistungsstaat
impact	Einwirkung
implementing administration	Vollzugsverwaltung, Hoheitsverwaltung
implementing arm of the state	Ausführungsstab des Staates
implementing legitimation	betriebliche Legitimation
law-enforcement administration	Eingriffsverwaltung
location attractiveness factor	Standortfaktor
one-line budget	Globalbudget
organisational capacity	Potential
outcome	Auswirkung / Wirkung
Outcome-oriented Public Management	Wirkungsorientierte Verwaltungsführung
output	Leistungen, Produkte
output—outcome	Leistung—Wirkung
output buyer	Leistungskäufer
output funder	Leistungsfinanzierer
output *or* service	Leistung
(output) provider	Leistungserbringer
output provision *or* service provision	Leistungserstellung
performance agreement	Leistungsauftrag, -vereinbarung

Outcome-Oriented Public Management, pages 233–234
Copyright © 2010 by Information Age Publishing
233

performance objective	Leistungsziel
policy-making	Politikvorbereitung
principles of governance	staatsleitende Grundsätze
productive state	Leistungsstaat
ratio of government expenditure to the GDP	Staatsquote
results	Leistungen und Wirkungen zusammen
right to initiate legislation	Initiativrecht
right to initiate referendum	Referendumsrecht
service recipient	Leistungsempfänger
service-provision administration	Leistungsverwaltung
social contract on which civil society and the state are based	staatlicher Grundkonsens
structuration theory	Strukturierungstheorie
three-layered legitimation	gestufte Legitimation
welfare state	Sozialstaat

References

Adamaschek, B. (Hrsg.). (1997). *Interkommunaler Leistungsvergleich. Leistung und Innovation durch Wettbewerb* (2. Aufl.). Gütersloh: Bertelsmann Stiftung.

Aucoin, P. (1990). Administrative Reform in Public Management: Paradigms, Principles, Paradoxes and Pendulums. *Governance: An International Journal of Policy and Administration, 3,* 115–137.

Badelt, Ch. (1987). *Marktanreize im öffentlichen Sektor, Strategien zur Effizienzsteigerung mit Beispielen aus den USA.* Wien: Signum.

Baldersheim, H. (1993). Die „Free Commune Experiments" in Skandinavien: Ein vergleichender Überblick. In G. Banner & C. Reichard (Hrsg.), *Kommunale Managementkonzepte in Europa: Anregungen für die deutsche Reformdiskussion* (S. 27–41). Köln: Deutscher Gemeindeverlag GmbH und Verlag W. Kohlhammer GmbH.

Bangemann, M. (1995). *Europa und die globale Informationsgesellschaft.* Vaduz: Verwaltungs- und Privat-Bank AG.

Banner, G. & Reichard, C. (Hrsg.). (1993). *Kommunale Managementkonzepte in Europa. Anregungen für die deutsche Reformdiskussion.* Köln: Deutscher Gemeindeverlag GmbH und Verlag W. Kohlhammer GmbH.

Banner, G. (1995). Mit dem „Neuen Steuerungsmodell" zur dezentralen Ergebnisverantwortung. In D. Berchtold & A. Hofmeister (Hrsg.), *Die öffentliche Verwaltung im Spannungsfeld zwischen Legalität und Funktionsfähigkeit: Schnittstellen Verwaltungsrecht und -management* (S. 41–59). Bern: SGVW.

Barzelay, M. (1992). *Breaking through bureaucracy a new vision for managing in government.* Berkeley, Calif.: University of California Press.

Barzelay, M. (2001). *The New Public Management: Improving Research and Policy Dialogue.* Berkeley, Calif.: University of California Press.

Becker, B. (1989). *Öffentliche Verwaltung. Lehrbuch für Wissenschaft und Praxis.* Percha: Schulz.

Outcome-Oriented Public Management, pages 235–254
Copyright © 2010 by Information Age Publishing

Behn, R. D. (1995). The Big Questions of Public Management. *Public Administration Review, 55,* 313–324.

Bellamy, C. & Taylor J. A. (1998). *Governing in the Information Age.* Buckingham: Open University Press.

Belz, C., Bircher B. & Büsser, M. (1991). *Erfolgreiche Leistungssysteme. Anleitungen und Beispiele.* Stuttgart: Schäffer.

Berchtold, D. & Hofmeister, A. (Hrsg.). (1995). *Die öffentliche Verwaltung im Spannungsfeld zwischen Legalität und Funktionsfähigkeit: Schnittstellen Verwaltungsrecht und -management.* Bern: SGVW.

Berg-Schlosser, D. & Schissler, J. (1987). Politische Kultur in Deutschland. In D. Berg-Schlosser & J. Schissler (Hrsg.), *Politische Kultur in Deutschland. Bilanz und Perspektiven der Forschung* (S. 11–26). Opladen: Westdeutscher Verlag.

Bertelsmann Stiftung (Hrsg.). (1993). *Carl-Bertelsmann-Preis 1993: Demokratie und Effizienz in der Kommunalverwaltung: Bd. 1. Dokumentation zur internationalen Recherche.* Gütersloh: Bertelsmann Stiftung.

Bertelsmann Stiftung & Saarländisches Ministerium des Inneren (Hrsg.). (1996). *Kommunales Management in der Praxis, Bd. 1. der Veröffentlichungsreihe des Projektes „Modern & Bürgernah—Saarländische Kommunen im Wettbewerb": Gesamtkonzeption des Wettbewerbs.* Gütersloh: Bertelsmann Stiftung.

Bertelsmann Stiftung & Saarländisches Ministerium des Inneren (Hrsg.). (1997). *Kommunales Management in der Praxis, Bd. 4. der Veröffentlichungsreihe des Projektes „Modern & Bürgernah—Saarländische Kommunen im Wettbewerb": Budgetierung und dezentrale Ressourcenverantwortung.* Gütersloh: Bertelsmann Stiftung.

Bertelsmann Stiftung (Hrsg.). (1998). *Computer für die Stadt der Zukunft, Internationale Fallbeispiele.* Gütersloh: Bertelsmann Stiftung.

Bertot, J. C. (1998-99). Challenges and Issues for Public Managers in the Digital Era. *The Public Manager, 27*(4), pp. 27–31.

Bieger, T. (1998). *Dienstleistungsmanagement—Einführung in Strategien und Prozesse bei persönlichen Dienstleistungen.* Bern/Stuttgart/Wien: Haupt.

Blanke, B., von Bandemer, S., Nullmeier, F. & Wewer, G. (Hrsg.). (2005). *Handbuch zur Verwaltungsreform.* Wiesbaden: Verlag für Sozialwissenschaften.

Bleicher, K. (1991). *Das Konzept Integriertes Management.* Frankfurt a.M.: Campus.

Blume, M. (1993). Tilburg: Modernes, betriebswirtschaftlich orientiertes Verwaltungsmanagment. In G. Banner & C. Reichard (Hrsg.), *Kommunale Managementkonzepte in Europa: Anregungen für die deutsche Reformdiskussion* (S. 143–160). Köln: Deutscher Gemeindeverlag GmbH und Verlag W. Kohlhammer GmbH.

Bogumil, J. (1997). Das Neue Steuerungsmodell und der Prozess der politischen Problembearbeitung - Modell ohne Realitätsbezug?. In J. Bogumil & J. Kißler (Hrsg.), *Verwaltungsmodernisierung und lokale Demokratie. Risiken und Chancen eines Neuen Steuerungsmodells für die lokale Demokratie* . Baden-Baden: Nomos.

Bogumil, J. (2003). Politische Rationalität im Modernisierungsprozess. In K. Schedler & D. Kettiger (Hrsg.), *Modernisieren mit der Politik: Ansätze und Erfahrungen aus Staatsreformen* (S.15–42). Bern/Stuttgart/Wien: Haupt.

Bogumil, J., Holtkamp, L. & Kissler, L. (2001). *Verwaltung auf Augenhöhe. Strategie und Praxis kundenorientierter Dienstleistungspolitik.* Berlin: Edition Sigma.

Bogumil, J. & Jann, W. (2005). *Verwaltung und Verwaltungswissenschaft in Deutschland. Einführung in die Verwaltungswissenschaft.* Wiesbaden: Verlag für Sozialwissenschaften.

Bolz, U. (Hrsg.) (2005). *Public Private Partnerships in der Schweiz.* Zürich: Schulthess.

Bolz, U. & Klöti, U. (1996). Parlamentarisches Steuern neu erfinden? NPM-Steuerung durch die Bundesversammlung im Rahmen des New Public Management (NPM)—Ein Diskussionsbeitrag. *Schweizerisches Zentralblatt für Staats- und Verwaltungsrecht, 97,* 145–182.

Bolz, U. & Lienhard, A. (2001). Staatsrechtliche Kernfragen der wirkungsorientierten Steuerung in den Kantonen. *Schweizerisches Zentralblatt für Staats- und Verwaltungsrecht, 102,* 1–30.

Borins, S. (1998a). *Innovating with Integrity: How local heroes are transforming American government.* Washington, D.C.: Georgetown University Press.

Borins, S. (1998b). Lessons from the New Public Management in Commonwealth Nations. *International Public Management Journal, 1,* 37–58.

Boston, J., Martin, J., Pallot, J. & Walsh, P. (1996). *Public management—The New Zealand Model.* Auckland: Oxford University Press.

Boyne, G. A. (1998). Bureaucratic Theory meets Reality: Public Choice and Service Contracting in U.S. Local Government. *Public Administration Review, 58,* 474–484.

Brede, H. (2001). *Grundzüge der öffentlichen Betriebswirtschaftslehre.* München: Oldenbourg.

Brede, H. & Buschor, E. (Hrsg.). (1993). *Das neue öffentliche Rechnungswesen. Betriebswirtschaftliche Beiträge zur Haushaltsreform in Deutschland, Österreich und der Schweiz, Schriften zur öffentlichen Verwaltung und öffentlichen Wirtschaft, Bd. 133.* Baden-Baden: Nomos.

Brinckmann, H. (1994). Strategien für eine effektivere und effizientere Verwaltung. In F. Naschold & M. Pröhl (Hrsg.), *Produktivität öffentlicher Leistungen.* Gütersloh: Bertelsmann Stiftung.

Brown, K. (2004). Human resource management in the public sector. *Public Management Review, 6,* 303–309.

Brühlmeier, D., Haldemann, T., Mastronardi, P. & Schedler, K. (1998). New Public Management für das Parlament: Ein Muster-Rahmenerlass WoV. *Schweizerisches Zentralblatt für Staats- und Verwaltungsrecht, 99,* 297–316.

Brühlmeier, D., Haldemann, T., Mastronardi, P. & Schedler, K. (2001). *Politische Planung. Mittelfristige Steuerung in der wirkungsorientierten Verwaltungsführung.* Bern/Stuttgart/Wien: Haupt.

Brun, M. E. (2003). *Adressatengerechte Berichterstattung bei Leistungsaufträgen.* Bern: Haupt.

Buchanan, J. M. (1967). *Public Finance in Democratic Process: Fiscal Institutions and Individual Choice.* Chapel Hill: University of North Carolina Press.

Buchwitz, R. (1998). Überblick und vergleichende Bewertung der internationalen Reformen anhand der OECD-PUMA Forschungspublikationen. In H. Neisser & G. Hammerschmid (Hrsg.), *Die innovative Verwaltung. Perspektiven des New Public Management in Österreich* (S. 167–199). Wien: Signum.

Budäus, D. (1987). Betriebswirtschaftslehre - Controlling - öffentliche Verwaltung. In R. Koch (Hrsg.), *Verwaltungsforschung in Perspektive.* Baden-Baden: Nomos.

Budäus, D. (1995). *Public Management. Konzepte und Verfahren zur Modernisierung öffentlicher Verwaltungen* (3. Aufl.). Berlin: Edition Sigma.

Budäus, D. (1999). Neues öffentliches Rechnungswesen - Notwendigkeiten, Probleme und Perspektiven. In D. Budäus & P. Gronbach (Hrsg.), *Umsetzung neuer Rechnungs- und Informationssysteme in innovativen Verwaltungen: 1. Norddeutsche Fachtagung zum New Public Management* (S. 321–341). Freiburg/Berlin/München: Haufe.

Budäus, D. (2004). Modernisierung des öffentlichen Haushalts- und Rechnungswesens. In W. Jann, J. Bogumil & G. Bouckaert (Hrsg.), *Status-Report Verwaltungsreform - eine Zwischenbilanz nach zehn Jahren* (S. 75–86). Berlin: Edition Sigma.

Budäus, D. & Gronbach, P. (Hrsg.). (1999). *Umsetzung neuer Rechnungs- und Informationssysteme in innovativen Verwaltungen.* Freiburg: Haufe.

Budäus, D. & Grüning, G. (1996). Public Private Partnership, Notwendigkeit und Ansatz einer begrifflichen Strukturierung. *Verwaltung und Management, 2,* 278–282.

Budäus, D. & Grüning, G. (1997). Public Private Partnership—Konzeption und Probleme eines Instruments zur Verwaltungsreform aus Sicht der Public-Choice-Theorie. In D. Budäus & P. Eichhorn (Hrsg.), *Public Private Partnership. Neue Formen der Aufgabenerfüllung* (S. 25–66). Baden-Baden: Nomos.

Buschor, E. (1992). Controlling in öffentlichen Verwaltungen und Betrieben. In P. Weilenmann & R. Fickert (Hrsg.), *Strategie-Controlling in Theorie und Praxis* (S. 205–221). Bern / Stuttgart /Wien: Haupt.

Buschor, E. (1993). Zwanzig Jahre Haushaltsreform—Eine verwaltungswissenschaftliche Bilanz. In H. Brede & F. Buschor (Hrsg.), *Das neue öffentliche Rechnungswesen. Betriebswirtschaftliche Beiträge zur Haushaltsreform in Deutschland, Österreich und der Schweiz, Schriften zur öffentlichen Verwaltung und öffentlichen Wirtschaft, Bd. 133* (S. 199–269). Baden-Baden: Nomos.

Buschor, E. (1994). Introduction: From Advanced Public Accounting via Performance Measurement to New Public Management. In E. Buschor & K. Schedler (Hrsg.), *Perspectives on Performance Measurement and Public Sector Accounting* (S. vii–xviii). Berne/Stuttgart/Vienna: Haupt.

Buschor, E. (1994). *Organisationsmodelle für ein wirksameres öffentliches Gesundheitswesen* (2. Aufl.). Zürich: Direktionen des Gesundheitswesens und der Fürsorge des Kantons Zürich.

Czybulka, D. (1989). *Die Legitimation der öffentlichen Verwaltung unter Berücksichtigung ihrer Organisation sowie der Entstehungsgeschichte zum Grundgesetz.* Heidelberg: C.F. Müller.

Damkowski, W. & Precht, C. (1995). *Public Management. Neuere Steuerungskonzepte für den öffentlichen Sektor.* Stuttgart: Kohlhammer.

Demsetz, H. (1988). *The organization of economic activity.* Oxford: Blackwell.

Donahue, A. K., Selden, S. C. & Ingraham, P. W. (2000). Measuring Government Management Capacity: A Comparative Analysis of City Human Resources Management Systems. *Journal of Public Administration Research & Theory, 10,* 381–412.

Downs, A. (1967). *Inside Bureaucracy.* Boston: Little Brown and Company.

Drucker, P. F. (1980). The Deadly Sins in Public Administration. *Public Administration Review, 40,* 103–106.

Drucker, P. F. (1990). *Managing the Non-Profit Organization.* Oxford: Butterworth-Heinemann Ltd..

Dubs, R. (1996). *Schule, Schulentwicklung und New Public Management.* St. Gallen: Institut für Wirtschaftspädagogik.

Dyson, K. (1980). *The State Tradition in Western Europe.* Oxford: Robertson.

Egli, H.-P. & Käch, U. (1995). Instrumente der neuen Verwaltungsführung im Projekt Wirkungsorientierte Verwaltung (WOV) des Kanton Luzern. In P. Hablützel, T. Haldemann & K. Schedler (Hrsg.), *Umbruch in Politik und Verwaltung. Ansichten und Erfahrungen zum New Public Management in der Schweiz* (S. 165–184). Bern/Stuttgart/Wien: Paul Haupt.

Eichhorn, P. (1997). *Öffentliche Betriebswirtschaftslehre. Beiträge zur BWL der öffentlichen Verwaltungen und öffentlichen Unternehmen.* Berlin: Verlag Arno Spitz.

Eichhorn, P., Böhret, C., Derlien, H., Friedrich, P., Püttner G. & Reinermann, H. (1991). *Verwaltungslexikon* (2. Aufl.). Baden-Baden: Nomos.

Eilsberger, R. & Leipelt, D. (1994). *Organisationslehre der Verwaltung. Ziele und Strukturen.* Heidelberg: R. v. Decker's.

Evers, A., Rauch, U. & Stitz, U. (Hrsg.). (2002). *Von öffentlichen Einrichtungen zu sozialen Unternehmen. Hybride Organisationsformen im Bereich sozialer Dienstleistungen.* Berlin: Edition Sigma.

Fairbanks, F. (1994). Verschiedene Aspekte von Leistungsvergleichen. In Bertelsmann Stiftung (Hrsg.), *Carl-Bertelsmann-Preis 1993. Demokratie und Effizienz in der Kommunalverwaltung, Bd. 2* (S. 115–131). Gütersloh: Bertelsmann Stiftung.

Felix, J. (2003). *Besonderheiten eines Qualitätsmanagements in der öffentlichen Verwaltung.* Bamberg: Difo-Druck.

Finanzdepartement Solothurn (2003). *Botschaft und Entwurf zur Änderung der Kantonsverfassung und zum Gesetz über die Wirkungsorientierte Verwaltungsführung.* Solothurn: Regierungsrat.

Finger, M. (1997). Die Rolle des Parlaments beim New Public Management, Entflechtung von strategischen Entscheidungen und operativer Führung. *Der Schweizer Treuhänder, 1–2,* 47–51.

Finger, M. & Ruchat, B. (1997). Le New Public Management: etat, administration et politique. In M. Finger, M. & B. Ruchat (Hrsg.), *Pour une nouvelle approche du management public* (S. 33–56). Paris: Seli Arslan.

Finger, M. (2002). Dynamique de la Nouvelle Gestion Publique et Rôle du Parlement. In F. Bellanger & T. Tanquerel (Hrsg.), *Les Contrats de Prestations* (S. 95–104). Genève: Helbling und Lichtenhahn.

Fischer, G. & Thierstein, A. (1995). Der Staat als Partner in der Regionalpolitik. In Brandenberg, A. (Hrsg.), *Standpunkte zwischen Theorie und Praxis. Handlungsorientierte Problemlösung in Wirtschaft und Gesellschaft* (S. 653–669). Bern/Stuttgart/Wien: Haupt.

Fischer, M. (1995). *Wirksames Kostenmanagement im Staatsspital—chancenlos? Einige spitze Bemerkungen eines Ex-Spitalpräsidenten zur betriebswirtschaftlichen Problematik öffentlich-rechtlicher Spitäler,* Referat an der Fachtagung Verwaltungsmanagement 1995 des IFF-HSG von 9. März 1995.

Fleiner-Gerster, Th. (1980). *Allgemeine Staatslehre.* Berlin: Springer.

Flury, R. (2002). *Gestaltungsregeln für eine Kosten- und Leistungsrechnung der Kantone und Gemeinden.* Bern/Stuttgart/Wien: Haupt.

Flynn, N. (2002). Explaining the New Public Management: the importance of context. In K. McLaughlin, S. Osborne & E. Ferlie. (Eds.), *New Public Management. Current trends and future prospects* (pp. 57–76). London: Routledge.

Fountain, J. (2001). *Building the Virtual State. Information Technology and Institutional Change.* Washington DC: Brookings.

Frese, E. (1993). *Grundlagen der Organisation. Konzepte-Prinzipien-Strukturen* (5. Aufl.). Wiesbaden: Gabler.

Freudenberg, D. (1997). Das Neue Steuerungsmodell in einer Landesverwaltung. Vorschläge zur Modernisierung der hessischen Landesverwaltung. *Verwaltung und Management, 3,* 76–83.

Frey, B. & Kirchgässner, G. (1994). *Demokratische Wirtschaftspolitik, Theorie und Anwendung* (2. Aufl.). München: Vahlen.

Frey, H.-E. (1994). Agonie des Bürokratiemodells? Wo fehlt der politische Wille, wo hemmen die Vorschriften die Reform des öffentlichen (kommunalen) Sektors?. In U. Steger (Hrsg.), *Lean Administration. Die Krise der öffentlichen Verwaltung als Chance* (S. 23–47). Frankfurt a.M.: Campus.

Germann, N. (2004). *Faktoren des Kundenempfindens von Stellensuchenden gegenüber den Regionalen Arbeitsvermittlungszentren Darstellung aus der Sicht der bei den RAV Lugano und Solothurn registrierten Stellensuchenden.* Dissertation, Universität St. Gallen, Nr. 2875. St. Gallen: Universität St. Gallen.

Gerstlberger, W., Grimmer, K. & Kneissler, T. (1998). Netzwerke als unbeabsichtigte Folge des Kontraktmanagements?. *Verwaltung und Management, 4,* 282–287.

Gerstlberger, W., Grimmer, K. & Wind, M. (1999). *Innovationen und Stolpersteine in der Verwaltungsmodernisierung.* Berlin: Edition Sigma.

Giddens, A. & Turner, J. H. (Hrsg.). (1990). *Social theory today.* Cambridge: Polity Press.

Gomez, P. (1981). *Modelle und Methoden des systemorientierten Managements, Schriftenreihe des Management-Zentrums St. Gallen, Bd. 2,* Bern/Stuttgart/Wien: Haupt.

Gore, A. (1993). *Creating a Government that Works Better and Costs Less: Reengineering Through Information Technology, Report of the National Performance Review.* Washington DC: Government Printing Office.

Gregory, R. (2001). Getting better but feeling worse? Public sector reform in New Zealand. In L. R. Jones, J. Guthrie & P. Steane (Hrsg.), *Learning from international public management reform* (S. 211–232). Oxford: Elsevier Science.

Grimmer, K. (1995). Verwaltungsreform und Informationstechnologie: Ein Blick über Grenzen. In H. Reinermann (Hrsg.), *Neubau der Verwaltung. Informationstechnische Realitäten und Visionen* (S. 161–178). Heidelberg: R. v. Decker's.

Grünenfelder, P. (1997). *Die Rolle der politischen Führung im New Public Management: am Beispiel von Christchurch.* Bern/Stuttgart/Wien: Haupt.

Grüning, G. (2000). *Grundlagen des New Public Management. Entwicklung, theoretischer Hintergrund und wissenschaftliche Bedeutung des New Public Management aus Sicht der politisch-administrativen Wissenschaften der USA.* Münster: LIT.

Güntert, B. (1988). *Managementorientierte Informations- und Kennzahlensysteme für Krankenhäuser. Analyse und Konzepte,* Dissertation, Universität St. Gallen. Konstanz: Hartung-Gorre.

Hablützel, P. (1995). New Public Management als Modernisierungschance - Thesen zur Entbürokratisierungsdiskussion. In P. Hablützel, T. Haldemann & K. Schedler (Hrsg.), *Umbruch in Politik und Verwaltung. Ansichten und Erfahrungen zum New Public Management in der Schweiz* (S. 499–507). Bern/Stuttgart/Wien: Paul Haupt.

Hablützel, P., Haldemann T. & Schedler, K. (Hrsg.). (1995a). *Umbruch in Politik und Verwaltung. Ansichten und Erfahrungen zum New Public Management in der Schweiz.* Bern/Stuttgart/Wien: Paul Haupt.

Häfelin, U. & Müller, G. (1998). *Grundriss des Allgemeinen Verwaltungsrechts* (3. Aufl.). Zürich: Schulthess.

Haldemann, T. (1995). *New Public Management: Ein neues Konzept für die Verwaltungsführung des Bundes, Schriftenreihe des Eidg. Personalamtes, Bd. 1.* Bern: Eidgenössisches Personalamt.

Hartmann, K. & Pesendorfer, S. (1998). Organisations- und dienstrechtliche Rahmenbedingungen von NPM-Massnahmen im österreichischen Kontext. In H. Neisser & G. Hammerschmid (Hrsg.), *Die innovative Verwaltung. Perspektiven des New Public Management in Österreich* (S. 337–361). Wien: Signum.

Harringer, R. (2000). Das Globalbudget als Zentral- und Schwachstelle im Modell der „Wirkungsorientierten Verwaltung". *Schweizerisches Zentralblatt für Staats- und Verwaltungsrecht, 10*, 505–525.

Heeks, R. (1999). *Reinventing Government in the information age.* New York: Routledge.

Hendriks, F. & Tops, P. (1999). Between democracy and efficiency: trends in local government reform in the Netherlands and Germany. *Public Administration, 77*, 133–153.

Herbig, G. (1997). Personalwirtschaft. In K. König & H. Siedentopf (Hrsg.), *Öffentliche Verwaltung in Deutschland* (2. Aufl.) (S. 559–593). Baden-Baden: Nomos.

Herweijer, M. & Mix, U. (1996). *10 Jahre Tilburger Modell - Erfahrungen einer öffentlichen Verwaltung auf dem Weg zum Dienstleistungscenter, Praxis Reihe Verwaltungsreform.* Bremen/Boston: SachBuchVerlag Kellner.

Hilb, M. (1997). *Integriertes Personal-Management Ziele - Strategien - Instrumente.* Neuwied: Luchterhand.

Hill, H. (1994). Staatskonzeption. Auf dem Weg zu einem neuen Staat. *In VOP, 5*, 301–309.

Hill, H. (1996). Vom Ergebnis zur Wirkung des Verwaltungshandelns. In H. Hill & H. Klages (Hrsg.), *Modernisierungserfolge von Spitzenverwaltungen. Eine Dokumentation zum 3. Speyerer Qualitätswettbewerb 1996.* Stuttgart: Raabe.

Hill, H. (1997). *Verwaltung im Umbruch, Speyerer Arbeitshefte 109.* Speyer: Hochschule für Verwaltungswissenschaften.

Hill, H. (1997a). Vergesst die Bürger nicht!: Entwicklung einer bürgerorientierten Kommunalverwaltung, In H. Hill (Hrsg.), *Verwaltung im Umbruch, Speyerer Arbeitshefte 109* (S. 101–117). Speyer: Hochschule für Verwaltungswissenschaften.

Hill, H. (1997b). Reengineering im öffentlichen Bereich. In H. Hill (Hrsg.), *Verwaltung im Umbruch, Speyerer Arbeitshefte 109* (S. 53–66). Speyer: Hochschule für Verwaltungswissenschaften.

Hill, H. (1998). *Politik und Gesetzgebung im Neuen Steuerungsmodell, Speyerer Arbeitshefte 114.* Speyer: Hochschule für Verwaltungswissenschaften.

Hill, H. (1998a). Gesetzgebung und Verwaltungsmodernisierung. In H. Hill (Hrsg.), *Verwaltung im Umbruch, Speyerer Arbeitshefte 114* (S. 61–79). Speyer: Hochschule für Verwaltungswissenschaften.

Hill, H. (1998b). Verwaltungsmodernisierung als Demokratiechance in der Kommune. In H. Hill (Hrsg.), *Verwaltung im Umbruch, Speyerer Arbeitshefte 114* (S. 3–14). Speyer: Hochschule für Verwaltungswissenschaften.

Hill, H. & Klages, H. (Hrsg.). (1993). *Qualitäts- und erfolgsorientiertes Verwaltungsmanagement: aktuelle Tendenzen und Entwürfe, Schriftenreihe der Hochschule Speyer.* Berlin: Dunker & Humblot.

Hill, H., Dearing, E., Hack, H. & Klages, H. (Hrsg.). (2005). *Spitzenleistung zukunftsorientierter Verwaltungen. 7. Internationaler Speyerer Qualitätswettbewerb.* Wien: Neuer Wissenschaftlicher Verlag.

Hoch, D. (1995). Voraussetzungen für die erfolgreiche Implementierung moderner Management-Informationssysteme. In R. Hichert & M. Moritz (Hrsg.), *Management-Informationssysteme. Praktische Anwendungen* (2. Aufl.) (S. 158–167). 2. Auflage, Berlin: Springer.

Hoffmann, H., Hill, H. & Klages, H. (1996). *Motor Qualität. Verwaltungsmodernisierung in der Landeshauptstadt Saarbrücken.* Düsseldorf: Raabe.

Hood, C. (1991). A Public Management for all seasons? *Public Administration, 69,* 3–19.

Hristova, R. (2005). *Digitales Aktenmanagement, Konzeptionelle Grundlagen, Entwicklungsstand auf kantonaler Verwaltungsebene in der Schweiz und internationale Initiativen.* St. Gallen: Institut für öffentliche Dienstleistungen und Tourismus der Universität St. Gallen.

Hubmann Trächsel, M. (1995). *Die Koordination von Bewilligungsverfahren für Bauten und Anlagen im Kanton Zürich.* Zürich: Schulthess.

Hughes, O. E. (1994). *Public management and administration. An introduction.* Houndmills: Macmillan Press.

International Group of Controlling (Hrsg.). (1999). *Controller-Wörterbuch. Deutsch–Englisch, Englisch–Deutsch.* Stuttgart: Schäffer-Poeschel.

Ipsen, J. (1997). *Staatsrecht* (9. Aufl.). Berlin: Luchterhand.

ISO 9000 (1999). SN ISO/CD2 9000-2000. *Qualitätsmanagementsysteme—Grundlagen und Begriffe. SNV Schriftenreihe, Publikation 1.* Zürich: Schweizerische Normen-Vereinigung.

Jann, W. (1983). *Staatliche Programme und „Verwaltungskultur": Bekämpfung des Drogenmissbrauchs und der Jugendarbeitslosigkeit in Schweden, Grossbritannien und der Bundesrepublik Deutschland im Vergleich.* Opladen: Westdeutscher Verlag.

Jann, W. (2005). Hierarchieabbau und Dezentralisierung. In B. Blanke & S. Plass (Hrsg.), *Handbuch zur Verwaltungsreform* (S. 154–162). Wiesbaden: VS Verlag für Sozialwissenschaften.

Jann, W., Röber, M. & Wollmann, H. (Hrsg.). (2006). *Public Management - Grundlagen, Wirkungen, Kritik. Modernisierung des öffentlichen Sektors.* Berlin: Edition Sigma.

Johnson, N. (2000). State and Society in Britain. Some Contrasts with German Experience. In H. Wollmann & E. Schröter (Hrsg.), *Comparing public sector reform in Britain and Germany: key traditions and trends of modernisation* (S. 27–46). Aldershot: Ashgate.

Jones, L. (2004). International Public Management Network Symposium: "New Public Management has been completely discredited, thank God!." *International Public Management Review, 5*(2), 148–172.

Jones, L. R., Guthrie, J. & Steane, P. (2001). Learning from international public management reform experience. In L. R. Jones, J. Guthrie & P. Steane (Hrsg.), *Learning from international public management reform* (S. 1–28). Oxford: Elsevier Science.

Jones, L. & Thompson, F. (1999). *Public Management: Institutional Renewal for the twenty-first century.* Stamford: JAI Press.

Ju, E.-J. (1986). *Max Webers Bürokratiekonzeption als Ausgangspunkt für eine vergleichende Studie der chinesischen und deutschen Bürokratie* (Dissertation). Speyer: Deutsche Hochschule für Verwaltungswissenschaften.

Kanton Zürich (1999). *Voranschlag des Kantons Zürich.* Zürich: Kant. Materialzentrale.

Kaplan, R. S. & Norton, D. P. (1997). *Balanced Scorecard. Strategien erfolgreich umsetzen.* Stuttgart: Schäffer-Poeschel.

Kettiger, D. (Hrsg.). (2000). *Wirkungsorientierte Verwaltungsführung und Gesetzgebung. Untersuchungen an der Schnittstelle zwischen New Public Management und Gesetzgebung.* Bern/Stuttgart/Wien: Haupt.

Kettl, D. F. (1991). Searching for Clues about Public Management: Slicing the Onion Different Ways. In B. Bozeman (Hrsg.), *Public Management - The State of the Art* (S. 55–70). San Francisco: Jossey-Bass.

Kettl, D. F. (1993). *Sharing power. Public governance and private markets.* Washington DC: Brookings Institution.

KGSt (1989). *Aufgabenkritik: Neue Perspektiven auf der Grundlage von Erfahrungen. Bericht Nr. 9/1989.* Köln: Kommunale Gemeinschaftsstelle für Verwaltungsvereinfachung.

KGSt (1992). *Wege zum Dienstleistungsunternehmen Kommunalverwaltung. Fallstudie Tilburg. Bericht Nr. 19/1992.* Köln: Kommunale Gemeinschaftsstelle für Verwaltungsvereinfachung.

KGSt (1993). *Das Neue Steuerungsmodell. Begründung, Konturen, Umsetzung. Bericht Nr. 3/1993.* Köln: Kommunale Gemeinschaftsstelle für Verwaltungsvereinfachung.

Kickert, W. M. (Hrsg.). (1997). *Public Management and Administrative Reform in Western Europe.* Cheltenham: Edward Elgar.

Kickert, W. J. M. (2000). *Public Management Reforms in The Netherlands - Social Reconstruction of Reform Ideas and Underlying Frames of Reference.* CW Delft: Eburon.

King, C. S., Feltey, K. M. & O'Neill Susel, B. (1998). The Question of Participation in Public Administration. *Public Administration Review,* 317–326.

Klages, H. (1998). *Verwaltungsmodernisierung. „Harte" und „weiche" Aspekte II* (2. Aufl.). Speyer: Forschungsinstitut für öffentliche Verwaltung bei der Deutschen Hochschule für Verwaltungswissenschaften Speyer.

Klages, H., Hayn, M. & Witzmann M. (1998). *Abschlussbericht (vorläufige Fassung) zum Forschungsprojekt: Evaluierung von Budgetierungsansätzen bei Schulen in kommunaler Trägerschaft.* Speyer: Forschungsinstitut für öffentliche Verwaltung bei der Deutschen Hochschule für Verwaltungswissenschaften Speyer.

Klages, H., Hippler, G., Haas, H. & Franz, G. (1989). *Führung und Arbeitsmotivation in Kommunalverwaltungen. Ergebnisse einer empirischen Untersuchung.* Gütersloh: Bertelsmann Stiftung.

Klages, H. & Hippler, G. (1991). *Mitarbeitermotivation als Modernisierungsperspektive. Ergebnisse eines Forschungsprojektes über „Führung und Arbeitsmotivation in der öffentlichen Verwaltung".* Gütersloh: Bertelsmann Stiftung.

Kleindienst, A. (1999). *Controlling-Konzept im integrierten Gemeindemanagement-Modell für Gemeinden ohne Parlament unter besonderer Berücksichtigung der vertikalen Integration. Schriftenreihe des Instituts für Öffentliche Dienstleistungen und Tourismus: Beiträge zum Öffentlichen Management, Bd. 1.* Bern/Stuttgart/Wien: Haupt.

Klingebiel, N. (Hrsg.). (2001). *Performance Measurement & Balanced Scorecard.* München: Vahlen.

Knill, C. (2002). *The Europeanisation of National Administration.* Cambridge: Cambrigde University Press.

Knoepfel, P. (1995). New Public Management: vorprogrammierte Enttäuschungen oder politische Flurschäden - eine Kritik aus der Sicht der Politikanalyse. In P. Hablützel, T. Haldemann & K. Schedler (Hrsg.), *Umbruch in Politik und Verwaltung. Ansichten und Erfahrungen zum New Public Management in der Schweiz* (S. 453–470). Bern/Stuttgart/Wien: Paul Haupt.

Koci, M. (2005). *Servicequalität und Kundenorientierung im Öffentlichen Sektor eine Untersuchung personenbezogener Dienstleistungen.* Bern: Haupt.

Kommission der Europäischen Gemeinschaften (2004). *Grünbuch zu öffentlichen und privaten Partnerschaften und den gemeinschaftlichen Rechtsvorschriften für öffentliche Aufträge und Konzessionen.* Brüssel: Kommission der Europäischen Gemeinschaften.

König, K. & Siedentopf, H. (Hrsg.). (1997). *Öffentliche Verwaltung in Deutschland* (2. Aufl.). Baden-Baden: Nomos.

Kooiman, J. (1999). Governance. A social-political perspective. *Public Management: an International Journal of Research and Theory, 1*(1), 67–92.

Kraemer, K. L. (1995). Verwaltungsreform und Informationstechnologie: Von neuem betrachtet. In H. Reinermann (Hrsg.), *Neubau der Verwaltung. Informationstechnische Realitäten und Visionen* (S. 181–202). Heidelberg: R. v. Decker's.

Krueger, A. O. (1974). The Political Economy of the Rent-Seeking Society. *American Economic Review, 64,* 291–303.

Kuhlmann, S. (2004). Interkommunaler Leistungsvergleich in Deutschland: Zwischen Transparenzgebot und Politikprozess. In S. Kuhlmann, J. Bogumil & H. Wollmann (Hrsg.), *Leistungsmessung und -vergleich in Politik und Verwaltung* (S. 94–120). Wiesbaden: VS Verlag für Sozialwissenschaften.

Kuhlmann, S., Bogumil, J. & Wollmann, H. (Hrsg.). (2004). *Leistungsmessung und Leistungsvergleich in Politik und Verwaltung.* Berlin: Verlag für Sozialwissenschaften.

Lane, J.-E. (2000). *New Public Management.* London: Routledge.

Laux, E. (1993). *Vom Verwalten. Beiträge zur Staatsorganisation und zum Kommunalwesen.* Baden-Baden: Nomos.

Lenk, K. (1992). Servicebündelung in der Kommunalverwaltung durch „BürgerBüros". *Wirtschaftsinformatik, 34,* 567–576.

Lienhard, A. (2005). *Staats- und verwaltungsrechtliche Grundlagen für das New Public Management in der Schweiz. Analyse - Anforderungen - Impulse.* Bern: Stämpfli.

Lienhard, A., Ritz A. & Steiner R. (Hrsg.). (2005). *10 Jahre New Public Management in der Schweiz. Bilanz, Irrtümer und Erfolgsfaktoren*. Bern/Stuttgart/Wien: Haupt.

Linder, W. (1983). Entwicklung, Strukturen und Funktionen des Wirtschafts- und Sozialstaats in der Schweiz. In A. Riklin (Hrsg.), *Handbuch Politisches System Schweiz, Bd. 1 Grundlagen* (S. 255–382). Bern/Stuttgart/Wien: Haupt.

Löffler, E. (1996). *The Modernization of the Public Sector in an International Comparative Perspective—Implementation Strategies in Germany, Great Britain and the United States*. Speyerer Forschungsberichte 174. Speyer: Forschungsinstitut für öffentliche Verwaltung.

Luhmann, N. (1993). *Das Recht der Gesellschaft*. Frankfurt a. M.: Suhrkamp.

Lüder, K. (1991). Konzeptionelle Grundlagen für die Ausgestaltung des staatlichen Rechnungswesens. In K. Lüder (Hrsg.), *Staatliches Rechnungswesen in der BRD vor dem Hintergrund neuerer internationaler Entwicklungen* (S. 165–182). Schriftenreihe der Hochschule Spreyer. Berlin: Duncker & Humbolt.

Lüder, K. (1996). *Konzeptionelle Grundlagen des neuen kommunalen Rechnungswesens (Speyerer Verfahren)*. Stuttgart: Staatsanzeiger für Baden-Württemberg.

Lüder, K. (1999). Entwicklung des öffentlichen Rechnungswesens im internationalen Vergleich. In D. Budäus & P. Gronbach (Hrsg.), *Umsetzung neuer Rechnungs- und Informationssysteme in innovativen Verwaltungen* (S. 39–54). Freiburg/Berlin/München: Haufe.

Lüder, K. & Kampmann, B. (1993). *Harmonisierung des öffentlichen Rechnungswesens in der Europäischen Gemeinschaft*. Speyer: Forschungsinstitut für öffentliche Verwaltung.

Lütolf, P. (1997). *Wirtschaftsförderung im Modell der wirkungsorientierten Verwaltungsführung*. Luzern: Rüegger.

Lynn, L. E. (1996). *Public Management as Art, Science, and Profession*. Chatham, NJ: Chatham House Publishers Inc.

Lynn, L. E. (2005). Public Management: A concise history of the field. In E. Ferlie, L. E. Lynn & Ch. Pollitt (Hrsg.), *The Oxford Handbook of Public Management* (S. 27–50). Oxford: Oxford University Press.

Mäder, Ch. (2001). Der moralische Kreuzzug des New Public Management in der Schweiz. *Sozialer Sinn: Zeitschrift für hermeneutische Sozialforschung, 2*, 191–204.

Mäder, H. & Schedler, K. (1994). Die Entwicklungen des öffentlichen Rechnungswesens in der Schweiz vor dem Hintergrund der spezifischen nationalen Rahmenbedingungen. In K. Lüder (Hrsg.), *Öffentliches Rechnungswesen 2000* (S. 49–68). Berlin: Duncker & Humblot.

Maier, P. (1999). *New Public Management in der Justiz. Möglichkeiten und Grenzen einer wirkungsorientierten Gerichtsführung aus betriebswirtschaftlicher und rechtlicher Perspektive. Schriftenreihe des Instituts für Öffentliche Dienstleistungen und Tourismus: Beiträge zum Öffentlichen Management, Bd. 2*. Bern/Stuttgart/Wien: Haupt.

Mastronardi, Ph. (1998). New Public Management im Kontext unserer Staatsordnung. Staatspolitische, Staatsrechtliche und verwaltungsrechtliche Aspekte der neuen Verwaltungsführung. In Ph. Mastronardi & K. Schedler (Hrsg.), *New Public Management in Staat und Recht. Ein Diskurs.* (S. 47–120). Bern/Stuttgart/Wien: Haupt.

Mastronardi, Ph. (1999). Gewaltenteilung unter NPM. *Schweizerisches Zentralblatt für Staats- und Verwaltungsrecht, 9,* 449–464.

Mastronardi, Ph. (2000). Die staatspolitische Erweiterung des NPM-Konzeptes aus rechtlicher Sicht. *Verwaltung und Management, 6,* 222–227.

Mastronardi, Ph. & Schedler, K. (1998). *New Public Management in Staat und Recht - Ein Diskurs.* Bern: Haupt.

Mauch, S. (2005). Neue Wege der Personalrekrutierung. In B. Blanke, S. von Bandemer, F. Nullmeier & G. Wewer, (Hrsg.), *Handbuch zur Verwaltungsreform* (S. 260–270). Wiesbaden: VS Verlag für Sozialwissenschaften.

McGregor, D. (1960). *The Human Side of Enterprise.* New York: McGraw Hill.

McLaughlin, K., Osborne, S. P. & Ferlie, E. (Hrsg.). (2002). *New Public Management. Current trends and future prospects.* London: Routledge.

Metcalfe, L. & Richards, S. (1987). Evolving public management cultures. In J. Kooiman & K. Eliassen (Hrsg.), *Managing Public Organizations - Lessons from Contemporary European Experience* (S. 65–86). London: Sage.

Milward, H. B. & Provan, K. G. (2003). Managing the hollow state. *Public Management Review, 5*(1), 1–18.

Moore, M. H. (1995). *Creating Public Value: Strategic Management in Government.* Cambridge, MA: Harvard University Press.

Müller, G. (1995). Funktionen des Legalitätsprinzips im Organisationsrecht i.w.S. (Haushalts-, Personal- und Organisationsrecht). In D. Berchtold & A. Hofmeister (Hrsg.), *Die öffentliche Verwaltung im Spannungsfeld zwischen Legalität und Funktionsfähigkeit: Schnittstellen Verwaltungsrecht und -management* (S. 15–25). Bern: SGVW.

Myburgh, S. (2005). Records Management and Archives: Finding Common Ground. *The Information Management Journal, 39*(2), 24–29.

Nagel, E. (1999). *New public management (k)ein Wandel ohne Kulturentwicklung(!).* Basel: Wirtschaftswissenschaftliches Zentrum der Universität Basel.

Nagel, E. (2001). *Verwaltung anders denken.* Baden-Baden: Nomos.

Nagel E. & Müller W. R. (1999). *New Public Management: (k)ein Wandel ohne Kulturentwicklung. Reihe WWZ-Forschungsberichte, Jan. 1999.* Basel: Wirtschaftswissenschaftliches Zentrum der Universität Basel.

Naschold, F. (1995). *Modernisierung des Staates. Zur Ordnungs- und Innovationspolitik des öffentlichen Sektors* (3. Aufl.). Berlin: Edition Sigma.

Naschold, F. (1995a). *Ergebnissteuerung, Wettbewerb, Qualitätspolitik. Entwicklungspfade des öffentlichen Sektors in Europa.* Berlin: Edition Sigma.

Naschold, F. (1997). Umstrukturierung der Gemeindeverwaltung: eine international vergleichende Zwischenbilanz. In F. Naschold, M. Oppen & A. Wegener (1997), *Innovative Kommunen. Internationale Trends und deutsche Erfahrungen* (S. 15–48). Stuttgart: Kohlhammer.

Naschold, F., Budäus D., Jann, W., Mezger, E., Oppen, M., Picot, A., Reichard, C. ... Simon, N. (1996). *Leistungstiefe im öffentlichen Sektor. Erfahrungen, Konzepte, Methoden.* Berlin: Edition Sigma.

Naschold, F., Oppen, M. & Wegener, A. (Hrsg.). (1997). *Innovative Kommunen. Internationale Trends und deutsche Erfahrungen.* Stuttgart: Kohlhammer.

Naschold F., Jann, W. & Reichard, C. (1999). *Innovation, Effektivität, Nachhaltigkeit—Internationale Erfahrungen zentralstaatlicher Verwaltungsreform, Reihe: Modernisierung des öffentlichen Sektors, Bd. 16.* Berlin: Edition Sigma.

Neisser, H. & Hammerschmid, G. (Hrsg.). (1998). *Die innovative Verwaltung. Perspektiven des New Public Management in Österreich.* Wien: Signum.

Niskanen, W. A. (1971). *Bureaucracy and representative government.* Chicago, IL: Aldine Atherton.

NSW Government (1997). *An Internet Strategy for NSW.* Sidney: Department of Public Works and Services.

OECD (1995). *Public Management Developments, Update 1995.* Paris: OECD.

OECD (Ed.). (1996). *Responsive Government - Service Quality Initiatives.* Paris: OECD.

OECD (1997). *In Search of Results: Performance Management Practices - Key Performance Management Issues: Sweden.* Paris: OECD.

OECD (2001). *Understanding the Digital Divide.* Paris: OECD.

Öhlinger, Th. (1997). *Verfassungsrecht* (3. Aufl.), Wien: WUV-Universitätsverlag.

Oppen, M. (1995). *Qualitätsmanagement. Grundverständnisse, Umsetzungsstrategien und ein Erfolgsbericht.* Berlin: Edition Sigma.

Osborne, D. & Gaebler, T. (1997). *Der innovative Staat. Mit Unternehmergeist zur Verwaltung der Zukunft.* Wiesbaden: Gabler.

Ösze, D. (2000). *Managementinformationen im New Public Management.* Bern/Stuttgart/Wien: Haupt.

Parasuraman, A., Zeithaml, V. A. & Berry, L. L. (1985). A conceptual model of service quality and its implications for future research. *Journal of Marketing, 49*(4), 41–50.

Parkinson, C. N. (1957). *Parkinsons's law or the pursuit of progress.* London: Murray.

Pallot, J. (1998). The New Zealand Revolution. In O. Olson, J. Guthrie and C. Humphrey (Hrsg.), *Global warning! Debating international developments in new public financial management* (S. 156–184). Oslo: Cappelen Akademisk Forlag.

Pede, L. (2000). *Wirkungsorientierte Prüfung der öffentlichen Verwaltung.* Bern/Stuttgart/Wien: Haupt.

Pollitt, Ch. (1990). *Managerialism and the Public Service: An Anglo-American Experience.* Oxford: Blackwell.

Pollitt, C. & Bouckaert, G. (2004). *Public Management Reform. A Comparative Analysis* (2nd ed.). Oxford: Oxford University Press.

Proeller, I. (2002). *Auslagerung in der hoheitlichen Verwaltung. Interdisziplinäre Entwicklung einer Entscheidungsheuristik.* Bern/Stuttgart/Wien: Haupt.

Proeller, I. (2006). Wirkungsorientierung - Vision oder Utopie der schweizerischen Verwaltungsmodernisierung. In K. Birkholz, CH. Maass, P. von Maravić & P. Siebart (Hrsg.), *Public Management - Eine neue Generation in Wissenschaft und Praxis* (S. 153–170). Potsdam: Universitätsverlag.

Proeller, I. & Schedler, K. (2005). Change and Continuity in the Continental Tradition of Public Management. In E. Ferlie, L. E. Lynn & C. Pollitt (Hrsg.), *The Oxford Handbook of Public Management* (S. 695–719). Oxford: Oxford University Press.

Proeller, I. & Zwahlen, Th. (2003). *Kundenmanagement in der öffentlichen Verwaltung.* Zürich/St. Gallen: Mummert Consulting und IDT-HSG.

Promberger, K., Niederkofler, C. & Bernhart, J. (2001). *Dienstleistungscharters. Was kann sich der Bürger von der öffentlichen Verwaltung erwarten?.* Wien: Linde Verlag.

Reichard, C. (1987). *Betriebswirtschaftslehre der öffentlichen Verwaltung* (2. Aufl.). Berlin: DeGruyter.

Reichard, C. (1993). Internationale Trends im kommunalen Management. In G. Banner & C. Reichard (Hrsg.), *Kommunale Managementkonzepte in Europa. Anregungen für die deutsche Reformdiskussion* (S. 3–24). Köln: Deutscher Gemeindeverlag GmbH und Verlag W. Kohlhammer GmbH.

Reichard, C. (1994). *Umdenken im Rathaus - Neue Steuerungsmodelle in der deutschen Kommunalverwaltung.* Berlin: Edition Sigma.

Reichard, C. (1995). *Umdenken im Rathaus. Neue Steuerungsmodelle in der deutschen Kommunalverwaltung* (4. Aufl.). Berlin: Edition Sigma.

Reichard, C. (1996). Die 'New Public Management'-Debatte im internationalen Kontext. In C. Reichard & H. Wollmann (Hrsg.), *Kommunalverwaltung im Modernisierungsschub?* (S. 241–274). Basel: Birkhäuser.

Reichard, C. (1997). Deutsche Trends der kommunalen Verwaltungsmodernisierung. In F. Naschold, M. Oppen, & A. Wegener (Hrsg.). (1997). *Innovative Kommunen. Internationale Trends und deutsche Erfahrungen* (S. 49–74). Stuttgart: Kohlhammer.

Reichard, C. (1997a). Neue Ansätze der Führung und Leitung. In K. König, & H. Siedentopf (Hrsg.), *Öffentliche Verwaltung in Deutschland* (2. Aufl.) (S. 641–660). Baden-Baden: Nomos.

Reichard, C. (1998). Institutionelle Wahlmöglichkeiten bei der öffentlichen Aufgabenwahrnehmung. In D. Budäus (Hrsg.), *Organisationswandel öffentlicher Aufgabenwahrnehmung* (S. 121–153). Baden-Baden: Nomos.

Reichard, C. (1998a). Zur Naivität aktueller Konzepttransfers im deutschen Public Management. In T. Edeling, W. Jann & D. Wagner (Hrsg.), *Öffentliches und privates Management* (S. 53–70). Opladen: Leske + Budrich.

Reichard, C. & Schröter, E. (1993). Verwaltungskultur in Ostdeutschland—Empirische Befunde und personalpolitische Ansätze zur Akkulturation ostdeutscher Verwaltungsmitarbeiter. In R. Pitschas (Hrsg.), *Verwaltungsintegration in den neuen Bundesländern: Vorträge und Diskussionsbeiträge der verwaltungswissenschaftlichen Arbeitstagung 1992 des Forschungsinstituts für Öffentliche Verwaltung bei der Hochschule für Verwaltungswissenschaften Speyer* (S. 191–222). Berlin: Duncker und Humblot.

Reinermann, H. (Hrsg.). (1991). *Führung und Information - Chancen der Informationstechnik für die Führung in Politik und Verwaltung, Schriftenreihe Verwaltungsinformatik.* Heidelberg: Decker & Müller.

Reinermann, H. (1993). *Ein neues Paradigma für die öffentliche Verwaltung?—Was Max Weber heute empfehlen dürfte. Speyerer Arbeitshefte 97.* Speyer: Deutsche Hochschule für Verwaltungswissenschaften.

Reinermann, H. (Hrsg.). (1995). *Neubau der Verwaltung. Informationstechnische Realitäten und Visionen.* Heidelberg: R. v. Decker's.

Reinermann, H. (1995a). Anforderungen an die Informationstechnik. In H. Reinermann (Hrsg.), *Neubau der Verwaltung. Informationstechnische Realitäten und Visionen* (S. 382–403). Heidelberg: R. v. Decker's.

Reinermann, H. & von Lucke, J. (Hrsg.). (2000). *Portale in der öffentlichen Verwaltung - Internet, Call Center, Bürgerbüro, Speyerer Forschungsberichte 205.* Speyer: Forschungsinstitut für öffentliche Verwaltung.

Remer, A. (1989). Kompetenz und Verantwortung. In K. Chmielewicz & P. Eichhorn (Hrsg.), *Handwörterbuch der öffentlichen Betriebswirtschaft* (S. 789–795). Stuttgart: C. E. Poeschel.

Rhodes, R.A.W. (1991). The New Public Management. *Public Administration, 69,* 1–2.

Richli, P. (1996). *Öffentliches Dienstrecht im Zeichen des New Public Management. Staatsrechtliche Fixpunkte für die Flexibilisierung und Dynamisierung des Beamtenverhältnisses.* Bern: Stämpfli.

Ridley, F. F. (2000). The Public Service in Britain From Administrative to Managerial Culture. In H. Wollmann & E. Schröter, E. (Hrsg.), *Comparing public sector reform in Britain and Germany: key traditions and trends of modernisation* (S. 132–149). Aldershot: Ashgate.

Rieder, L. (2004). *Kosten-/Leistungsrechnung für die Verwaltung.* Bern: Haupt.

Rieder, S. (2006). Bilanz der wirkungsorientierten Steuerung in der Schweiz - ein Erfahrungsbericht. In Bertelsmann Stiftung (Hrsg.), *Strategische Steuerung - Dokumentation eines Expertendialoges im Rahmen der Projektinitiative "Staat der Zukunft"*(S. 22–28). Gütersloh: Bertelsmann.

Rieder, S. & Furrer, C. (2000). *Evaluation des Pilotprojekts Leistungsauftrag mit Globalbudget im Kanton Solothurn.* Luzern: Interface Politikstudien.

Rieder, S. & Lehmann, L. (2002). Evaluation of New Public Management Reforms in Switzerland. In *International Public Management Review, 3*(2), 25–43. Retrieved from www.ipmr.net

Riklin, A. (Hrsg.). (1983). *Handbuch Politisches System Schweiz, Bd. 1 Grundlagen.* Bern/Stuttgart/Wien: Haupt.

Riklin, A. & Möckli, S. (1983). Werden und Wandel der schweizerischen Staatsidee. In A. Riklin (Hrsg.), *Handbuch Politisches System Schweiz, Bd. 1: Grundlagen* (S. 9–118). Bern/Stuttgart/Wien: Haupt.

Riklin, A. (1997). *Vom Sinn der Verfassung, Beiträge und Berichte 256/1997*. St. Gallen: Institut für Politikwissenschaft.

Ritz, A. (2003). *Evaluation von New Public Management*. Bern/Stuttgart/Wien: Haupt.

Röber, M. (1996). Germany. In D. Farnham, S. Horton, J.Barlow & A. Hondeghem (Eds.), *New Public Managers in Europe. Public Servants in Transition* (S. 169–193). Houndmills: Macmillan.

Sachverständigenrat „Schlanker Staat" (1997). *Abschlussbericht, Bd. 1*. Bonn: Bundesministerium des Inneren.

Savas, E. S. (2000). *Privatization and Public-Private Partnerships*. New York: Chatham House.

Schäfer, W. (1995). Perspektiven für die Soziale Marktwirtschaft: Anthropologische Grundlagen. In F. Quaas & Th. Straubhaar (Hrsg.), *Perspektiven der Sozialen Marktwirtschaft* (S. 135–149). Bern/Stuttgart/Wien: Haupt.

Schauer, R. (1993). Die Eignung verschiedener Rechnungsstile für den managementorientierten Informationsbedarf in öffentlichen Verwaltungen. In H. Brede & E. Buschor (Hrsg.), *Das neue Öffentliche Rechnungswesen* (S. 143–166). Baden-Baden: Nomos.

Schauer, R. (2000). Output-orientierte Steuerung in öffentlichen Verwaltungen - Ansätze und Erfahrungen in Österreich. In D. Budäus (Hrsg.), *Leistungserfassung und Leistungsmessung in öffentlichen Verwaltungen* (S. 59–72). Wiesbaden: Gabler.

Schedler, K. (1995). *Ansätze einer Wirkungsorientierten Verwaltungsführung*. Bern/Stuttgart/Wien: Haupt.

Schedler, K. (2001). eGovernment und neue Servicequalität der Verwaltung?. In M. Gisler & D. Spahni (Hrsg.), *eGovernment: eine Standortbestimmung* (S. 33–51). Bern/Stuttgart/Wien: Haupt.

Schedler, K. (2005). Denkanstösse zur Wirkungsorientierten Verwaltungsführung. In A. Lienhard, A. Ritz & R. Steiner (Hrsg.), *10 Jahre New Public Management in der Schweiz. Bilanz, Irrtümer und Erfolgsfaktoren* (S. 223–235). Bern/Stuttgart/Wien: Haupt.

Schedler, K. & Felix, J. (1998). Quality in Public Management: the Customer Perspective. *International Public Management Journal, 3*(1), 125–143.

Schedler, K. & Reichard, C. (Hrsg.). (1998). *Die Ausbildung zum Public Manager*. Bern/Stuttgart/Wien: Haupt.

Schedler, K. & Siegel, J. P. (2005). *Strategisches Management in Kommunen*. Düsseldorf: Hans Böckler Stiftung.

Schedler, K., Summermatter, L. & Schmidt, B. (2003). *Electronic Government einführen und entwickeln. Von der Idee zur Praxis*. Bern/Stuttgart/Wien: Haupt.

Schedler, K. & Weibler, J. (1996). Personalcontrolling in der öffentlichen Verwaltung. In J. Goller, H. Maack & B. Müller-Hedrich (Hrsg.), *Verwaltungsmanagement. Handbuch für öffentliche Verwaltungen und öffentliche Betriebe* (S. 1–32). Stuttgart: Raabe.

Schein, E. (1985). *Organizational Culture and Leadership*. San Francisco: Jossey-Bass Publishers.

Schick, A. (1996). *The Spirit of Reform. Managing the New Zealand State Sector in a Time of Change*. Wellington: State Service Commission.

Schick, A. (1998). Why most developing countries should not try New Zealand Reforms. *The World Bank Research Observer, 13*, 123–131.

Schneider, H.-P. (1974). *Die parlamentarische Opposition im Verfasssungsrecht der Bundesrepublik Deutschland, Bd. I: Grundlagen*. Frankfurt a. M.: Vittorio Klostermann.

Schuppert, G. F. (1989). Markt, Staat, Dritter Sektor—oder auch noch mehr? Sektorspezifische Steuerungsprobleme ausdifferenzierter Staatlichkeit. In Th. Ellwein, J.J. Hesse, R. Mayntz & W.F. Scharpf (Hrsg.), *Jahrbuch zur Staats- und Verwaltungswissenschaft, Bd. 3* (S. 47–88). Baden-Baden: Nomos.

Schuppert, G. F. (1995). Rückzug des Staates?—Zur Rolle des Staates zwischen Legitimationskrise und politischer Neubestimmung. *Die Öffentliche Verwaltung, 51*, 761–770.

Schuppert, G. F. (1998). Die öffentliche Verwaltung im Kooperationsspektrum staatlicher und privater Aufgabenerfüllung: zum Denken in Verantwortungsstufen. *Die Verwaltung, 31*, 415–447.

Schwarz, P., Purtschert, R. & Giroud, C. (1995). *Das Freiburger Management-Modell für Nonprofit-Organisationen (NPO)* (2. Aufl.). Bern/Stuttgart/Wien: Haupt.

Schweizerischer Bundesrat (1974). *Richtlinien für die Verwaltungsführung im Bunde*. Bern: EDMZ.

Seghezzi, H.-D. (1996). *Integriertes Qualitätsmanagement: das St. Galler Konzept*. München: Hanser.

Shleifer, A. (1998). *State versus Private Ownership*. Cambridge, MA: National Bureau of Economic Research (NBER).

Siegel, J. Ph. (2006). Probleme und Defizite bei der Reform der US-Bundesverwaltung: Erste Ergebnisse einer meta-analytischen Untersuchung. In K. Birkholz, C. Maass, P. von Maravic & P. Siebart (Hrsg.), *Public Management - Eine neue Generation in Wissenschaft und Praxis* (S. 201–220). Potsdam: Universitätsverlag.

Shand, D. & Arnberg, M. (1996). Chapter 1, Backgroundpaper. In OECD (Ed.), *Responsive Government—Service Quality Initiatives* (S. 15–38). Paris: OECD.

Sprenger, R. (1992). Mythos Motivation. Wege aus einer Sackgasse. Frankfurt a.M.: Campus.

Stainback, J. (1999). Position of Strength. Can Government Officials Structure and Negotiate Public/Private Partnerships. *PA Times, 22*(7), 1–2.

Stünck, C. & Heinze, R. G. (2005). Public Private Partnerships, In B. Blanke, S. von Bandemer, F. Nullmeier & G. Wewer (Hrsg.), *Handbuch zur Verwaltungsreform* (S. 120–128). Wiesbaden: Verlag für Sozialwissenschaften.

Sutter-Somm, Th. (1998). Legalitätsprinzip und New Public Management (NPM). *Gesetzgebung heute* 1998/2/3, Bern: Schweizerische Bundeskanzlei, S. 47–61.

Tannenbaum, R. & Schmidt, W. H. (1958). How to Choose A Leadership Pattern. *Harvard Business Review, 36*(2), 95–101.

Thalmann, H. (1999). *Uster zum Beispiel. Neue Wege politischer Führung.* Bern/ Stuttgart/Wien: Haupt.

Thompson, F. & Jones, L. R. (1986). Controllership in the Public Sector. *Journal of Policy Analysis and Management, 5,* 547–571.

Thompson, F. & Jones, L. R. (1994). *Reinventing the Pentagon. How the New Public Management Can Bring Institutional Renewal.* San Francisco: Jossey Bass Publishers.

Thom, N. & Ritz, A. (2000). *Public Management.* Wiesbaden: Gabler Verlag.

Thom, N., Ritz, A. & Steiner, R. (Hrsg.). (2002). *Effektive Schulführung. Chancen und Risiken des Public Managements im Bildungswesen.* Bern/Stuttgart/ Wien: Haupt.

Tondorf, K., Bahnmüller, R. & Klages, H. (2002). *Steuerung durch Zielvereinbarungen. Anwendungspraxis, Probleme, Gestaltungsüberlegungen.* Berlin: Edition Sigma.

Tullock, G. (1967). The Welfare Costs of Tariffs, Monopolies, and Theft. *Western Economic Journal (heute: Economic Inquiry), 5,* 224–232.

Ulrich, H. (1990). *Unternehmenspolitik* (3. Aufl.). Bern/Stuttgart/Wien: Haupt.

Van Wart, M. (1998). *Changing Public Sector Values.* New York: Garland.

Virtanen, T. (2000). Changing competences of public managers: tensions in commitment. *International Journal of Public Sector Management, 13,* 333–341.

Von Bandemer, St., Blanke, B., Hilbert, J. & Schmid, J. (1995). Staatsaufgaben - Von der „schleichenden Privatisierung" zum „aktivierenden Staat". In F. Behrens, R. G. Heinze, J. Hilbert, S. Stöbe, & E. M. Welsken (Hrsg.), *Den Staat neu denken. Reformperspektiven für die Landesverwaltungen* (S. 41–60). Berlin: Edition Sigma.

Walsh, K. (1995). *Public Service and Market Mechanisms. Competition, Contracting and the New Public Management.* New York: St. Martins's Press.

Walsh, K. et al. (1997). *Contracting for Change: Contracts in Health, Social Care, and Other Local Government Services.* New York: Oxford University Press.

Weber, M. (1985). *Wirtschaft und Gesellschaft. Grundriss der verstehenden Soziologie* (5. Aufl.). Tübingen: J. C. B. Mohr.

Wegener, A. (1997). Wettbewerb zwischen öffentlichen und privaten Dienstleistungsanbietern. In F. Naschold, M. Oppen & A. Wegener (Hrsg.), *Innovative Kommunen. Internationale Trends und deutsche Erfahrungen* (S. 77–106). Stuttgart: Kohlhammer.

Wettenhall, R. & Kimber, M. (o.J.). *One Stop Shopping: Notes on the Concept and Some Australian Initiatives.* Canberra: Center for Research in the Public Sector Management at the University of Canberra.

Wildavsky, A. (1974). *The Politics of the Budgetary Process.* Boston/Toronto: Little Brown and Company.

Williamson, O. E. (1985). *The economic institutions of capitalism: firms, markets, relational contracting.* New York: The Free Press.

Winter, (1998). www.help.gv.at—Ein Bürgerinformationssystem, Die österreichische Verwaltung im Internet. *Verwaltung und Management, Zeitschrift für allgemeine Verwaltung, 4,* 136–139.

Wissenschaftlicher Beirat der Gesellschaft für öffentliche Wirtschaft (2004). *Public Private Partnership. Positionspapier.* Berlin: Gesellschaft für öffentliche Wirtschaft.

Wollmann, H. (2000). Comparing Institutional Development in Britain and Germany: (Persistant) Divergence or (Progressive) Convergence?. In H. Wollmann & E. Schröter (Eds.), *Comparing public sector reform in Britain and Germany: key traditions and trends of modernisation* (S. 1–26). Aldershot: Ashgate.

Wollmann, H. (2001). Germany's trajectory of public sector modernisation: continuities and discontinuities. *Policy & Politics, 29,* 151–169.

World Bank (2001). *Diagnostic Surveys of Corruption in Romania.* Washington D.C.: World Bank.

World Bank (2003). *Philippines Pilot E-Procurement System.* Washington D.C.: World Bank.

Wunderer, R. & Grunwald, W. (1980). *Führungslehre I. Grundlagen der Führung.* Berlin: DeGruyter.

Wunderer, R. (1997). *Führung und Zusammenarbeit: Beiträge zu einer unternehmerischen Führungslehre* (2. Aufl.). Stuttgart: Schäffer-Poeschel.

Würtenberger, Th. (1996). *Die Akzeptanz von Verwaltungsentscheiden.* Baden-Baden: Nomos.

Zehnder, M. (1989). *Die heutige Kritik an Max Webers Bürokratie-Begriff angesichts des raschen gesellschaftlichen Wandels (Diplomarbeit).* St. Gallen: Universität St. Gallen.

Zifcak, S. (1994). *New Managerialism. Administrative Reform in Whitehall and Canberra.* Buckingham: Open University Press.

Zimmermann, G. (1993). Die Leistungsfähigkeit von Kostenrechnungssystemen für den managementorientierten Informationsbedarf. In H. Brede & F. Buschor (Hrsg.), *Das neue öffentliche Rechnungswesen. Betriebswirtschaftliche Beiträge zur Haushaltsreform in Deutschland, Österreich und der Schweiz, Schriften zur öffentlichen Verwaltung und öffentlichen Wirtschaft, Bd. 133* (S. 167–197). Baden-Baden: Nomos.